Twayne's United States Authors Series

EDITOR OF THIS VOLUME

David J. Nordloh

Indiana University, Bloomington

American Literary Criticism, 1860-1905

Volume II

TUSAS 340

AMERICAN LITERARY CRITICISM, 1860–1905

VOLUME II

By JOHN W. RATHBUN

California State University, Los Angeles

and

HARRY H. CLARK

TWAYNE PUBLISHERS
A DIVISION OF G. K. HALL & CO., BOSTON

Published in 1979 by Twayne Publishers,
A Division of G. K. Hall & Co.
All Rights Reserved

Printed on permanent/durable acid-free paper and bound
in the United States of America

First Printing

Library of Congress Cataloging in Publication Data

Rathbun, John Wilbert, 1924-
American literary criticism.

(Twayne's United States authors series ;
TUSAS 339-341)
Vol. 2 by J. W. Rathbun and H. H. Clark;
v. 3 by A. L. Goldsmith.
Includes bibliographies and indexes.
CONTENTS: v. 1. 1800-1860.—v. 2. 1860-1905.
—v. 3. 1905-1965.
1. Criticism—United States—History. I. Clark,
Harry Hayden, 1901-1971, joint author. II. Gold-
smith, Arnold L., joint author. III. Title
PN99.U5R37   801'.95'0973   79-9903

ISBN 0-8057-7264-2 (v. 2)

Contents

About the Authors

Harry Hayden Clark taught in the American Literature section of the Department of English at the University of Wisconsin, Madison, from 1928 until his death in 1971. During that period he directed over one hundred doctoral dissertations and achieved an outstanding reputation as one of the country's leading scholars. He served as President of the Wisconsin Academy of Sciences, Arts and Letters (1965–1966) and as President of the American Literature section of the Modern Language Association (1952–1953). Among honors and awards he was the recipient of a Guggenheim fellowship (1931–1932), a Library of Congress fellowship (1945–1946), the Certificate of Merit (1953) and Centennial Award (1955) from Michigan State University, an LL. D. from Bowling Green State University (1951), and a Litt. D. from Trinity College (1963). Author of *American Literature: Poe Through Garland* (1970), he was also editor of eight books on American authors and literary movements, including the Modern Language Association edition of *Transitions in American Literary History* (1954). He was General Editor of the prestigious American Writers Series published by the American Book Company between 1934 and 1947, as well as of that company's American Literature and American Fiction series. Between 1924 and 1971 he was the author of nineteen contributions to books, twenty-nine articles, and numerous book reviews.

Professor Clark was born in New Milford, Connecticut, in 1901, and received his B.A. from Trinity College in 1923 and his M.A. from Harvard University in 1924. He was instructor in English at Yale University (1924–1925), and Assistant Professor of English at Middlebury College (1925–1928). A Smith-Mundt visiting professor at the University of Uppsala and University of Stockholm (1953–1954), he was also at various times visiting professor at Stanford University, Northwestern University, the University of Iowa, the University of Southern California, and the Bread Loaf School of English.

John W. Rathbun is Professor of English at California State University, Los Angeles, where he divides his teaching duties between the Department of English, in which he offers courses in nineteenth-century American literature, and the Department of American Studies, in which he teaches courses in intellectual history and Los Angeles area urban history. Active in professional groups, he has been a member of the National Council of the American Studies Association, President of the College English Association of Southern California, and President of the American Studies Association of Southern California. He has presented papers before various professional associations, has published articles on American literary figures and intellectual movements in such journals as *Modern Fiction Studies, American Quarterly, International Philosophical Quarterly,* and *Nineteenth-Century Fiction,* and has contributed chapters to two books on American culture. He is presently at work on a book on American avant-garde movements.

Dr. Rathbun was born and raised in Sioux City, Iowa, and during World War II served in the Field Artillery and Combat Engineers of the U.S. Army. He received his Ph.B., with twin majors in Philosophy and English, and his M.A. in English from Marquette University in 1951 and 1952 respectively. In 1956 he received his Ph.D. in English from the University of Wisconsin. Between 1969 and 1975 he served as Chairman of the Department of American Studies.

Preface

This book is the second in a three-volume survey of American literary criticism from 1800 to 1960; the other two volumes are *American Literary Criticism, 1800–1860*, by John W. Rathbun, and *American Literary Criticism, 1905–1965*, by Arnold L. Goldsmith. The intention in all three volumes, insofar as possible, is to emphasize origins and basic principles of critical schools and movements, combined with a close analysis of the major critics associated with them. The various critical schools and methodologies are ordinarily discussed according to the chronology of their beginnings.

Whereas pre–Civil War literary criticism is distinguished by types of critical principles rather than schools or critics, American literary criticism between 1860 and 1905 testifies to a sharpened awareness of how the thought and work of critics demonstrate common influences and unifying beliefs. This fact has made it possible to organize the chapters in this book according to editorial intentions by concentrating on the premises and directions of particular critical schools. Yet individual figures tended less to join such schools than to share critical positions, and so within the chapters there is greater emphasis on the distinctive contributions of particular critics than would be necessary in a discussion of either antebellum or twentieth-century literary criticism. In two cases—Henry James and George Santayana—the men so far surpass the critical schools with which they are commonly linked that they have been granted separate chapters.

In order to focus on the schools and major trends, some selection has been necessary. The lesser critics, important in their day, perhaps, but largely forgotten in ours, appear only infrequently or not at all: George Parsons Lathrop, W. C. Wilkinson, J. H. Morse, Richard Watson Gilder, Richard Burton, and others. In addition, the academic historians—people like Moses Coit Tyler most notably, but also William P. Trent, Charles F. Richardson, Barrett Wendell, John S. Hart, Henry A. Beers—receive little distinct attention because their critical orientation is covered in the chapter on "Historical and Evolutionary Criticism."

The American social setting in the post–Civil War period was witness to an accelerated industrial and urban expansion that extended the psychology of the city, enhanced the practical and social sciences as instruments of national purpose, and ratified the already great authority of a middle-class urban culture. Critical theory was readily adapted to the new circumstances. Intellectuals emphasized description and objective exposition, scholars patterned their literary studies on the supposed thoroughness and meticulous procedures of scientific study, and everyone put primary stress on method. Many critics were uneasy with or openly opposed to the new values and concepts of public function that seemed to emerge as a consequence of social change, but taken collectively practically all of them reflect a middle-class bias in respect to two assumptions: that American society was a single social system, the parts of which were functionally interdependent; and that all professions, including the arts, were subsumed in the more comprehensive national purpose. The first assumption closed off any discussion of cultural pluralism and of the legitimate needs of minorities, especially when the social system was tied to the racial motif of Anglo-Saxonism; while the second assumption reduced the autonomy of the arts by making them a basic social resource. Together, these two views help to explain why historical criticism was integral to the theories of most critical schools, and why so many critics concentrated on the "truth" of the works they were examining. For if writers erred in describing human nature and social character, the social utility of their work was diminished.

Professor Clark and I have had separate roles in the book. He was awarded the original contract, and intended to survey twelve spokesmen whose critical work may be said to have reached its peak during these years. His unfortunate death left the manuscript in an early stage of development, and the contract was renegotiated to include me. I have relied on portions of Professor Clark's manuscript, but I have completely reorganized the book into a study of the critical schools of the period, and have used a considerable quantity of new material that I myself gathered together. In addition, I have expressed judgments and emphasized salient points according to my own reading in the critics under study for which I alone should accept responsibiltiy.

Both Professor Clark and I consulted the resources of the University of Wisconsin Memorial Library and the Wisconsin State Historical Library. In addition, I have consulted materials in the Los Angeles Public Library, the Huntington Library, the Library of the

Preface

University of California at Los Angeles, and the Library of the California State University, Los Angeles. Their staffs have all been courteous and helpful. Expenses were met in part by a grant-in-aid from the Office of Research and Governmental Relations of the California State University, Los Angeles. Paul Hurley and Charles Nelson assisted Professor Clark on some of the essays in his manuscript. My colleague, Professor John Bushman, read chapters in manuscript and gave helpful advice. Professors Arnold Goldsmith of Wayne State University and David J. Nordloh of Indiana University read the entire manuscript and made extremely valuable recommendations for revision. I am grateful to Nancy Craven and Lyle Waters for their expert typing of the manuscript.

JOHN W. RATHBUN

California State University, Los Angeles

Chronology

1860   Emerson's, *The Conduct of Life*. William T. Coggeshall's *The Poets and Poetry of the West: with Biographical and Critical Notices*. John Lothrop Motley begins seven-year publication of *History of the United Netherlands*. Henry Adams begins writing essays and reviews for the *Boston Courier* and the *Boston Daily Advertiser*.

1863   Lowell becomes joint editor of the *North American Review* with C. E. Norton. Harriet Beecher Stowe's *A Reply . . . in Behalf of the Women of America*.

1865   E. L. Godkin founds the *Nation* as a journal of political and social reform. *The Knickerbocker Magazine* ceases publication.

1867   John Burroughs' *Notes on Walt Whitman as Poet and Person*. W. T. Harris establishes the *Journal of Speculative Philosophy* in St. Louis as an organ for neo-Hegelianism.

1868   *Lippincott's* established in Philadelphia as a rival to the *Galaxy* and *Atlantic Monthly*.

1870   Lowell's *Among My Books*. Emerson's *Society and Solitude*. Harriet Beecher Stowe's *Lady Byron Vindicated*. Lucy Stone establishes the *Woman's Journal* under auspices of National American Woman Suffrage Association.

1871   Lowell's *My Study Windows*. Whitman's *Democratic Vistas* and *Passage to India*. Howells becomes editor-in-chief at the *Atlantic Monthly*. Horace Howard Furness begins publication of his monumental New Variorum edition of Shakespeare. Oliver Wendell Holmes' *Mechanism in Thought and Morals*. Hubert Howe Bancroft begins publication of the 28-volume *History of the Pacific States*.

1872   T. S. Perry's "American Novels" in the *North American Review*, part of the general discussion of what an American novel should be. John S. Hart gives one of the first courses in American literature at Princeton University. *Appleton's Journal* begun with Oliver Bell Bunce as editor.

1874   The Chautauqua Assembly founded by Lewis Miller and John

H. Vincent to foster cultural and educational values, leading to Chautauqua societies throughout the country. John Fiske's *Outlines of Comic Philosophy*.

1875   Edmund Clarence Stedman's *Victorian Poets*. James McCosh's *The Scottish Philosophy of Common Sense*.

1876   Lowell's *Among My Books, Second Series*. Emerson's *Letters and Social Aims*.

1878   Moses Coit Tyler's *The Literary History of the American Revolution, 1763–1783*.

1879   Bayard Taylor's *Studies in German Literature* published posthumously. Henry James's *Hawthorne*. James A. Herne, in collaboration with David Belasco, produces one of first plays of realism, *Hearts of Oak*. John Fiske's *Darwinism and Other Essays*. Henry George's *Progress and Poverty*.

1880   Bayard Taylor's *Critical Essays and Literary Notes* published posthumously. Sidney Lanier's *The Science of English Verse*.

1882   Francis James Child begins publication of the five-volume standard reference work, *The English and Scottish Popular Ballads*.

1883   W. H. Browne edits and publishes Sidney Lanier's *The English Novel and the Principle of its Development*.

1885   Holmes' *Ralph Waldo Emerson*. Henry James's *The Art of Fiction*. Edmund Clarence Stedman's *Poets of America*.

1886   Howells begins the "Editor's Study" in *Harper's*, to continue until 1892.

1887   E. P. Whipple's *American Literature and Other Papers*.

1888   James's *Partial Portraits*. Edmund Clarence Stedman and Ellen M. Hutchinson begin two-year publication of eleven-volume *A Library of American Literature from the Earliest Settlement to the Present Time*.

1889   William Crary Brownell's *French Traits: an Essay in Comparative Criticism*.

1890   Hamilton Wright Mabie's *My Study Fire*. Mabel Loomis Todd and T. W. Higginson's *Poems by Emily Dickinson, Edited by Two of Her Friends*.

1891   Howells' *Criticism and Fiction*.

1892   Lowell's *The Old English Dramatists* published posthumously, Hjalmar Hjorth Boyesen's *Essay on German Literature*. Edmund Clarence Stedman's *The Nature and Elements of Poetry*. William P. Trent establishes *The Sewanee Review* as a Southern journal.

1893   Henry James' *Essays in London and Elsewhere*.
1894   Hjalmar Hjorth Boyesen's *A Commentary on the Writing of Henrik Ibsen* and *Literary and Social Silhouettes*. Hamlin Garland's *Crumbling Idols*.
1895   E. L. Godkin's literary contributions to the *North American Review* and other journals are published as *Reflections and Comments, 1865–1895*. Hjalmar Hjorth Boyesen's *Essays on Scandinavian Literature*.
1896   Brander Matthews' *An Introduction to the Study of American Literature* and *Aspects of Fiction and Other Ventures in Criticism*. Hamilton Wright Mabie's *Books and Culture*. Santayana's aesthetic theories are developed in *The Sense of Beauty*.
1899   Hamilton Wright Mabie's *The Life of the Spirit*.
1900   Edmund Clarence Stedman's *An American Anthology, 1787–1900*. George Woodberry's *Makers of Literature*. Barrett Wendell's *A Literary History of America*. Lewis E. Gates's *Studies and Appreciations*. Santayana's *Interpretations of Poetry and Religion*. Josiah Royce's *The World and the Individual*.
1901   William Crary Brownell's *Victorian Prose Masters*. Charles Moulton begins his four-year publication of the eight-volume *Library of Literary Criticism of English and American Authors*.
1902   Henry W. Lanier edits two volumes of Sidney Lanier's *Shakespeare and His Forerunners: Studies in Elizabethan Poetry from Early English*.
1903   Richard Henry Stoddard's *Recollections, Personal and Literary*. George Woodberry's *America in Literature*. Brander Matthews' *The Development of the Drama*. Frank Norris' *The Responsibilities of the Novelist* published posthumously. William P. Trent's *A History of American Literature, 1607–1865*.
1904   Paul Elmer More begins publication of *Shelburne Essays*.
1905   Henry James' *The Lesson of Balzac*. George Woodberry's *The Torch* and *Swinburne*. James Gibbon Huneker's *Iconoclasts* and *Visionaries*. Santayana begins publication of the five-volume *The Life of Reason or the Phases of Human Progress* with publication of *Reason in Common Sense*.

CHAPTER 1

Critical Idealism

CRITICAL idealism has survived on the margin of literary criticism as a rather dull, somewhat devitalized movement painfully adrift in the main currents of a period it could not understand. As a result, students of the period have been forced to read of critical idealism through a screen of personal predilections and pejorative terms: Parrington's "The Great Barbecue"; Van Wyck Brooks' "New England: Indian Summer"; Santayana's "The Genteel Tradition." It is time, however, to dispense with such expressions.[1] The critical idealists were individual men, even while they collectively constituted a movement that in its day was powerful and influential. Some of them, George Woodberry particularly, betray on occasion a hesitant and genteel tone that unmans their criticism. But others, like Brander Matthews, provide such a balanced and thoroughly judicious appraisal of writing that they persuade us that we are in the presence of minds to whom it is profitable to pay attention.

Throughout the period 1860–1905, critical idealism was in main positions of power. Three factors contributed to its authority. It was in a direct line of descent from Emerson and Lowell, and benefitted from their prestige. Lowell especially, by virtue of the esteem he enjoyed, helped materially in promoting the careers of men who came to his attention. Secondly, through a succession of editors the movement had access to the pages of the *Atlantic Monthly* and *Century Magazine,* two prestigious magazines that enjoyed wide circulation. Finally, by the 1880s the critical idealists found themselves in conflict with new energetic literary movements like realism and naturalism, and labored hard to sharpen critical tenets, to more precisely define the boundaries of the conflict, and in general to deepen sentiment with persuasive argument.

In the end, inevitably it seems now, realism and naturalism triumphed. The better writers embraced those movements and slighted the idealists. In 1894, William R. Thayer could cite only

Caine, Doyle, Zangwill, Weyman, Crockett, and Du Maurier as "proof" that romanticism was reasserting itself over realism.[2] In exploring why critical idealism exercised a fading hold over American writers, Floyd Stovall finds that the frontier, the Civil War, and the advance of science were primary influences in changing the attitudes of writers, while the general decline in church authority, the expansion of public education, and foreign literary influences played subordinate roles.[3] One might also cite two interrelated facts. Throughout its career, the movement was largely devoted to the perpetuation and encouragement of poetry at a time when prose fiction was in the ascendant. Mark Twain was the national storyteller, and public attention was almost exclusively devoted to the novel. And secondly, the movement lacked a representative author of any stature and ability. At the century's end, as Jay Martin points out in *Harvests of Change*, there was no "standard" American poet to replace those of New England.[4] Whitman might have served this purpose, if only the movement's leaders had not been so timid in accepting and promoting him.

Critical idealism favored literature of the romantic past, as well as the "masters" of Western literature like Shakespeare, Milton, and Cervantes, and the classical poetry of Virgil and Horace. It tended to be uncertain and defensive about contemporary literature. Regionalism, realism, and naturalism, in their commitment to observed experience, all seemed to deny the active shaping powers of the imagination. In this respect contemporary literature appeared to be on a par with the culture—too materialistic. To the critical idealists (as well as any number of other intellectuals), America was bent on a materialistic orgy that simply dispensed with humane values. The new middle class was unlettered, indifferent to the arts, vulgarly greedy and extravagant, crudely energetic in its pursuit of money. The indictment is familiar. Emerson had said it first. But how could poetry save such untutored souls?

In its general orientation, critical idealism can be characterized by an aversion to moral evaluation, preferring instead to judge the "completeness" of a literary work; an historical approach to literature that owes much to the nineteenth-century infatuation with social evolution and national progress; a concept of the imagination indebted to Emerson and of beauty indebted ultimately to Plato; an elitist approach to books somewhat akin to Matthew Arnold's faith in the best that has been thought and said; and a critical fastidiousness most often found in a discreet skirting of issues raised by the opposi-

tion. The strength of these principles was on occasion eroded by the
movement's respect for propriety and the Brahmin masters of New
England. Stedman's critical acumen, for instance, was sturdy enough
to recognize the distinctive contribution that Whitman was making to
American literature.[5] But in his critical remarks on Longfellow and
Bayard Taylor, he evaded the main issue of their lack of depth and
dwelt instead on safe biographical data.

I   *Ralph Waldo Emerson (1803–1882)*

Emerson and Lowell were productive until their deaths in 1882
and 1891. Together they served as the "masters" under whom the
younger critical idealists alternately wrote and chafed.[6] In the early
parts of their careers, the two men had been considered radical
innovators not entirely to be countenanced. Emerson's early concern
for the "infinitude of the private man," which he phrased as
self-reliance, and his early faith in the goodness of nature and of the
natural man, which went unbalanced by the kind of inductive
historical knowledge "The American Scholar" was supposed to have
attacked, were regarded as naive. But the misgivings of Emerson's
readers of *Nature* in 1836 were partially eliminated by his subsequent
development. By the time *The Conduct of Life* (1860) and *Society
and Solitude* (1870) were published, it seemed apparent to many that
Emerson urged a mediation between the needs of the private man
and the uses of tradition as an ethical guide.[7] On these grounds
Emerson's contemporaries tended to domesticate him to the prevailing attitudes of the time. His moral reserve was translated into moral
reticence, his social distance into dignified stuffiness, and his intellectual discretion into a diluted form of literary conservatism.

This image of Emerson even today continues to substitute for the
real Emerson, so that few students voluntarily turn to his work for
inspiration and insight. And yet it is in his work that Emerson
continues to make his own good case. He consistently held that the
apprehension of beauty was inseparable from the good life. It is one
way to put all life under contribution. Most men, he thought, live
fragments of experience. But there were some, a "company of the
wisest and wittiest men," who have touched and understood the
authentic strands of common experience. He felt that these were the
men to consult, since they set "in the best order the results of their
learning and wisdom."[8] Emerson realized that most of us, in our
faintheartedness, conceive of the good as a series of limitations on the

active life. We elaborate moral codes which function as a restraint on behavior. Wise men, on the other hand, have learned to avoid the dowdiness of this moral good. They are psychologically healthy persons who can lend their good offices to our instruction. What they consistently teach us, Emerson held, is that wisdom is superior to knowledge and virtue is to be preferred to the moral. When men restrict themselves to knowledge, they experience the intellectual poverty of the "practical" or positivist mind. When they are "moral," they affirm a series of taboos which close the individual off from certain kinds of experience. Men need to "delimit" experience. Emerson offered wisdom and virtue as a series of possibilities which could open up life. In our fallow moments, when we are visited by no direct inspiration of our own, the office of criticism was to acquaint us with how "well used" books can be an inspiring way of living broadly.

Emerson thus saw criticism as a vehicle for conveying to readers insights that might otherwise remain obscure. Consequently the touchstones for his criticism are his idealistic distinctions between the law-abiding imagination and the capricious fancy, between inspired genius and poetic talent, and between intuitive reason and the discursive understanding—distinctions adopted and in the main followed by the next generation of critical idealists.

As the distinctions suggest, Emerson was not so much interested in the mode taken to communicate a thought as in the quality of the thought itself. "Criticism is an art," he concluded in "Art and Criticism," "when it does not stop at the words of the poet, but looks at the order of his thoughts and the quality of his mind. 'Tis a question not of talents but of tone; and not particular merits, but the mood of mind into which one and another can bring us."[9] Just as to Emerson God is revealed directly, without mediator or advocate, whenever anyone has a psychological impulse to do something good, so whenever anyone enters into the spirit of a great book he becomes akin to its author and partakes of his inspiration.

II   *James Russell Lowell (1819–1891)*

By the time of his death in 1882 Emerson had become a citizen of the world, acknowledged as one of its intellectual lights. Wherever he went, England, the Continent, men attended the intellectual gatherings to which he had been invited, noting later in their journals the simple observation, "Mr Emerson was in attendance." James Russell Lowell, sixteen years Emerson's junior, and destined to outlive him by nine, shared in the ethical and imaginative idealism of Emerson, whose influence he gratefully acknowledged. Together the two men had an incalculable influence on younger critics like Hamilton Wright Mabie, George Woodberry, and Edmond Clarence Stedman. In comparison to Emerson, Lowell had a much deeper and more comprehensive knowledge of criticism, and he was much more concerned with strictly literary matters such as the history of language, style, and form. All things considered, Lowell is in certain respects superior to Matthew Arnold.

In his early period, Lowell, like Emerson, was radically inclined, especially in urging an antitraditional literature of didacticism devoted to furthering racial and social reform. From this early interest in humanitarian reform, he moved successively to a strong nationalism, occasioned by the Civil War, and then to an international traditionalism based on the classics of Western literature.[10] He was founder and editor of the *Atlantic Monthly* (1857–1861) and coeditor beginning in 1864 of the *North American Review,* magazines which provided him a forum to extend himself. His career from 1867 to his death in 1891 was marked by the publication of a long series of fine critical essays which grew out of two decades of Harvard teaching and his experience as minister to Spain (1877–1880) and to England (1880–1885).

The mutations in Lowell's critical ideals enabled him to touch the history of American literary taste at a great number of points. Overly austere and even unfair in his essays on Thoreau and Percival, he reviewed Howells and James in a very sympathetic and encouraging manner, and as editor of the *Atlantic Monthly* he discovered and published such pioneers of realism as Harriet Prescott Spofford, Rose Terry Cooke, and Rebecca Harding Davis, whose "Life in the Iron Mills" can still strike a reader as ultrarealistic. Later, as a liberal transcending age and nation, and sensitive to excellence in whatever race, place, or time, Lowell did much to broaden the narrow taste of people who, in their ignorance of or contempt for what they regarded as a "feudal" European past, were starving themselves aesthetically. In this later period he insisted that literature "must be judged . . . absolutely, with reference, that is, to the highest standard, and not relatively to the fashions and opportunities of the age."[11]

Lowell derived this standard form from the "immutable principles" he found in the Greek critical tradition. The standard was useful if for no other reason than that it provided a "determinate point of view" or strategy for approaching literary works. Furthermore, the standard was applicable because so much Western literature bore the Greek stamp. The Greek legacy to Western civilization had encouraged a literature of such "purity of outline and harmony of parts" that those attributes could safely be taken, when found in subsequent literary works, as demonstrative of their excellence. Hence one of the principles that Lowell accepted for his critical theory was the doctrine of organic form, which he defined as the "artistic sense of decorum controlling the coordination of parts and insuring their harmonious subservience to a common end." The doctrine subsumed even style.[12]

Like Emerson, Lowell gave his concept of organic form a modern color by his admiration for the critical principles of Coleridge and, partly through him, of the Germans. He regarded Coleridge as a "main influence" in teaching the modern mind "to recognize in the imagination an important factor not only in the happiness but in the destiny of man. In criticism he was, indeed, a teacher and interpreter whose service was incalculable."[13] Among others who influenced Lowell's critical position were Carlyle, whom Lowell thought at one point in Carlyle's career "the first in insight of English critics," and Goethe, whom Lowell termed the "most widely receptive of critics."[14]

Lowell's criticism, as Richard H. Fogle points out,[15] is most successful when it deals with established masters. He is thus excellent on Keats and on such great figures as Dante, Shakespeare, and Cervantes. Temperamentally Lowell was simply more attracted to richly rewarding proven writers, even while he could be responsive to new literary talent like Howells and James. But he was not receptive to realism as a literary theory. Realism did not encourage artists to present anything more than the cluttered incoherency of the mundane scene. There was no *discovery*. When at their best, literary realists seemed to transcend their own theory to approach the unseen world of universal values, so that theory was of almost no help in the literary exploration of experience.

To Lowell, man simply floundered about when he lacked literary and human values. The business of life, he thought, was to discover our own selves. In this respect, the affirmation of certain values was almost synonymous with the discovery of self. The entire range of human observation and experience could be put under contribution. But more particularly there was the utility of literature, especially when criticism had already sifted out what seemed to be productive of the good life. In time, and armed with the values fostered by explored experience, the individual man could become "sole sponsor of himself." "Every high example of virtue, though it led to the stake or scaffold, becomes a part of the reserved force of humanity, and from generation to generation summons kindred natures to a standard of righteousness as with the sound of a trumpet."[16] The statement is inflated, and has led some to charge Lowell with being a bookish Brahmin who expressed the traditionalist's faith in the ideal of emulation. But the charge does not take into consideration Lowell's own emphasis on self-reliant and selective reading. Nor does it consider, really, the fact that his critical essays grew out of his classroom expositions of the liberal imagination. The kindled imagination illuminates the reason and leads to a sharpened awareness of the intimate relation between intelligence, human value, and artistic symmetry.

III *The Younger Critical Idealists*

Emerson and Lowell provided the younger men who followed in their critical tradition with a solid belief in the humanistic character of criticism. George Woodberry, Edmund Clarence Stedman, Hamilton Wright Mabie, and to some extent Brander Matthews, continued to believe that the best literature dealt with the essential and lasting characteristics of human beings, and that these characteristics were discovered and elaborated through the imaginative exploration of experience. Human behavior, when inquired into and regularized by the imagination, was found to contain the highest wisdom of which man was capable, and that wisdom, as Stedman said, was ethical.[17] Beauty was absolute and objective, genius was the means for extracting its essential character from experience, and subjective taste provided genius with the means for developing new and ideal structures of literary expression.

Their idealism, then, was not fleshless and visionary, although often enough this has been the accusation leveled against them. It was rather a heightened form of realism with a sufficiently large perspective to distinguish between the superficial and true character of reality. According to Mabie, the defect of a good deal of literature that Howells admired lay in its lack of veracity: "it is essentially untrue and it is, therefore, fundamentally unreal."[18] The critical idealists believed that the good writer must of necessity have recourse to the obvious facts of life. But the good writer orders these facts in a sequence which both explains and interprets. The fact is observed, but the truth is discerned, for the truth lies beyond mere observation. It is in this sense, just as Emerson had said, that true idealism is true realism, for idealism moves beyond the provisional nature of prosy experience to provide us an interpretation of experience. If in its essentials the work of art is equal to the interpretation, then we have one more truth as a tool for working out our own lives. Men increasingly benefit from this aspect of art, for artistic culture is cumulative, slowly but irresistibly building toward a definition of life. "Every great new truth compels, sooner or later," said Mabie, "a readjustment of the whole body of organized truth as men hold it."[19]

As the critical idealists saw it, then, the true artist must possess two strengths. He must first of all be astute in his selection from experience. And he must put his selection in perspective. Art depends on nature, as Charles Dudley Warner observed, but in opposition to the realists the idealists argued that art is not limited to nature.[20] Indeed, when one immerses himself in the period and examines the tedious quantity of work produced by second-rate realists, regional writers, and Western wits, it is possible to see what the critical idealists were arguing against. To Stedman the entire country was being "flooded, deluged, swamped, beneath a muddy tide of slang, inartistic bathers [bathos], impertinence and buffoonery that is not wit."[21] It was once again time, the idealists thought, to recall readers to the fact that real literature deals with human sentiments and ideas, spiritual rather than material values, imaginative rather than literal experience. In this sense all the great writers, said Mabie, are idealists "in the fundamental if not the technical sense".[22]

The practical criticism of the idealists was not always equal to their theory. And their efforts at poetry were unsuccessful counters to the rising popularity of realism. They were not really artists. The tinkling rhythms and refined prose technique of Thomas Bailey Aldrich did not catch on even in his own day, prompting him to foresake both his editorship of the *Atlantic Monthly* and the New York scene. Richard Henry Stoddard modeled his poems on Keats, as did George Woodberry later, and Stedman found his inspiration in a number of romantic poets, including Tennyson. But the poetry they produced was insignificant. Bayard Taylor was one of the most widely known of these men, publishing poetry, travel books, and translations that were both respected and emulated. But even Stedman, as sympathetic as he was, recognized the thinness of his work. Except for such figures as Whitman and Emily Dickinson, poetry was in the doldrums, and would not revive until Edwin Arlington Robinson and Robert Frost began to publish. In the meantime, the critical idealists protected the field by continuing to exalt the saving powers of the poet, the permanence of traditional values expressed in formally satisfying language, and the important role of beauty in fleshing out an adjustment to human experience.

The views of the critical idealists were based upon an unswerving belief in the permanent unalterable order of existence. Hence the ideal critic attended both to the specific truths embodied in litera-ture, isolating them for the benefit of readers, and to the degree of harmony between truth and beauty found in single works of art. This kind of critical task transcended the fashions of time and place. No matter the age or culture, good literature was thought to be uniformly characterized by soundness of substance, perfection of form, and vitality, the latter always a tricky matter for criticism. For these reasons the critical idealists were inclined to prize works that echoed the sentiments of the great literary past and to downgrade attempts at literary contemporaneity and muckraking.

Literature, then, was the expression of beauty based upon the unchanging nature of reality. But just as Emerson and Lowell also provided for an idealist conception of the historical role of literature, the critical idealists who followed them viewed literature as the cumulative record of man's intellectual and spiritual growth. In accord with their times, they viewed history in evolutionary and progressive terms, even while they maintained that human or moral values were timeless and universal. Change was therefore benign, for it occurred within a structured whole. Change could be accepted, even embraced, for it took the form of a progressive line of develop-ment that was clearly rational.

To the critical idealists, literature shared in this historical de-velopment. While fixed and final standards were necessary to the study and evaluation of literature, a more comprehensive view based on historical analysis could place literary works within the contexts of literary movements in order to discover how they shared, as Mabie said, in "some fresh energy of conviction" of a "race or an epoch."[23] Not consciously steered by individual artists, literature moved in directions that were "inevitable and beneficent." Its study could be broadened to include historical and psychological analysis. The view was not limited to the critical idealists. Practically everyone in the post–Civil War period believed in some form of evolutionary or historical criticism. Of the critical idealists, Mabie was the most enthusiastic, Woodberry the most single-minded, in promoting the idea of the historical relevance of literature. The climactic era for criticism, Mabie thought, was his own. Such vast resources of data had been accumulated that the "comparative method" could be used on a scale never before possible. Critics had canvassed the full range of literature. They knew the diverse conditions under which it had been composed. They had intensively studied historical backgrounds. Now a summit had been reached. It was possible to glimpse the entire "range and significance" of literature as the "vital outcome of all human experiences."[24]

A. George Woodberry (1855–1930)

Mabie's attraction to "modern criticism" was shared by George Woodberry, a man trained and recommended by Harvard teachers like Lowell, Henry Adams, and Charles Eliot Norton. Woodberry lacked Stedman's faculty for precise statement and defensive maneuvering, and his critical tone was different from Mabie's exultant sense of critical power. But Woodberry was a prudent and careful critic and, on the testimony of students like Joel Spingarn and John Erskine, an inspiring teacher.

Woodberry taught briefly at the University of Nebraska, then accepted a professorship at Columbia University, where he headed its Department of Comparative Literature for thirteen years (1891–1904). Little known today, Woodberry is commonly described as the anemic end to his literary tradition, who with colleagues like Barrett Wendell of Harvard and Henry Van Dyke of Princeton secured the remnants of critical idealism in the universities. But Woodberry and his colleagues were neither escapists nor managers of a withdrawal to the monastic academy. They may have been impracticably visionary in their program. According to Robert Falk, Woodberry and others "maintained the old-fashioned belief that the frictions of an increasingly industrialized and stratified society might be assuaged by a literature which, without sacrificing the authenticity which a realistic and analytic method could bring, still upheld a broad standard of ethical and aesthetic decorum."[25]

In his own time Woodberry was a public figure of some consequence. Harvard bracketed him with no less a person than Henry James in awarding an honorary doctorate. His *America in Literature* (1903) is credited by Howard Mumford Jones with being wiser, subtler, and more comprehensive than the views of Richardson and

Wendell in encouraging American critics to explore American kin-
ship with the European and classical traditions.

Woodberry was a poet of mild competence and at his best a critic
whose style, often grave and noble and lyrical, is equal in appeal to
that of Santayana and P. E. More. The same qualities were apparently to be found in his teaching, in which he developed in students
like Spingarn and Erskine an appreciation for the autonomy of art.
The central focus of his own critical studies, however, was his theory
of "Race-Power," a somewhat subtle combination of earlier
traditionalism as represented by Lowell and the later evolutionary
stress on the inexorable continuity of human culture. The idea
resembles Emerson's concept, expressed in "History," that the
"mind is one in all ages," so that "past, present, and future are triple
blossoms from one root." But in his book on Emerson, Woodberry
does not recognize this aspect, and includes antitraditionalism as one
of Emerson's limitations. The concept of "Race-Power" anticipates in
broad terms T. S. Eliot's belief that a vital tradition is more alive and
important than individuality. And as one finds the concept expressed
in the first two lectures in *The Torch* (1905) and elsewhere, Woodberry's emphasis on archetypal patterns and mythic recurrence puts him
in the company of such modern critics as Maud Bodkin and Northrop
Frye.

Not so much an ethnic entity as a spiritual quality, the racial mind is
a shorthand way of describing how the stored memories and experiences of man constitute tradition. It is the race that makes literature.
The individual is merely a participant in the nobility of the race.
Artists draw from the "continuing growing fund" of the race,
transform the material imaginatively through a process of refinement
and clarification, and produce work that is truth in its "simplest, most
vivid and vital form."

Woodberry illustrated the process in *The Torch* in a three-pronged
analysis. He first discussed at some length how mythology, chivalry,
and the Scriptures may be seen as three sources of spiritual power in
the past. He then described how the reappearing myth of the Titans
in these three early forms of civilization revealed the continuing
power of "race-images and race-ideas." Finally he examined some of
the poetry of Spenser, Milton, Wordsworth, and Shelley to demonstrate that their "essential greatness and value" was proportional to
the extent that they availed themselves of the "race-store." But
Woodberry was specifically opposed to the celebration of the race as
the ultimate object of loyalty. He pushed through to the ideal of

humanity by solemnizing the sacrificial destiny of the race. "Nay, if the aristocracy of the whole white race is to melt in a world of the colored races of the earth, I for one should only rejoice in such an approach to the sacrificial idea in history; for it would mean the humanization of mankind."[26]

His emphasis, obviously, is less on the delight that literature might inspire—although, like Aristotle and Coleridge, Woodberry admitted that delight was the "direct aim" of literature—than on the human uses that literature serves. Literature provides enjoyment in the sense that pleasure derives from the form. But instruction comes from the matter, and this is primary, because the intention of literature is to present truth under the guise of a social instrument. Ideally, since they are collaborators in the effort to understand our own selves and our own experiences, both the reader and the artist should possess a lively curiosity, sensitivity, and interest in life. And both should understand that the end of literature is to explain experience. "The material is still experience, but it is experience transformed by being newly arranged and it is life expressed rather in its function of power than in its operation of reality."[27] Woodberry admitted that there were other ways to observe human beings. But outside of direct observation and experience he held that literature is "the principal means of obtaining knowledge of human life."[28]

His own critical tastes are illustrated by the attitudes that Woodberry took toward Lowell and Matthew Arnold. In his review of Lowell's *Democracy and Other Addresses*, Woodberry not only defended Lowell against the current charge of distrusting democracy but, in associating Lowell's critical principles with those of Coleridge, distinguished Lowell from the realists—since an acceptance of Coleridge's theory of imagination helped one to hold that universal experience was the only genuine reality that we might hope to understand. Rephrasing Lowell, Woodberry pointed out that if experience is too particular, central only to the psychology of one individual, it might be interesting as a social aberration. But otherwise it is of little account, since the only significant form of human communication is shared experience. In this position of Lowell, according to Woodberry, it was possible to discover "the whole organon of the higher criticism," for "the type is the only thing real in an exact sense, and . . . art consists in identifying the individual with the type." Woodberry's argument is a semi-Platonic one of long ancestry, and he argued it with considerable skill in pushing Lowell as the "only critic of the highest rank that our country has produced."[29]

Woodberry was critical of Matthew Arnold. Despite Arnold's obvious social orientation, the English critic showed no real awareness of the evolutionary nature of literature. He was incapable of applying psychological or aesthetic methods to literature with any degree of precision. And his small store of ideas, surprising in view of Arnold's popularity, when combined with a "stiffly didactic" evangelizing style, became monotonous in its "ceaseless iteration."[30] As a critic Arnold's scale was meager. Woodberry felt that the critic should have an abiding interest in human nature, and he should prize the art work as itself final. On both counts Arnold failed. The power, range, and discrimination that Woodberry attributed to Lowell and Coleridge were remarkably lacking in Arnold, who in his work on education and politics and on theological and religious tendencies seemed more a cultural critic than a critic of imaginative literature. Part of Arnold's popularity, Woodberry felt, might be attributed to making his readers respect the few ideas he did have, and in directing his readers toward worthwhile continental writers. A less attractive reason for Arnold's popularity, in Woodberry's mind, was Arnold's habit of making the reader party to his "malicious pleasure" in visiting the "chastisement of irony" on men he disliked.

Arnold's famous indictment of Shelley may also account for Woodberry's reservations about his critical judgment. An early admirer of Wendell Phillips, Woodberry adored liberty to the point where it verged upon license. He was outraged by the plight of the Indian and Negro in this country, and was in sympathy with all reform efforts to alleviate their condition. Shelley he celebrated as preeminently the spokesman for the idealized spirit of the French Revolution. He wrote in all six essays on Shelley, and in 1892 published an edition of the poems and the Harvard *Shelley Notebook,* both of which still have some objective value. This work tends to confirm Julia Power's observation that "Woodberry's contribution to Shelley criticism far exceeds both in quality and quantity that of any other American of the century."[31] To the often stated charge that Shelley's artistic and practical instincts frequently worked at cross-purposes, Woodberry replied that it is in the tension between these two that we encounter such fine poems as "Ode to the West Wind" and "Adonais." For the rest, Shelley's love of liberty, his fusion in such poems as "Prometheus Unbound" of the Greek idea of commitment and the Christian idea of love, his mythmaking ability in general, and his revolutionary but peaceful fervor in anticipating a future when men might live together in love, all seemed to Woodberry so connected with his own concept of the race mind that in "A New Defense of Poetry" he urged his readers to "idealize your masters and take Shelley and Sidney to your bosom, so shall they serve you nobly."

Woodberry's criticism of American literature is uneven. *America in Literature*, ostensibly written to gain perspective on "the recent and rising world of letters," is really a collection of essays published at different times. It is chiefly interesting for its sectional approach, with essays on the Knickerbockers, literary Boston, the South, and the West. Elsewhere Woodberry had reviewed books of Howells and James, but he omits consideration of them in this book. He was not sympathetic to Howells' concern with "minute felicities," and his general objections to realism, while muted and tactful, are clear enough. The discussion of Western writers is limited to Harte, Joaquin Miller, and Lew Wallace, who are described as "three romancers." There is nothing on Mark Twain beyond a sentence dismissing him as a humorist and a "type of popular celebrity." Two pages are devoted to Whitman as the author of "a few fine lyrics." But Woodberry was uneasy before Whitman's "democratic crudity" and the "pure primitiveness" of his idealism. Having stressed romanticism along with its European parallels, and having practically omitted the solid literature of his own day, Woodberry found it relatively easy to reproach later American writers for the "inadequacy" of their achievement.

Woodberry's coolness toward Emerson is also troublesome, especially since most commentators have stressed Woodberry's great debt to New England individualism and to Platonism. Owning in *Emerson* (1907) that he had "little intellectual sympathy" for the man in any way, Woodberry charged that "no modern mind can abide his ideas." Yet he was forced to conclude that Emerson was perhaps the "only great mind" that America had produced. Among some seven of "Emerson's limitations," which included "blindness to the life of humanity" and denial of the significance of "institutional life," the one most serious to Woodberry was the charge that Emerson "slighted history, science, art and letters, and religion, the entire recorded life of the race." Emerson's inspiring doctrine of the emancipation of the individual could account, Woodberry thought, for his "broad and profound" influence. But to Woodberry the individual, no matter what the strength of his "faculty and fortune," added little to the total sum of civilization. It would appear that in 1907 when Woodberry was engaged in publishing his essays on great writers, such as the excellent one on Virgil, Emerson had the misfortune to run afoul of Woodberry's strong and central regard for the "race-mind" as embodied in tradition.

Woodberry's books on Poe and Hawthorne, however, are both in their ways impressive biographical interpretations. His 1909 revision of the biography of Poe, first published in 1885, uses new data from both the Griswold and the Poe-Chivers papers, and makes about twenty-five corrections in the correspondence prepared by J. A. Harrison. In both the biography and *America in Literature* Poe is pictured as a literary loner, a critic with "well-reasoned standards of taste and art who wrote a few excellent pieces of criticism," and an original in lyric tone and mood in selected poems and stories. The affliction that prevented Poe from realizing his full potential was his southern heritage. To Woodberry, the South was "outside the current of the age." It consequently lacked any coherent body of ideas, and was intellectually stifled by those morbid, dark, and gruesome characteristics of mood Woodberry located in southern regions of the world. Needless to say, they were characteristics in which Poe was thought to share profoundly.

Hawthorne was published in 1902, and *Hawthorne, How to Know Him* in 1918. Both reveal a masterly approach to the short stories, to the symbolism, and to *The Marble Faun*, which Woodberry rated higher than *The Scarlet Letter*. Generally sympathetic to Hawthorne's achievement, Woodberry was especially helpful in pointing out how Hawthorne's imagery reinforced thematic concerns without "loss of distinctness" in his vision. Woodberry found a progressive deepening and sophistication in Hawthorne's handling of imagery, from the early and "obvious" imagery in "The Minister's Black Veil" through stories like "Lady Eleanor's Mantle," "The Birthmark," and "Rappaccini's Daughter." "The Artist of the Beautiful" was the culmination of Hawthorne's craftsmanship. In this story, Woodberry said, image and idea were fused so completely as to constitute an identity. The story itself could stand as the crown of Hawthorne's achievement in subtlety, thought, and artistic workmanship. Woodberry's whole discussion is well argued, and aptly illustrates that he was perfectly capable at his best of combining a concern for specific literary problems with reflection on the broader substantive development of a writer's thought and art.

B. *Brander Matthews (1852–1929)*

Brander Matthews disliked what he termed Woodberry's diluted idealism, and as academic colleagues relations between the two men were often strained. But Matthews too may be viewed as a critical idealist—in many respects its most attractive personality. A wonderfully sophisticated man, Matthews was for thirty-two years professor of English at Columbia University, where he informed his teaching with an unusual hedonism provided him by his native New Orleans background, considerable travel, and many literary friendships, including a very close one with Mark Twain. In his fondness for abstract literary standards, his commitment to the skills and purposes of literary history, his instinctive attraction to problems of technique, and his distaste for the overtly moral and didactic, Matthews shared in the critical views of the idealists. But he paradoxically combined these interests with a lifelong regard for Jules Lemaitre, which made Matthews markedly susceptible to impressionistic criticism.

In his autobiographic recollections, *These Many Years* (1919), Matthews listed four qualifications of a critic: insight, scholarly equipment, disinterestedness, and sympathy.[32] As a scholar, he sought to put himself in the author's time and place and to adopt the author's point of view, to select truly representative quotations, and to stick to the text under analysis rather than write a parallel essay. These points, modest enough in intent, have not been well observed by critics in practice, and it is to Matthews' credit that he reiterated them. Too often, he thought, critics were so partial to one literary view that they could not sympathetically enjoy works outside their self-imposed limits. One of the reasons Mark Twain succeeded as an author but failed as a critic, Matthews wrote, was that Twain insisted on "applying the standards of today to the fiction of yesterday." Furthermore, Twain was really defending various theses based on the principles of critical realism, and was thus not properly objective in dealing with such issues as Sir Walter Scott's views on chivalry or Fenimore Cooper's use of diction and dramatic coincidence. The more broadly sympathetic critic, on the other hand, was unencumbered by loyalty to a single literary movement and could help readers understand and enjoy the most diverse forms of literature. Most importantly, the reader could be brought to some sharpened awareness of the literary styles of writers and to the best of contemporary literature.

Matthews' emphasis on technique foreshadows some important

trends in modern criticism. He was a pioneer in urging more attention to form at a time notorious for stressing the nebulous idea of "soul" in literature. His essay on the short story shrewdly extended the views of Poe to encompass the short story as a literary form. Matthews also pointed out that the author is not always the best guide to his intentions, since frequently the author's best effects are subconscious.[33] He sided with Lowell and Lounsbury in attacking "Briticisms" and Oxford artificialities as manifestations of social snobbery. And in his discussion of drama, a form that he found continually intriguing, he antedates G. P. Baker and others in approaching dramatists, especially Shakespeare, from the standpoint of the actual staging of the plays.

In "Literature in the New Century," an address presented before the Belles-lettres Section of the International Congress of the Arts and Sciences in 1904, Matthews compressed into half a dozen pages most of the current thinking about the nature of literature and its relation to his time. The essay centers on "four legacies from the nineteenth to the twentieth century: first, the scientific spirit; second, the spread of democracy; third, the assertion of nationality; and fourth, that stepping across the confines of language and race, for which we have no more accurate name than 'cosmopolitanism.' "[34] He was especially intrigued by the way that science might stimulate art and criticism, though he felt that we should remain suspicious of the "sterile application of scientific formulas" and scientific findings, or the use of scientific theories in art. Here he thought the evolutionary criticism of Brunetière proved helpful. Matthews does not seem to have been bothered by the solemn moralizing in Brunetière that so provoked Huneker. Brunetière, in tracing changes in the morphology of literary forms, had shown how such forms "may cross-fertilize each other." And the writers themselves were representative voices of their cultures, since the material they used was "the whole complex of conceptions, religious, imaginative and ethical," which formed their "mental atmosphere."[35] Evolutionary concepts like these directed Matthews toward a criticism which was relative, descriptive, and dominated by appreciative sympathy, even while he continued to maintain that past literary masters might serve as judicial yardsticks against which the critic could measure instead of merely describe.

Matthews knew that too exclusive an attention to modern literature could finally numb a critic's judgment. He acknowledged that "few contemporary writings are masterpieces," and that it was best to remain a moderate spokesman for the better aspects of tradition. But Matthews was just as much a mediator and advocate of modernism. He recognized the genius of *Huckleberry Finn* and claimed that Twain should be regarded as a match for Cervantes and Molière rather than simply a Western wit. He thought Howells' *The Rise of Silas Lapham* a masterpiece. He respected James' criticism and consistently maintained that James was one of our leading writers of fiction. He followed the fortunes of writers like Stevenson, Daudet, Zola, and Maupassant. And he promoted the work of younger men like Elmer Rice.

An author himself of stories and dramas, Matthews' interest in recent literature was spurred by the quality of craftsmanship he detected in his contemporaries. The technical advances he found in Turgenev, Howells, and Garland pointed to a continuing growth in the creative process that criticism should welcome. Earlier, in 1874, George Parsons Lathrop had explored the growth of the novel and its future in two companion essays in *The Atlantic Monthly* which also revealed a deep interest in contemporary fiction. Lathrop's major interest was in the dramatic quality of fiction, phrased in terms he had inherited from the critical idealists. But Lathrop could not invest the terms with as much meaning as could Matthews, who also used various Coleridgean terms like imagination and fancy, creativity and invention, to describe the successes that authors had in combining style and thought to achieve intellectual depth.[36] But it is in Matthews's emphasis on the technical dimension that his criticism is distinctive, pointing the way to the subtler explications of literature in the twentieth century.

C. *Edmund Clarence Stedman (1833–1908)*

Granting the grace, charm, and sophistication of Matthews, Edmund Clarence Stedman is still by all odds the most significant of the critical idealists who came after Emerson and Lowell, and the most representative of that critical tradition. Woodberry's criticism was most apt when dealing with classicists like Virgil and romantics like Shelley. Then the tone and quality of his writing lose their discursiveness and become charged with an eloquent style that helps to explain his contemporary popularity. At these times Woodberry's criticism warrants more than antiquarian interest, just as Matthews's graceful tone of personal intimacy with literary personalities like Twain, Howells, and Kipling increases the credibility of his criticism.

But if one comes down to the important matter of the range and acumen of the critical mind itself, its accuracy in apprehending literary value in writing, and its ability to forthrightly state its critical standards, then for critical idealism one considers Stedman.

Stedman is a sort of "dean" of post–Civil War critical idealism. After Emerson and Lowell one of the first to uphold the tradition they had helped to initiate, Stedman formed part of a literati in New York City that came to have considerable power. Plagued through a good bit of his life by ill-health, which may have been partly psychosomatic, and forced to devote much of his time to his Wall Street brokerage house, he nevertheless was able to be an active member of the Author's Club, a practicing poet, and a productive critic.

The sturdiness of Stedman's criticism partly derives from the fact that he clearly defined to himself the reasons for his literary preferences. Partly it derives from an early acquaintance with Poe's work, which resulted in a collaboration with Woodberry to write Poe's biography. In general, his critical principles are based on a somewhat ingenious blending of the critical views of Emerson and Poe—not so unusual when one remembers the Platonic idealism of those two men. He shared Emerson's taste for poetry as the highest form of literature, together with a disinclination to see much of value in current fiction. And from Poe he got the example of a careful formulation of critical criteria for the judgment of literary works. Stedman questioned the prevailing equation of beauty and moral statement, and emphasized craftsmanship. And like most of his contemporaries, he was influenced by the current respect for a theory of "progressive" history, which is to be chiefly found in his *Victorian Poets* (1887), based on the historical methods of Taine; his edition of *A Library of American Literature* (1888–1890), an eleven-volume set edited by Stedman and Ellen Hutchinson; and *An American Anthology* (1900), a book unusual in the fact that it included poems by Melville, Dickinson, and E. A. Robinson at a time when practically all critics and anthologists were ignoring these people. But along with his theories of historical literary development, Stedman consistently held that the real world was found in the ordered mind, in which values had their origin and validity.

One finds elements of puffery in Stedmen's critical references to friends, and he certainly was deferential to the point of servility when confronted with the New England tradition. But his editorship of the *Century* accounted for some first-rate writing, including that of many realists, and when compared to the more conservative policy of

Joseph Gilder and James H. Morse in the *Critic*, Stedman's balance and perspicuity become all the more evident. He was simply incapable of the sentimental preference for romance over realism advocated by a person like Twain's old collaborator, Charles Dudley Warner.[37] According to Willard Thorp, Stedman's instincts were true if sometimes disguised: "If we peel off his elaborate praise of the elder poets as kind neighbors and good citizens, we come, time and again, on the hard core of a valid judgment."[38]

Stedman's dislike of realism was of long standing, and based on literary preferences. He simply adhered to the primacy of poetry at a time when fiction dominated the scene—a poignant position with which many today can be in sympathy. The fiction itself and the Western ballads which often appealed to principles of realism were scarcely uniformly high in quality. The poor presentation of dialect, the frequent lapses into the most turgid writing (about which even Howells complained), and the overripe sentimentality were enough to disenchant a sensitive critic like Stedman. Realism as a critical theory did not seem to have much to offer, since it apparently affirmed a "servilely accurate imitation of nature" that resulted in writing that was not very perceptive. Writers should be realists in knowledge, Stedman thought, but they should be idealists in interpretation. That is, the real assessment of a writer must be based on how he *handles* the material he knows: "the quality of the writer, his power of expression, the limits of his character."[39] If these criteria are impartially applied, Stedman said, then the presumed antagonism between realist and idealist is seen as a "forced one," for all differences finally devolve upon the inherent power of the writer himself.

Stedman's squeamishness is another matter. His continuing appreciation of Whitman and Swinburne at a time when these poets were largely unacceptable and his later attraction to Mark Twain indicate that Stedman could step aside from his "gentility" to dispassionately assess a writer's ability. He was not prudish, as many would have it. It was simply that the ideal world had no place for the processes of generation and decay. His devotion was to beauty, to the healing power of poetry, the excellence of passion—all of them qualities of man's spiritual impulses. He did not always understand the full spirit of these principles. His lyrical impulses resulted only in poems of a thin and tenuous strain, while his prose reveals too often a self-conscious indulgence in flowers of rhetoric too delicate to carry much intellectual effect.

The Nature and Elements of Poetry, the published result of his Turnbull lectures at John Hopkins in 1891, is in a sense the final summing up of Stedman's critical position and an exceedingly good presentation of the tenets that formed his critical idealism. His two major points are neo-Platonic in origin: the poet is possessed by the *furor divinus*, or divine fury of inspiration; and this inspiration provides him insight into the quintessence of nature. The artist thus possesses an "inward vision" or "second sight" that amounts to a prophetic gift. For this reason the essential spirit of poetry is indefinable, Stedman thought, even though it is to be apprehended by a "faculty" that all people possess, though in varying degrees.[40] But if the spirit of poetry is not reducible to critical formulation—a position which Stedman developed with some skill—it does nevertheless point to the intimate union of two aspects of poetry: its rhythmical, imaginative quality, and its revelation of the "invention, taste, thought, passion, and insight" of the author himself. Consequently, the poetic spirit in its "absolute and primal" sense becomes a particular means for expressing an "art-ideal" or creative idea that embodies both beauty and truth. Our first response is to beauty in terms of our reaction to the cadences of rhythmic construction of the artist's language, which become more urgent in proportion to intensity of emotion. The mark of the great poem, then, and indirectly of the poet, is the rhythmical sophistication of the language, a position that I. A. Richards would later develop at length and with persuasive force.

Going on, Stedman defined beauty as a quality that "lies in a vibratory expression of substance." This definition would seem to concentrate on the expressive nature of beauty, a position later adopted by Joel Spingarn in his aesthetic criticism. But Stedman also held that beauty inhered in the substance itself, and the substance of literature was drawn from human experience. When expressed honestly and well, the truth that underlay experience was perceived by both the writer and reader. Hence truth and beauty ultimately become "equivalent terms," an insight we come to accept when we appreciate the power of imagination. By itself, experience is inert and discrete. But subjected to the transforming power of the imagination, the inert becomes vital and the discrete becomes part of nature's harmony. And since the imagination is uniquely a faculty of man, a creature whose every action necessarily has some moral implication, imaginative wisdom is in essence ethical.[41] The ethical is real insight, real understanding, as these result from a deliberate exploration of experience. A prosaic moral or "pedagogic formulas of truth," on the other hand, are tedious and uninformative precisely because they are imposed on experience from without. "Affective conviction, affectation of any kind, and even sincere conviction inartistically set forth, are vices in themselves,—are antagonistic to truth."[42]

Stedman's emphasis on beauty in art is probably indebted to Poe, while his emphasis on the truthful and imaginative depiction of experience is indebted to the New England romantic tradition, and particularly to Emerson and Lowell. His conviction that real life includes the commonplace but is not confined to it, developed in opposition to the advocates of realism, is sound and defensible, as is his belief that the primary qualifications of the critic are accuracy, taste, and honesty. The idea that an extraneous moral, or a didactic purpose, is injurious to good literature is one that has found common acceptance. Stedman's entire focus is on the integrity of the work of art itself, its vitality, its understanding of the complex nature of real experience. His misfortune was an excessive veneration of tradition, mainly because it inhibited his judgment and because it encouraged him to develop a "model" of the perfect piece of literature which could be used for comparative purposes. The expense was too great, for the model often came to substitute for Stedman's own perspicuity and good sense. The result was that he failed to give the particular work its just due. Yet in being the first to anthologize Emily Dickinson and Herman Melville, and in heralding the genius of Whitman and later of Mark Twain, Stedman's perception was true.

D. Walt Whitman (1819–1892)

Walt Whitman too represents the continuance of critical idealism, though not with the cultivated good manners of Stedman, Mabie, Woodberry, and Matthews. In his critical work, Whitman's tone as the guru of idealistic nationalism is impressively prophetic in celebrating the virtues of democratic freedom, of science, and of the primacy of the self. But in his application of critical principles to existing authors, Whitman tends to be brief and generally unimpressive. As a critic he is important for critical principles which are chiefly significant for their oracular concern for a new kind of national literature. Partly transcendental if not mystical, Whitman associated his doctrine of organic expression and development with his favorite themes, immense evolutionary time and progressive growth. His tone was frequently eschatological as he theorized about the "divine literatus" who would breathe new life and taste into the republic. He found little in his own time to support his optimism. In *Democratic Vistas* he scornfully posed the question: "Do you call those genteel little creatures American poets? Do you term that perpetual, pistoreen, paste-pot work, American art, American drama, taste, verse?"[43]

Whitman obviously did not. He had his ear tuned to the mountaintop laughter of the "Genius of these States." Despite the tremendous volume of printed matter, America continued without anything that could genuinely be called literature. He lamented the self-indulgence which used writing as a "stimulus" for the "sensational appetite," while the "endless thread of tangled and superlative" love stories seemed intended only "to amuse, to titillate, to pass away time."[44] America, he thought, was floundering in a sea of "copious dribble." The country longed for but was unable to imagine a poetry that, inspired by "science and the modern," would be "all-surrounding and kosmical."[45] Whitman insisted that science and the modern meant "exposure in everything," a point which he tried to illustrate in "I Sing the Body Electric" and other poems grouped in *Leaves of Grass* under the "Children of Adam" and "Calamus" subheadings. More particularly, it could mean that the details of sexual intercourse might serve as major material in literature, as his nine-page latter to Emerson in 1856 indicates.[46] But beyond *Democratic Vistas*, Whitman in his actual criticism of others does not seem to have given much emphasis to sex.

Unlike Lowell, who could prepare long and rounded critical essays for an audience with academic tastes, Whitman was primarily a journalist whose conversational short papers usually took the form of "melanged cogitations . . . hap-hazard." He is, of course, of considerable historical significance as a literary theorist urging new literary ideals. But, like most critics who single out one thing from the full circumference of the literary world, Whitman's criticism often involves misplaced emphasis. He did not entirely ignore art, form, and beauty, but his remarks on technique and related matters are usually obvious and trite, and are subordinated to an attempt to ascertain an author's attitude toward democracy. For instance, he disliked Scott for his "principles of caste," and even Shakespeare's art, he thought, suffered from a feudal orientation. His essay on Tennyson, on the other hand, is more appreciative and expressionistic than most of Whitman's essays, for he liked Tennyson's personal character, the "vital and genuine" if conventional nature of his morality, and his personal integrity, even though finally Tennyson was a spokesman for "non-democracy."[47] Similarly, Whitman qualified his criticism of Carlyle, whom he considered feudal to the core, with admiration for a strong personality that "refused any compromise to the last."[48]

It is possible to partially excuse Whitman's practical criticism by acknowledging that he did not consider the role of critic very important. Besides commenting on a few well-known authors and writing three anonymous reviews of his own work, Whitman devoted most of his time to the writing and rewriting of his poetry. In his condescending manner he assigned the job of critic to those who do not possess either "passion or imagination or warp or weakness, or any pronounced cause of specialty."[49]

CHAPTER 2

Critical Realism

AS wars are apt to do, the Civil War ended the authority of one literary movement and occasioned the emergence of several rival movements each aspiring to cultural leadership. One of these movements was realism, armed to the teeth with its attendant theories, interdictions, and lines of action. We see now that the movement produced the period's best literature, and that its theories were most apt for the changing texture of the country's culture. But its progress in the early postwar years was slow and often resisted. The critical idealists, committed to literary guidelines formulated in the romantic period, continued to control the major avenues of publication. Furthermore, the venerated "schoolroom" poets—Longfellow, Bryant, Whittier, Emerson, Lowell, and Holmes—dominated the sales charts, though, as Jay Martin suggests, reading them may well have been an exercise in cultural piety designed to reassure the faltering self of "traditional values and aspirations."[1] The realists thus had two tasks: to disabuse readers of their little stock of literary expectations; and to develop fresh tactics to reinforce in them an unwavering commitment to the present.

To the realists, the literary "establishment" seemed too devoted to an abstract beauty that had little to do with the factual nature of people's existence. Beauty seemed an easily surrendered norm when intellectuals were sick to the core of Tammany Society politics and the business practices of General Robert C. Schenck, Daniel Drew, Jay Gould, and Jim Fisk. And of what utility was beauty in describing the convergence on our cities within a three-decade period of six million Germans, Irish, English, and eastern Europeans. Nor did it appear that beauty could provide any decent instrumental frame for seeing the dimensions of the failure of Reconstruction, the opening of the West by mining and cattle interests, or the increasingly regional character of the country. Mark Twain, a realist, had little use for beauty. But he delighted in the invention of the typewriter in 1867.

Somehow the typewriter, as well as the light bulb (1879) and the telephone (1876), seemed much more consequential for literature and for the world at large than abstruse considerations of beauty in one's private chamber. Thomas Bailey Aldrich, who was on the side of beauty, forlorn as that allegiance appeared to be, indicted the new age thus: "Today we breathe a commonplace, / Polemic, scientific air."[2]

As a literary movement, realism was a response to increased interest in prose fiction, the literary needs and interests of all sections of the country, the secularization of the country following social and economic expansion, the wide diffusion of the concepts of popular science, and a general shift in interest, on the part of writers, from English to European authors like Sainte-Beuve, Turgenev, Musset, Taine, Balzac, Maupassant, Brunetière, Scherer, and Flaubert. Of special consequence for literary realism was the rise of a type of genre fiction based on regional prototypes. This fiction, drawing on the diversity of American cultural experience as well as a presentiment that time was running out for those people not part of the mainstream culture, helped to foster a documentary psychology that encouraged writers to pay more attention to specific detail in setting and characterization. Under the new dispensation of objective accuracy, writers were free to record the slang and colloquialisms and idiomatic forms of the language of common folk, with the violence to a "literary" concept of language that one might expect. In *The Story of a Country Town* (1883), for instance, Edgar Watson Howe depicted Kansas life so accurately and grimly that even Mark Twain was moved to approbation, while William Dean Howells, who as much as any critic of the time kept genre writers in the public eye, praised its realism and remarked that it was noteworthy in avoiding the superficial sentimentality that often marred descriptions of regional manners.[3]

Realist theory stressed fidelity to observed experience, the primacy of the observed fact, and the accurate reproduction of the habitual behavior and voices of particular human beings. This emphasis on experience precisely transcribed meant in effect that behavior was broadly taken as an index to character, and that a person was the way he acted. The experience itself would be unveiled and recorded by a dispassionate observer, though some interpretation was allowed and even encouraged. And by putting a central character at the locus of action, as many writers did, there was an unacknowledged provision for registering moral purpose. But in the main, the intent was to describe behavior objectively, and through such description to subtly imply the subjective self within. Furthermore, there was to be little of the editorializing commonly found in romantic fiction. That is, the author would not interrupt the story in order to tell us how we should respond. Often affirmed in theory, the point proved difficult in practice. Edward Eggleston was not alone in pausing to instruct the reader in the interpretation of a scene.

The realists thus took as their literary task the conscious exploration and recording of the "new" age of physical and social mobility, scientific discovery, and increasing secularization of the mind. Complicating this task was a carryover of elements inherited from the romantic period: faith in the ideal destiny of America and in the cultural importance of the writer, moral restraint, sometimes a hyperactive idealism and sentimentality. At times, these disciples of the real found themselves working at cross-purposes. For example, regional writers were often divided between the impulse to "scientifically" record a peculiar way of life and the impulse to indulge in nostalgic regret because that way of life had fallen to the increasing standardization of American experience. Again, many realists were uncertain how to handle the question of the moral nature of art. Should one remain inflexibly clinical in his descriptions, or should certain "pointers" be scattered through the text? In the best work of Howells, Twain, and James, realism has come to stand as a sophisticated mediation between excessive romanticism, with its exalted view of the spiritual unencumbered by direct reference to the seamier circumstantial side of life, and naturalism with its fascination for the pathos of indeterminate and fruitless lives. And for certain scholars realism assumes a dimension so much larger than its historical setting that mediation is no longer a factor. In this view, realism is not only a visually accurate representation of human experience, but it somehow catches up those universal principles that make human experience sane. Realism is then one of two "counters" that seem to inform all literature, the other being romanticism, with naturalism a sort of side-channel for those who have lost their romantic faith.[4]

I   Bret Harte (1836–1902)

In his preface to *The Mystery of Metropolisville*, (1873) Edward Eggleston wrote that "I have at least rendered one substantial though humble service to our literature, if I have portrayed correctly certain forms of American life and manners." This reportorial idea of fiction informs the objectives of most realists of the period. Indeed, Mark Twain professed to rely so exclusively on experience that he consistently denied his status as an artist. With Bret Harte, however, we receive the first critical echoes of realism blending into art. Harte was sympathetic to the regionalists' aim of faithfully chronicling an area and its inhabitants. But while this was one of his chief literary objectives, in criticism his overall aim was to codify taste on a higher level.

Harte was an Easterner who actually spent little time in the West. Taciturn, aloof, financially improvident—personal failings that led Mark Twain to attack him in most savage and querulous ways— Harte's frontier spirit was veneer only. Yet the public persistently regarded him as an essentially Western product. Write as many poems as he wished, demand and recognition centered on his Western tales. And he was good in his craft. In "The Rise of the Short Story" (1899), he tallied his ideals: brevity, concision, no pointed moral, form evolved from the matter itself. Didacticism, excessive sentimentality, the violation by the writer of his own integrity are all literary sins. To the charge that he failed to keep his own house in order, Harte would have responded that his work revealed moral integrity and sentiment, not their pedantic excesses. He assumed that experience was man's educator, and he sought to transmute into art, seldom successfully, his own experience in the commonplaces of Western life.

In keeping with the spirit of the then popular Western story, Harte put much emphasis on humor as a means for gaining effect. He admitted that Artemus Ward's humor was not always artistic, but he pointed out that Ward did not really try for literary "elevation." The statement implies that the critic should not look for what is not there. Humor can be an end in itself. "The Showman has no purpose to subserve beyond the present laugh. He has no wrongs to redress in particular, no especial abuse to attack with ridicule, no moral to point."[5] This concentration on an immediate, limited objective was characteristic of American humor, he thought, and constituted a nationally distinct intellectual quality. Later, Harte broadened his inquiry to view humor as a universal quality that periodically surfaces in various periods and localities of man's history, as it had in the West. Mark Twain had the stature of a national humorist. But Harte speculated that America's "true humorist" was yet to come: "when he does come he will show that a nation which laughs so easily has still a great capacity for deep feeling, and he will, I think, be a little more serious than our present-day humorists."[6]

Later, Harte was to develop a thesis that humor was an essential weapon in emancipating American literature from the authority of Europe. Early American writers, especially Longfellow, Poe, and Hawthorne, followed literary tradition rather than social realities, and for this reason were "distinctly provincial." But in some indistinct fashion humor began to enter American writing. At first stories were transcribed from a rural oral tradition. Pulpits and camp meetings then gave the new writing a certain currency, the public press popularized the form even more, and ultimately the new writing was triumphant. It became known as "American" writing. The new writing had certain common characteristics. It was compact, and yet suggestive. It faithfully recorded the dialect, slang, and habits of thought of various sections of the country. It disdained fine writing but prized originality. It eschewed moral responsibility. In its concision it went directly to the point, and in a few lines could give a "striking photograph of a community or a section."[7]

Harte had hold of a small but striking point in explaining the prominence of the short story in his day. But while short stories were gaining in popularity, he wanted them better. Stories too often reveled in an eccentric mouthpiece useful for "smart sayings, extravagant incident, or political satire," but such gimmicks often undercut complete artistic success.[8] The seriousness which should be an added ingredient in the humorous story was lacking. Without deep intellectual and emotional feeling, humor is like Touchstone without Jacques. Part of the whole is missing. For after laughter we are inclined to be doubly serious. Moreover, such limp stories ultimately pall by their familiarity. They consequently resign what is their most important objective, to keep the reader absorbed in what is going on. The action of a story, Harte thought, should be "continuously and ably sustained," and in order to have the widest popular appeal it should be based upon "the prolonged struggle of man with his particular environment and circumstances."[9] Dumas, for example, moved from a "well-developed plot to a well-defined climax," which prompted Harte to call him "My Favorite Novelist."

Theoretically speaking, Harte could not condemn a writer who faithfully followed his premises to their conclusion, whether that writer wrote as a romanticist, realist, or naturalist. But he himself believed the reader most wants escape, action, and hope, and to be refreshed by lifting his limited horizon by "some specious act of heroism, endeavor, wrongs redressed, and faith rewarded."[10]

Such aims, which smack of more popular forms of writing, were counterbalanced by Harte's insistence upon form and technique. *The Count of Monte Cristo* was good because it interested as a story. A book like Disraeli's *Lothair,* on the other hand, belonged to the "Post-pliocene period of novel-writing" because of its vapid characterization, its self-conscious and inflated style, and the flatness of its diction.[11] As for the more syrupy concoctions of earnest but poor writers, Harte had no use for this "indigestible moral pie, sensational hot coffee, sentimental tea, and emotional soda water."[12] He looked, as he said, for an honest treatment of "characteristic American life, with absolute knowledge of its peculiarities and sympathy with its methods."[13] The conventional fastidiousness that avoided slang and folk expressions he thought unbearable, nor did he like any "moral determination" in excess of what the story itself might allow. Once all these criteria were observed and realized, however, Harte professed to be satisfied, and was even prepared to accept a story with an overt purpose or "moral."

II   *Mark Twain (1835–1910)*

Harte was born in New York state, as was Nasby, and Artemus Ward and Josh Billings were born in New England. But Mark Twain was born in the West and was part of the West. He became famous living in the West, and then, at the age of thirty-two, arrived in the East, married, settled in New England, and proceeded to acquire culture. If the East made him conscious of larger things than being a mere humorist, it was the West that gave him his materials and made the name of Mark Twain easily the most familiar of all American novelists.

Twain was paradoxically a realist and an idealist, a dreamer of dreams. He was not by temperament a sound and dispassionate critic, and most of his critical essays are really illustrative of his favored principles of writing, a defect noted by Brander Matthews when he remarked that Twain persistently applied modern literary standards to the literature of past periods. Most critical realists were ahistorical and had but a limited interest in past literature. Twain was no exception. The most noticeable trait about his literary taste is his keen aversion to feudalism and the type of chivalry glamorized by Malory and Walter Scott. He disliked the absence of humanitarian and equalitarian principles in the feudal caste system, and he thought that writers utilizing the conventions of feudalism betrayed deplorable stylistic weaknesses. On this latter ground, he indicted Scott for creating characters whose acts and speech patterns failed to specify station and origins, since the characters all used the same kind of speech. Twain himself placed great emphasis on a truly organic relation between the racial and geographical backgrounds and the social levels of fictional characters, and felt that there should be a corresponding individualization of their speech. This view was the subject of his brief "Explanatory" preface to *Huckleberry Finn:* "In this book a number of dialects are used, to wit: the Missouri Negro dialect; the extremist form of the backwoods South-Western dialect; the ordinary 'Pike-county' dialect; and four modified versions of this last. The shadings have not been done in a haphazard fashion, or by guess-work; but painstakingly, and with the trustworthy guidance and support of personal familiarity with the several forms of speech." Such a concern for the vernacular was related on one side to Twain's training in close observation, and on the other side to his belief in the democratic right of each individual to be himself, especially in the completely natural manner of expression. Hence his dislike for Scott's "nickel-plated artificial words," as well as for the mincing literary "cake-walk" that Twain detected in Dowden's biography of Shelley.[14]

In his own nonfictional passages, Twain sought a "strong, compact, direct, and unflowery" style. Especially concerned for the precise word in an individually precise emotional situation, Twain wittily indicted Scott for using the right word only when he could not think of another. He deplored Cooper's "literary offenses" sufficiently to write a sequel on "further" literary offenses. Cooper's language, he claimed, was a "flowing and voluminous and costly raiment" so overdone that the romances scarcely had anything real about them at all. But when Twain detected felicitous language, he was quick to appreciation. He admired Howells' handling of the drunkenness scene in *A Modern Instance.* And one reason for his admiration of Dickens, which he reported in the *Alta California* in 1868, was that despite the British accent and deficiencies in his oral presentation, Dickens was in control of his writing: he was a "puissant god" who "could create men and women and put the breath of life into them and alter all their ways and actions, elevate them, degrade them, murder them, marry them, conduct them through joy and sorrow, on their long march from the cradle to the grave, and never make a mistake."[15]

Since Twain is popularly known as a teller of humorous stories, his remarks on "How to Tell a Story" are especially interesting in revealing how self-conscious a craftsman Twain considered himself. He had lived, he says, "almost daily in the company of the most expert story-tellers for many years: men like Artemus Ward, Dan Setchell, Bill Nye, James Whitcomb Riley, all masters of the art." Twain had no hesitation in claiming his mastery of the theory, though he did not claim to be able to practice it. He regarded the humorous story, as did Harte initially, as a home-grown American product, "strictly a work of art—high and delicate art—and only an artist can tell it." To Twain, the essence of the storyteller's art is to seemingly ramble, to use the pause in the most delicate and dainty manner possible, and then casually drop the point or "snapper" so as to slur the impression and create a delayed reaction.

The counterpart to "How to Tell a Story" is Twain's constant rehearsing of his stories to gain an extemporaneous and immediate effect.[16] As Twain wrote Livy in 1871, his routine lecture-preparation involved "the same old practising on audiences" to feel their pulse and to accommodate to their mood. "The very same lecture that convulsed Great Barrington was received with the gentlest smiles in rippling comfort by Milford. Now we'll see what Boston is going to do."[17] As a public lecturer, Twain sought to respond to the expectations of successive "live" audiences composed largely of average rather than elite Americans. Delivering his individual story-episodes as public "lectures" before audiences provided him the live laboratory in which he could test the effects of various modes of expression. The lessons learned undoubtedly influenced his literary and critical theories.

Twain was reared in a faith that stressed the salvation of the elect through grace alone and a rigid moral code. He later abandoned this form of Calvinist Christianity. But his acceptance of Darwinism, in which he envisaged life as a struggle for existence and nature as "vicious, treacherous, and malignant," did not appreciably alter his generally deterministic views. Instead, he was prompted to emphasize the need for fictional characters who should reflect the interpenetration of character and environment, of ideals and the physical history of the race. In the essay "What Paul Bourget Thinks of Us," he suggested that a novelist should begin with a place that he knows best and then present his characters as developing and maturing in association with that place. Twain himself had an unusual devotion to what Walter Blair calls "the matter of Hannibal." And Twain tells us that the legacy of his riverboat piloting on the Mississippi, in which he had to learn every submerged rock and shoal in twelve hundred miles of river, disciplined his powers of observation, his memory and his self-dependence. On the river, too, he encountered and observed practically every type of human being. Retrospect, then, as well as an engrained determinism, played a large part in his work. Consequently such a foreigner as Bourget could not hope to understand the American people: "There is only one expert who is qualified to examine the souls and life of a people and make a valuable report—the native novelists. . . . Almost the whole capital of the novelist is the slow accumulation of *un*conscious observation—absorption."[18] Artists learned of people through living among them, and observation based simply on external vision uninformed by sympathetic understanding was of little account. So committed was Twain to this view that Bernard DeVoto concludes that "it is here [in the relation of character to environment] that Mark Twain's fiction attains his highest values. The community exists as it has never existed elsewhere in American fiction."[19]

Part of Twain's distaste for current romances and historical novels was based on this belief that the relationship between persons and places is organic. Writers respond best to their own deep-rooted memories. Writing to Livy in 1873, Twain praised his mother as the "best letter-writer in the world, because she threw such an atmosphere of her locality & her surroundings into her letters that the reader was transported. . . ."[20] Finally, Twain was led to deny that writers ever "created" a character. Fred Lorch quotes an 1895 interview with Twain in the *Oregonian* in which Twain argued that recollection and composite blending of real persons were the real capital of the writer: "Even when he is making no attempt to draw his character from life, when he is striving to create something different, even then, however ideal his drawing, he is yet unconsciously drawing from memory."[21]

The tendency of romance to drift into artificial and theatrical emotion for emotion's sake also accounts for Twain's aversion to that class of fiction. *Joan of Arc* has its share of sentimentality, and in much of his work Twain is the poet of nostalgia, but in general his Western origins, his own move to industrial Hartford, and his interest in technology conditioned a strong dislike for the romantic past. In *Huckleberry Finn* phony sentimentality is dismissed as "flapdoodle," and the manufactured graveyard elegy of the late Emmeline Grangerford is discounted in a parody of the whole graveyard school. He had little use for the antebellum glories popularly associated with the defeat of the agrarian South. "The History of a Campaign that Failed" plays down military heroics, and in a letter he attacked the correspondent Will Bowen for "drooling about the sweet yet melancholy past" which could not be restored: "My idea was to kill his nasty sham sentimentality once and forever."[22] And the famous attack on Walter Scott in *Life on the Mississippi* centers on Twain's sardonic claim that Scott's influence in perpetuating feudalism in the South had caused the Civil War.

Despite these apparently strong statements of belief, Twain remained ambivalent about his objectives as a writer throughout his career. He fluctuated between a simple intent to interest and an attempt to instruct. His intent to interest was partly temperamental, partly defensive. Disciplined, reserved intellectualism, which struck him as encouraging a roundabout, anemic approach to fiction, put him out of patience. Thus he thought that George Eliot, Henry James, and Hawthorne allowed the swift flow of narrative to be impeded while as would-be psychologists they analyzed "the guts out of their characters."[23] In a defensive mood, he wrote Andrew Lang in 1889 that his own program was entertainment for "the masses" rather than for the "cultivated classes." He was, he said, writing simply to amuse, catering to the "Belly and its Members." The great writer may be like a comet appearing once a century, but Twain imagined himself the warming and cheering sun which beams every day. And he warned Lang that the critic should observe such intentions in the writer. Given differences in objectives, it was wrong for the critic to bring all writers to one standard. Instead, the writer should follow his idiosyncratic bent. The critic, for his part, should judge these performances of the writers according to standards "proper to each."[24]

These views help to explain the tack of Twain's 1906 essay on William Dean Howells. In that essay he quotes Howells and Macaulay side by side to enforce his view of Howells' superiority in stylistic clarity, vigor, and avoidance of the artificial and the sentimental. Nowhere in the essay appears any consideration of Howells'

Altrurian or utopian humanitarianism, his concern for the psychology
of "The Heroines of Fiction," his interest in American manners and
the contrasts between classes in books like *A Chance Acquaintance*
(1873), or the great crusade for realism as opposed to the sentimental
and the romantic.[25] Yet at least in some respects these interests were
ones Twain shared. Until *The American Claimant* (1892), he wrote
primarily as a democratic humanitarian. He had been sympathetic to
the French Revolution.[26] And he conceived it his duty to attack
feudal stratification and to express warm sympathies for the advancement of the people. Part of his work had a clear social-political
didacticism (as Louis Budd and Phillip Foner have shown), as he tried
to pry "up to a higher level to manhood" readers addicted to habitual
acquiescence in their poverty and subordination. Twain's "To a
Person Sitting in Darkness" and his denunciation of King Leopold's
inhuman treatment of blacks in the Congo, among similar later
works, justify the judgments of George Bernard Shaw and others,
who have regarded Twain as a great writer who used satire to effect
beneficent social reforms and to excoriate departures from his form of
humanitarian belief.[27]

Twain moved a long way from humor for its own sake in the story of
the blue jay in *A Tramp Abroad* (1880) to the mordant satire of *The
Mysterious Stranger* (posthumously published in 1916). In the latter
book, Twain wrote that man's greatest weapon against wrong is the
power of ridiculing evil systems. Admitting that satiric laughter is the
"one really effective weapon" against evil, Satan adds that mankind so
far has lacked the sense and courage to use it. By 1898, groping for
some way to explain his personal misfortunes, Twain wrote that the
public should be weaned away from going to the theater for merely
light entertainment. He prescribed a "tragedy-tonic once or twice a
month" as a substitute.[28] His later view that all humanity is tainted
and that we all share a common doom moved him to react positively to
Wilbrandt's *Der Mesiter von Palmyra* (which he considered a "stately
metaphysical poem"), Edgar Watson Howe's *The Story of a Country
Town*, and Emile Zola's *La Terre*, all of which stress the dark
situations of men in this world. Twain always remained interested in
the vernacular and the differentiation of character through speech
shadings. But his turn to mordant satiric power to "ridicule, not
reverence" pretension, sham, and humbug moved him away, except
in occasional letters, from the freewheeling humorous expression of
his gustos and disgustos which so pleased H. L. Mencken.

III   *William Dean Howells (1837–1920)*

William Dean Howells was Twain's best friend and literary confidant. Born and raised in a small Ohio town, Howells' literary career was largely oriented toward journalism. In his 1901 essay on Mark Twain, Howells explained Twain's genesis and evolution (and presumably his own) by the fact that they were both reared according to frontier "values," came to the New England world of the "financier, the scholar, the gentleman," where they were first inclined to laugh at what seemed droll novelties, and in time were obliged to think over afresh "the whole field [and] conventions of the modern world." Like Twain, Howells had little formal education. His education was his reading. Irving, Cervantes, Heine, and Tennyson, whose early influence is chronicled in *My Literary Passions* (1895), introduced him to the world of fiction. Later influences such as Goldoni, Turgenev, and Taine helped him to expand his appreciation of the significance of literature for human life. And in *Heroines of Fiction* (1901), he documented his responses to Jane Austen, George Eliot, and a host of other women writers, all of whom he regarded as reinforcing his distinctive insights into feminine "psychology."

Upon his return to Boston following a four-year sojourn as consul in Venice, a reward for his campaign biography of Lincoln, Howells was "adopted" into the circle of Longfellow, who was at the time translating Dante. Lowell, Norton, and Holmes befriended him, leading James T. Fields to appoint him assistant editor to the *Atlantic Monthly*, of which he became chief editor (1871–1881). There he opened the doors to friends like James and Twain and wrote nearly fifty influential reviews of books in the cause of realism. But Howells' more belligerent crusade for realism, which gradually became colored by a concern for brotherhood and a semi-Christian socialism, was published after 1886, when he wrote brief editorials for "The Editor's Study" and "The Editor's Easy Chair" for *Harper's Monthly*. In a word, from his early apprenticeship on the *Ohio State Journal*, where he crusaded for such reforms as the abolition of slavery, to his work at *Harper's* until 1920, Howells as a critic was strongly conditioned by the higher journalism.

Literary Friends and Acquaintance (1900), on the New England leaders, and *My Mark Twain* (1910), written in a nostalgic mood, show his distinctive ability to present authors in their natural habitats, with partly impressionistic critical insights associated with their personalities. In other moods he responded to expanding political and economic interests and to the writings of Tolstoy, Gronlund, Garland, H. D. Lloyd, Bellamy, and Henry George. The result was a kind of criticism—perhaps not entirely characteristic—which was quite judicially severe, as when he claimed that three-fifths of the supposedly standard authors, such as Walter Scott, were intrinsically "dead" insofar as they had tended to defend feudalism and monarchy. But of all the advocates of realism, he was by far the most prolific, with nearly a hundred books of various sorts, and about eighteen hundred book reviews. He thus had an enormous influence in molding the literary tastes of great numbers of readers.

Howells was a good critic, though not a great critic like James. W. C. Brownell thought him too multifaceted. No man who engaged in discrete literary forms like criticism, fiction, poetry, and drama was apt to be successful in any. Another contemporary, Brander Matthews, took a different view. After noting that Turgenev and Flaubert had neglected criticism in favor of their art, and thus denied us the benefit of their thought, Matthews in what was on the whole a favorable review went on to praise Howells for the honesty and fidelity of his critical views.[29] Indeed, Howells, as Matthews suggests, not only delivered himself of his literary theory but went on to do the unpardonable, that is, to name names of literary offenders. Observing that "whatever is established is sacred for those who do not think," Howells wryly put a whole pantheon of authors to his test of critical realism, and found, to the discomfiture of many of his readers, that the authors were lacking.

A. *Howells in Theory*

Howells defined realism as "fidelity to experience and probability of motive," which is barely satisfactory in discriminating realism from other literary schools. It was his application of the definition that pinpointed its distinct characteristics. His basic method was to "truthfully" treat his material and to exactly interpret the "common feelings of commonplace people."[30] Unfortunately, he complicated this easy program by turning to the old critical concern for the "romance" as a point of departure. The romance, he said, dealt "allegorically and not representatively" with life. It located its characters in the ideal rather than the real. The realistic novel, on the other hand, sought nothing more than to mirror the particulars of life as they are encountered in this world in this time. Howells clung to the distinction long after it had ceased to be meaningful in literary

practice (James was much more astute here), and even himself
indulged on occasion in the earlier form. But realism had its hold on
Howells in terms of three intellectual commitments: democratic
theory, Victorian evolutionary optimism, and science. He would
have "our American novelists be as American as they unconsciously
can. . . . The arts must become democratic, and then we shall have
the expression of art in America."[31] Traditionalism was mere
"paralysis." He thought that the discovery of the principles of
evolution was "animating and shaping the whole future of criticism."[32] Thus the truth on which his realism was based was essentially nonqualitative and scientific rather than imaginative, which
constitutes the major difference between him and the critical
idealists. "The true realist," Howell said, "cannot look upon human
life and declare this thing or that thing unworthy of notice, any more
than the scientist can declare a fact of the material world beneath the
dignity of his inquiry."[33]

Howells would thus, in theory, minimize selection and even the
ordering and focusing of material which constitutes plot. Whereas the
critical idealists urged the artist to construct an imaginative synthesis
recreated from a selected "representative" reality, something universal derived from particulars, Howells ridiculed this doctrine of
idealization as analogous to reproducing a cardboard grasshopper
when a "real" grasshopper was available. Idealized character and
situation meant to him the removal of "lifelikeness" and the substitution of "booklikeness."[34] "The greatest achievement of fiction, in its
highest sense, is to present a picture of life; and the deeper the sense
of something desultory, unfinished, imperfect it gives, even in the
region of conduct, the more admirable it seems."[35]

Ultimately, perhaps, his view that the impersonal and unfocused
record of unselected experience will fulfill the aim of literature rests
on the early faith of Victorian evolutionists that "the beastman will be
so far subdued and tamed in us that the memory of him in literature
shall be left to perish."[36] Such a faith provides a context for an
otherwise unqualified remark he once made that "a great gulf, never
to be bridged, divides the ethical and the aesthetic intention." His
more characteristic view was that literature should help to make "the
race better and kinder," expressed in connection with Tolstoy: "If he
had represented the fact truly, as in his conscience and intelligence
he had known it really to be, he had treated it ethically and of
necessity aesthetically; for as you cannot fail to feel in every piece of

his fiction, the perfect aesthetics result from the perfect ethics. . . . Where the artist and the moralist work together for righteousness, there is the true art."[37]

In line with Taine, who praised *The Rise of Silas Lapham* and translated the novel into French, Howells partially accepted a deterministic interpretation of literature. One had to realize in the light of determinism that literature is like a plant, that it cannot be otherwise than it is, and therefore one has no right to evaluate it; one can only describe it and "place a book in such a light that the reader shall know its class, its function, its character."[38] The view intensified his general break with traditional approaches to literature, leading Howells to claim that "much if not most current criticism as practiced among the English and Americans is bad, is falsely principled, and is conditioned to evil."[39] The critic should proceed much as a botanist treats a plant. The attempt should not be to direct literature, but rather to dispassionately and scientifically analyze its relation to the people from whom it springs, since their "will and taste" determine its form. Criticism, hitherto judicial, had to "altogether reconceive its office." "It must reduce this to the business of observing, recording, and comparing; to analyzing the material before it, and then synthesizing its impressions."[40]

Howells was thus hostile to judicial evaluation. The botanist would not grind a plant underfoot because he did not find it pretty. It was just as absurd for the critic to deplore a poem or novel because he found it displeasing. Criticism should simply "identify the species," though Howells went on to say that the critic could also explain "how and where the specimen is imperfect and irregular."[41] Howells has been much censured for narrowing systematic criticism by trying to deprive it of its immemorial right to judge;[42] indeed, he himself violated his principle in this respect as much as anyone, for no one judged writers like Scott and Thackeray and Poe more harshly. He was followed in his approach by many theorists, however, who saw in science the gateway to a better criticism.[43]

B. *Howells in Practice*

In actual critical practice, Howells' essays on Longfellow, Lowell, and Mark Twain are doubtless his best work. Here, as a more dignified Boswell of impeccable good taste, he mingles personal reminiscence with literary appreciation of a broad sort. In *Literary*

Friends and Acquaintance (1900), a gently nostalgic book in method and point of view, Howells pictured the later New England atmosphere as really "too shy, and too lacking in high and striking contrasts" to be conducive to great fiction, a verdict which has stood up. He remarked of Lowell that his greatness was "somehow apart from the literary proofs of it," that Hawthorne's somber and brooding "look" was in keeping with a man who had "faithfully and therefore sorrowfully" dealt with the problem of evil, that Bayard Taylor's poetry "paid the inevitable allegiance to the manner of the great masters of the day." The book is a marvel of ambiguous tone, as the insights of a young man of twenty-three conflict with the later overview of the same man at sixty-three. There is a feeling of regret, of transience, an ambience of the dramatic elements of the present blended with memories of the past, each part of the book a soft dramatic episode. And there is a nice picture of the older Lowell failing to bound over a fence and being somewhat put out by it, which in its pathos reminds one of Jefferson suffering his broken wrist in showing off before the young Maria Cosway in Paris.

The assessment of Twain is balanced and perceptive. In one passage, Howells notes that Twain's best work revealed dramatic tension secured through a dual point of view, as when the present or adult point of view is brought into contrast with a sense of the charm of some period or region in the past. Howells himself in his early career, when the goal of poet was still before him, had been advised by Lowell, author of the attack on "Rousseau and the Sentimentalists," to sweat the sentimental Heine out of his bones, and Howells had done so. He was thus in a position to appreciate Twain's deflation of a morbid and theatrical sentimentalism, especially as associated with the purposeless baring of one's own bleeding heart. To Howells, Twain was the Lincoln of our literature, appraising Eastern civilization by standards of the Midwest, energizing his creative imagination by seeing the life of the populace through the point of view of boys, and criticizing feudal England from a supposedly humanitarian standpoint in *A Connecticut Yankee*.

And yet there were reservations about Twain. An intimate friend, Howells often read Twain's work from early draft to finished product. In fact, the finished product frequently betrayed Howells' discreet editing. A careful reading of *My Mark Twain* (1910), which Carl Van Doren calls "incomparably the finest of all the interpretations of Howells's great friend," suggests that Howells had misgivings about

Twain's impetuosity, frequent poor taste, and desultory reading. And when Howells was seeking to identify the pathfinders for later fiction, it was James and not Mark Twain that he coupled with George Eliot. One speculates on the reason for this. With his reverence for George Eliot's compassionate insights and ethical elevation as a novelist, Howells may have been privately dismayed by Twain's letter to him dismissing Eliot as a psychological novelist whose plot-development is impeded by too much psychologizing. Possibly Howells' own obsession with heroines as a test for greatness caused him to recall that Twain presented no sustained analysis of a mature woman beyond the part-Negro Roxy, while James was a kind of specialist on heroines. Possibly it was political. In 1881 Howells had accepted an exposure of H. H. Rogers and Standard Oil written by H. D. Lloyd for publication in the *Atlantic*, while Twain himself relied on Rogers in not following Howells into socialism.

Even on James, however, Howells had an occasional reservation. He admired James' early fiction, and he was sympathetic to James' attraction to the French theorists of realism. In sensibility and intelligence, he thought James incomparably one of the finest minds in literature that America had produced. At a time when George Woodberry in his final summing up of American literature omitted not only James and Twain but also Howells, and when Barrett Wendell in his huge *Literary History of America* nearly omitted them, it is instructive to see that Howells repeatedly pointed to Twain and James as the most promising American authors of the time. His review of James' *French Poets and Novelists* is typical.[44] The essay reveals considerable critical balance and tact in pointing to the "ease and brilliancy" of James' style, which Howells considered "irresistible," and the "felicity" with which James managed to evoke his own particular admirations. In particular Howells thought the chapter on Balzac "splendid," a verdict which has held up, although Howells himself was not prepared to regard Balzac so shapeless as James. He praised James' treatment of Turgenev and De Musset, but his critical insight failed him in agreeing with the "shrewd and trenchant" essay on Baudelaire. At the same time, Howells was as disconcerted as other reviewers of the book in noticing that James did not really seem to work out his problems to some forthright conclusions. "We find fault with Mr. James's attitude, judged as a critic, because it implies a certain nervousness that if he curtails his contradictory impressions he may not appear liberal enough."

C. *Limitations, Reservations, and Vitriol*

A major stumbling block in the acceptance of Howells has been the recurrent charge that he limited himself to the "smiling aspects of life" and virtually ignored evil. Everett Carter has ably put that phrase in perspective, by showing how the exigencies of writing prompted Howells to paste together material from various essays. The phrase, in other words, dropped into *Criticism and Fiction* almost accidentally.[45] Yet there is some justice to the charge. The truth is that Howells' sense of evil was really underdeveloped, though he was familiar enough with and reacted against its garden-variety growths—economic exploitation, sex, ambition. He was overly solicitous for New England gentility, certainly, and perhaps too concerned for the "innocence" of the young women increasingly making up the reading public.[46] Essentially a novelist of manners in the Jane Austen tradition until the late 1880s, Howells did pay insufficient attention to those elements of human perversity so difficult to fathom. Partly conditioned by Swendenborgianism and partly by the austerity of his idealistic parents, his interest centered on social imperfection. Evil resulted from the conflict between individual needs and divergent social standards, and could be alleviated through the "parental nurture" of goodness.

After 1889 he became ardently concerned with the evils associated with ruthless economic competition partly caused by giant corporations. The new concerns were less a shift in basic attitudes than a deepening of original views in response to social injustices of disturbing magnitude. These new concerns adversely affected his own writing. But they did have several salutary effects. His apprehension of the tangle of human affairs was deepened. And he was increasingly receptive to emerging young writers such as Hamlin Garland and Frank Norris, whose subjects offended a large number of critics, with the result that Howells was prone to approve writers and material his former skittishness would have avoided. Consequently he gave a turn to realism that advanced it in the direction of naturalism.

The strength of Howells' commitment to realism, and his own obvious integrity, sometimes provided him with strange allies. Richard Watson Gilder, who really was at odds with Howells on the matter of realism, nevertheless lamented the critical attacks on Howells that seemed so vicious and so uninformed, and he avoided accepting critical articles that were intended to dismiss Howells and realism generally. Lowell was also sympathetic to Howells, writing him that such critical attacks might be irritating but were scarcely formidable. Yet when W. R. Thayer, who later confessed to having read no more than one book of Howells, drove an earthmover over realism in "The New Story-Tellers and the Doom of Realism" in the *Forum* for 1894, and castigated *The Rise of Silas Lapham* as a filthy example of Howell's being enamored of Zola's filth, it was the realists who put Thayer in his place. Of the responses, H. H. Boyesen's "The Great Realists and the Empty Story-Tellers" was the most unrelenting counterattack. Boyesen argued that realism was the only feasible literary method for arriving at some truths about man and his situation, while opposing theories, such as romance, simply put unreal people into a never-never land in which the deep difficulties of man's predicament were avoided rather than confronted. [47]

The attacks on Howells did not deter him from publicizing a number of naturalist writers when most critics were shocked at such books as *Maggie, A Girl of the Streets*. [48] This championing of what other critics took to be the most repellent form of rancid realism serves as a sort of counterbalance to Howells' own more discreet fiction. At the end of *Criticism and Fiction* he called writers' attention to the fact that even in the United States "vast masses of men are sunk in misery that must grow every day more hopeless, or embroiled in a struggle for life that must end in enslaving and imbruting them."[49] According to W. F. Taylor, Howells courageously "presented, for the first time in the American novel, an economic criticism definitely based on collectivism instead of the older order of competitive, individual effort."[50] And in such novels as *A Hazard of New Fortunes* (1890), *The Quality of Mercy* (1892), *The World of Chance* (1893), *A Traveler from Altruria* (1894), and *Through the Eye of the Needle* (1907), he recognized very realistically in semisocialistic novels that aspects of American life were indeed quite unsmiling. Contrasted with his earlier standard of realism, which held that the author should impartially hold the mirror of art to life, Howells' later strong sense of justice and pity for the plight of the poor tempted him increasingly toward a reformer's didacticism. Of the fictional spokesmen of this trend, Edward Bellamy was closest to Howells' general taste.[51]

D. *The Breadth of Howells' Interests*

In general, then, there are two periods to Howells' criticism. Into the 1880s, he was largely engaged in illustrating his reasons for favoring the new realism, favorably reviewing such books as John De Forest's *Miss Ravenel's Conversion from Secession to Loyalty*, adroitly distinguishing between Dickens and Thackeray as personalities and the faintly antiquated nature of their styles, sturdily championing Mark Twain's various publications, pointing to Turgenev as a model for American realists, and adumbrating his reasons for linking James and George Eliot as pathfinders of the future.

In the later period, beginning roughly around 1885, Howells was much more reform-minded, and now included in his theory of critical realism a provision for reform.[52] Howells had spent much of his career to this point observing and recording the average in America. He had tended to celebrate that average as somehow the index to democratic republicanism. But as his experience deepened, and as he saw how shoddy and tawdry the average could be, not to speak of the corruption and arrogance that accompanied power, Howells' mood shifted. Less prone to accept what was clearly unacceptable, his new version of realism came to include a provision for changing the reality that was being described. He wished to describe experience in order to disturb men's acceptance of that experience. His intent was to encourage men to carefully examine their "social and moral opinions" and to change them.

Throughout his career, Howells noticed and brought to public attention most of the emerging writers of the period: Frank Norris, Hamlin Garland, various regional writers, Stephen Crane, Theodore Dreiser, Harold Frederic, Henry Blake Fuller, and others. In "The Editor's Easy Chair" in 1903, Howells ruefully admitted his own growing limitations in creating three-dimensional characters after he had "gone socialist." His own view of democratic society, he thought, was "incomparably less powerfully imagined" than the society delineated by Tolstoy. The long essay on Zola printed in the *North American Review* for 1902 reveals a certain weariness over the battle of realism. He had forcefully championed Zola ever since 1886, and now once again he was defending Zola against the old charges of indecency. But in the essay, Howells admitted that literary criticism had failed to sustain the new realism against the older romantic tradition. Zola, reared in the era of romanticism and sharing in the views of both the old romanticism and the new realism, had eventually been powerless in stemming a resurgence of romanticism. "It was the error of the realists whom Zola led, to suppose that people like truth better than falsehood; they do not; they like falsehood best;

and if Zola had not been at heart a romanticist, he never would have cherished his long delusion."[53] Partly it is this disillusion with the prospects of realism that helps to explain his own retrospective *My Literary Passions* and books in the Sainte-Beuve tradition like *Literary Friends and Acquaintance.*

But there were other reasons for his disillusionment. Some of the young men that he had helped to promote, such as Frank Norris, wrote disparagingly of Howells, and Howells himself, in his presidential address to the American Academy of Arts and Letters in 1909, acknowledged that "time will decide that some of us who are now here were not worthy to be here, and by this decision we must abide. But until it is rendered, we will suffer with what meekness, what magnanimity, we may the impeachments of those contemporaries who may question our right to be here."[54] To Larzer Ziff, Howells' later reservations had to do with one of the oldest complaints of American writers, that America simply did not possess sufficient "associations" to make the writer's task easy. Earlier, Howells had reacted against that very point in his review of James' *Hawthorne.* In addition, it seemed now that America was so broad that it was next to impossible to represent it fully, and therefore the American writer had to either go into depth in his characterization of a few, like James, or deal with regional manners in the way of Twain.[55] Howells himself felt that he had somehow come to the end of his possibilities. Yet a backward glance provided certain satisfactions. Together with James and Twain, he had helped to promote a kind of literature that was competitive with older, more established forms. All things considered, some of their works were of the first rank. Realism was established. And with the work of James especially, realism had been proven a useful tool for blending moral and social considerations in order to perceive the depth and meaning that can attach to human experience.

CHAPTER 3

Critical Realism: Henry James

HENRY James (1843–1916) tried his hand at practically every kind of literary composition. A distinguished master of fiction, he was as well a voluminous literary critic and a subtle student of literature, especially in matters of form. In the productivity of his enterprise, and in his observant and civilized concentration on human experience, James stands alone among the realists. He was a true cosmopolite. Divested of parochial prejudices, refined and deracinated, and endowed with a rich sensibility to literature, James was strategically situated to observe international differences in cultural needs and impulses, to which he thoughtfully responded in books and essays.

He was brought up in a remarkably sophisticated household. The father was intellectual, the family traveled widely in Europe, and all kinds of spokesmen of culture were graciously entertained to provide Henry and his brother William the pleasures of intellectual and artistic activity. Consequently James was not only personally familiar with and reacted to Americans such as Hawthorne, Emerson (a frequent house guest), Lowell (whose Harvard lectures on world masters he attended), Louis Agassiz, Poe, Norton (for whom he began book reviewing in 1864), and T. S Perry, who introduced him to Russian fiction, but to transatlantic authors as well: George Eliot, George Sand, De Musset, Flaubert, Turgenev especially, Balzac, Zola, Scherer, Sainte-Beuve, and many others.

This rich complex of experience had the effect of making James one of the most informed critics of his period, as well as one of the most discriminating. It is difficult to talk of particular "influences." Even while he responded to all kinds of intellectual stimuli, James seems to have always maintained a high degree of intellectual independence. Mainly he was his own man, emphasizing throughout his career the control of reason, of moral sensibility, and of artistic mastery of the materials artists use. At the same time, as he grew and pondered the nature of art, James became more flexible in his critical approach. Initially firm in his demand for good sense and delicate feeling, within a period of some twenty years James moved to a more open and dispassionate acceptance of an author's strong points, his critical judgment finally coming to rest in a consideration of what the artist had really achieved.

Except for the book on Hawthorne, written for the English reading public, the bulk of James' criticism was published as critical articles in various magazines. His apprentice articles, written between 1865 and 1874, were not gathered together in his lifetime. His own collections were published in four books: *French Poets and Novelists* (1878), *Partial Portraits* (1888), *Essays in London and Elsewhere* (1893), and *Notes on Novelists* (1914). The important *Art of Fiction* was published in 1885. *French Poets and Novelists* and *Notes on Novelists,* his first and last gathering of essays, emphasize continental writers, while *Partial Portraits* and *Essays in London and Elsewhere* are largely devoted to English and American writers.

James' critical career can be divided into three periods, corresponding roughly to the division introduced in Morris Roberts' *Henry James's Criticism* (1929). The first begins with his reviews for Norton in 1864, and ends with his move to Europe in the autumn of 1875 in the expectation of taking up permanent residence abroad. During this period the relative importance of intelligence and refined sensibility preoccupied him, and he examined and judged the traditional distinctions between the romance and the realistic novel, the imagination and fancy, and the morality of art. The second period, from 1875 to 1890, is a time of solid growth and development, which starts with the uneven *French Poets and Novelists* and culminates in the almost completely satisfying *Partial Portraits.* The final period includes *Essays in London and Elsewhere, The Lesson of Balzac,* the prefaces to the New York edition of his fiction (later published as *The Art of the Novel* by R. P. Blackmur), and *Notes on Novelists.*

I   *Early Criticism, 1864–1874*

A. *The Standard of Literary Truth*

Throughout his early career James steadily believed that the "measure" of a novel's merit lay in its truth: truth to character, to action, to situation. He did not ask for minute fidelity to fact, in the manner of Howells. Essentially he spoke for a modified form of realism. In the back of his mind was always the ideal writer, the one who possessed *all* qualities in abundance: imagination, brains, moral sensibility, a felicitous style. Discussing in 1865 the faults of cheap writers, James indirectly provided his own ideal for literature: the recognition of standards of truth or accuracy against which performance can be measured; the transcription of facts according to their relative merit and importance; the patient study of "nature" in order to establish the correct statement that describes it; the extraction of material from experiences rather than its elaboration through the imagination. The good writer, in other words, is economical and careful in the selection of material, constantly exercises the critical intelligence to determine what is necessary to his purposes, and avoids shortcuts based on stock responses.[1]

In this period James was absorbed in defining the nature of literary truth and the role of intellectual judgment. Whatever blocked this twin inquiry—for instance, allegiance to party, doctrine, principle, dogma, or theory—was discounted.[2] Eventually he came to the position that the "high ground" of criticism was "to make truth generally accessible, and not to apply it." Unlike philosophy and poetry, which deal with great truths directly, criticism deals in "contributions to truth." "Its business is to urge the claims of all things to be understood."[3] There are several implications in the statement. It assumes that literature particularly, and art generally, are forms of communication dealing, as he said, with both "plain facts" and "fancies," real and imaginative elements in other words, which it is the business of criticism to explicate. It assumes that criticism has quite done its task if the truth of matters is clearly presented. The application of that understanding is better left to others. And finally, it assumes that criticism itself, in its attempt to understand, must mainly rely on the discursive reason for success. The best critic is thus one who has cultivated his intelligence to deal sympathetically, broadly, and accurately with literature.

B. *The Types of Fiction*

A constant refrain in James's early reviewing was that second-rate novels seemed to be "the great literary feature of the day."[4] Most seemed to him to fall into one or another of three categories: romances, novels of manners, and what he called "photographic realism." Theoretically, James was inclined to accept whatever was put in front of him, without reference to type. But in practice, he found that type had a great deal to do with intention and management of material. Himself attracted to analysis of character and examination of motive within social context, James found, through sheer experience in reading, that these three types too often failed to convey some sense of the "truth" of life. Mostly descriptive or dramatic in their handling of material, they too often appeared to evade those elements of experience which most distinctively describe experience, "however questionable [those elements] may be in point of morals or of taste."[5]

The main problem with the novel of manners, the type with which James dealt least, was that it was too largely descriptive of the prevailing system or modes of social conduct of a specific society, period, or group. To that extent it relied more heavily that it should on circumstantial matter that had no primary significance to the inquiring reader. At its extreme, the novel of manners devolved into photographic realism, a type which put James out of all patience. Those who "get up" a photographic representation of experience could be shrewdly observant and widely experienced, and they might have a "turn for color," but the tendency, to his mind, was to overlay the canvas with too much detail.[6]

Of the "photographic realists" he put under review, James was most hostile to Trollope. Insisting that the "primary" function of a book is to "suggest thought," he accused Trollope of producing a kind of emasculated photographic transcription that missed the important elements of character and motivation.[7] "The photography lacks the supreme virtue of possessing a character. It is the detail alone that distinguishes one photograph from another."[8] James' scorn for Trollope approached white heat when he reviewed *The Belton Estate*. "It is essentially, organically, consistently stupid; stupid in direct proportion to its strength. It is without a single idea."[9] Fiction was not really a matter of counting how many details in a novel are imagined, how many based upon experience, since in any case they are destined to be converted into fiction. The real issue was how to manage the total bearing of a book, so that the integration of both imagined and real experience takes on one tone and color.[10]

James was consistently disappointed in the literary romances of his day. When sentimentalized, as in Mrs. D. M. M. Craik, every vestige of the work was destroyed through the falsifying of fact and truth, which in turn compromised the "appearance of reality" and inevitably impugned the "writer's sincerity."[11] The modern propensity for romances, he thought, may be "running away with the human mind, and operating as a kind of leakage in the evolution of thought."[12] Yet he could appreciate romances so long as they were "genuine and sincere." He enjoyed George Eliot's *The Spanish Gypsy* and *The Legend of Jubal*—which he regarded as romances rather than poems—he was very favorable in his views of Scott, and he always maintained an ambivalent interest in Hawthorne, whose work he admired for its "clearness of intellectual temper" and its "fantastic" handling of the romance genre, though he remained uneasy before lapses in form.

By 1874, James was less concerned with the types of fiction and the need to distinguish between them. In a significant review of Julian Hawthorne's *Idolatry,* he wrote that works of "purely imaginative art" are entirely to be accepted, provided only that the author makes such work entertaining (a point he would develop at greater length a decade later in *The Art of Fiction*). Any novel, no matter its "kind," can serve as a "possible vehicle of an infinite amount of wisdom," since all writing has something to communicate.[13] But there are levels of significance in human communication, and James was consistently for the highest.

C. *Imagination and Reason*

James' statements about the imagination are not wholly consistent. At rare times he used the term in its romantic sense, but imagination did not possess for him the strong semimystical import it had for romantics such as Emerson and Lowell.[14] That is, imagination did not reveal any central unified view of an ideal world. James pretty much restricted its application to literature. He generally ascribed two functions to the imagination: it was a "creative movement" which intensifies and animates a novelist's conception; and it was an inventive faculty which pulls fiction together into a functional whole. In addition, the imagination contributed a pictorial element to fiction in terms of charged language. Its presence in fiction was not essential. Trollope, for instance, had little imagination, but James immediately went on to add that Trollope had a "delicate perception of the actual which makes every whit as firm ground to work upon."[15]

Where imagination was in scarce supply, there could be offsetting factors: sharpness of perception, for instance, or sound sense, or ideally a combination of the two. It all had to do, James thought, with the usual manner of composition. One generally began writing rapidly, which often plunged one into error. Then a "sober second thought," related to judgmental intelligence, followed the creative impulse. Finally, the imagination, never wholly absent in a writer, could begin to function to complement the "natural or critical one," which in turn helped to animate the original conception.[16] Ideally, the writer should maintain some balance between sharpness of perception and imagined constructions. Perception provided those "minute and felicitous circumstances" which impart a sense of reality to fiction. Imagination contributed a "moral consciousness" and a "beauty and grace" that enlivened the whole work. Overarching both was the primacy of reason.[17]

James makes unmistakably clear in this early criticism that he prized intelligence as the *sine qua non* of the good writer. He insisted on probability, structure, organization, sensibility, all the offspring of the shaping powers of intelligence. Mind was broadly defined to include both intellectual power and mental responsiveness. Together, the rational and perceptive powers of the mind made life explicable by widening human awareness through the analysis of human experience. It was no accident, then, that thus early in his critical career James should have reminded his readers that "The only intensity worth anything in writing is intensity of thought."

This dedication to intelligence had implications for what James expected of literature. He looked for analysis, design, intellectual awareness, accurate and persuasive generalizations, "constant patience of facts, of linear divions, and of shades of meaning."[18] He disliked the tendency to sentimentalize the picturesque, as in Ruskin, or to substitute color for design, as in Swinburne.[19] He had reservations about both Thackeray and Dickens, because they seemed to him to have only a small stock of ideas and images.[20] His extravagant praise of George Sand was based at least in part on his belief that she combined the moral and philosophical senses to present us with the "most various" matters with "relative dignity."[21] He reacted favorably to George Eliot because the power of her scenes was "real" and finally so "intelligent," the latter point counting so much with James that he italicized the word.[22] Serious if not passionate in thought, George Eliot's central gift was the ripe reflective tendency of her intelligence, which always served to inform her observation.[23] If the novel was to be radical, he at least was prepared to welcome the kind of radical realism that was "so intelligent and so logical."

D. *Character and Moral Sense*

James was deeply concerned with problems of form. But finally, he thought, literature dealt with people, and it should do so in terms of their moral and psychological complexity. He explained his view in terms of the American temperament. Americans are "deeper, more substantial, more self-directing; they have, if not more virtue, at least more conscience; and when conscience comes into the game human history ceases to be a perfectly simple tale."[24] James could react warmly, as we still do today, to William Morris for his "healthy" view of experience. But there was a darker side to experience which it profits the artist to explore: "invalids learn so many secrets." One reason for his impatience with Trollope was that he gave us all the conventional sins against custom and propriety. James countered that such sins are essentially trivial in any overview of human experience, and the relatively untouched reader, asked to render his judgment, is tempted to say that the matter is of so little moment that it is solely the business of Trollope's characters.[25] Good authors, James maintained, deal with human nature, which is "as old as the hills." Poorer writers deal with society, which is a constantly changing scene, and indulge the public fancy for the exceptional and novel.[26]

In the early period of his criticism, James did not always keep these sensible views under control. Always inclined to reticence before what he considered gross, an inclination he carried throughout his life as a matter of fact, he sometimes gives the impression of overvaluing a safe moral tone. He was inclined to excuse the feeble dramatic construction, the halting gait, and the too large setting in George Eliot's *Romola* because of the "generous feeling and . . . elevated morality" of the novel.[27] Yet he appreciated Stendhal's *Chartreuse de Parma* as a good book which could be enjoyed for its "clear vision" and "magnificiently sustained pauses" despite its cynicism and "grossly immoral" characters. He was right in thinking that the moral atmosphere of Gautier was "unweighted with a moral presence." And he is perceptive—though his tone is a bit unsettling—in pointing out that *Madame Bovary* is a great work whose "elaborate picture of vice" can be used for "educational purposes." Not himself inclined toward the "physiological" interpretation of character, James' psychology asked that people be "interesting" because they have the "capacity to be tempted," for in the passions we encounter the depths that make fiction so rewarding.

E. *On Certain Critics*

James was fond of distinguishing the types of criticism and of classifying critics according to his estimate of their importance. Basically, he thought there were two forms of criticism. Great criticism had "more or less nearly" to do with philosophy and general principles, somewhat on the order of Goethe, whereas "small" criticism dealt in "pure" discussion of principles, observation of fact and result, individual works of art. The master of "great" criticism worked according to a "supreme object" and had a "deliberate theory of life, of nature, of the universe."[28]

For these reasons he tended to discount Sainte-Beuve, who was nevertheless the "first of living critics," and to accept Edmond Scherer. Later he would reverse the order. But at this point, he liked Scherer's "intellectual eclecticism" and his "moral conscience," and in a long catalog of Scherer's virtues really gave his own concept of the ideal critic:

The age surely presents no finer spectacle than that of a mind liberal after this fashion; not from a brutal impatience of order, but from experience, from reflection, seriously, intelligently, having known, relished, and appropriated the many virtues of conservatism; a mind inquisitive of truth and of knowledge, accessible on all sides, unprejudiced, desirous above all things to examine directly, fearless of reputed errors, but merciless to error when proved, tolerant of dissent, respectful of sincerity, content neither to reason on matters of feeling nor to sentimentalize on matters of reason, equitable, dispassionate, sympathetic.[29]

James was also attracted to Matthew Arnold and to Hippolyte Taine. Arnold had "delicate perceptions." But while "poetic feeling" can subserve "the end of criticism," it can also prompt occasional misreadings, which led James to distrust Arnold's specific judgments. He was tempted to set Taine before Scherer. But finally he concluded that Taine was more a philosopher and historian than a critic. Taine sought to synthesize literary experience, but he forgot to discriminate differences. Furthermore, Taine was "too passionate, too partial, too eloquent."[30]

II *Criticism, 1875–1890*

In the period 1875–1890 James published four books of criticism: *French Poets and Novelists* (1878), *Hawthorne* (1879), *The Art of*

Fiction (1885)—really a long essay—and *Partial Portraits* (1888). While the criticism is occasionally uneven, as a whole it is witness to the maturation of his literary and critical theory.

If we exclude *The Art of Fiction*, the most noticeable aspect of this period is James' increasing consciousness of the role of the historical imagination. In *French Poets and Novelists*, the apparent tutor is Taine, whereas in *Partial Portraits* a significant shift toward Sainte-Beuve has taken place. In discussing Balzac in the earlier book, James credits Taine with the best account of that great writer's career, and himself dwells less on analysis than on Balzac's general characteristics: his romantic idealism and incipient bourgeois feelings, his exquisite facility in giving us real persons and his coincident fatuity in making these persons generally odious, his social and philosophical conservatism, his descriptive ability, his marvelous pictures of women. Similarly, in the essay on George Sand, James begins with a reference to Taine as the apostle of milieu and moment. In subsequent pages James illustrates the historical approach in reference to her parentage, the consistency of her advocacy of the rights of love, her bohemianism, her tendencies to edification, didacticism, philosophizing, and preaching, all examples of her lineage from the military and aristocratic circumstances of her forebears. And in the review of James Elliott Cabot's two-volume *A Memoir of Ralph Waldo Emerson* (1887), James regrets that Cabot had not followed the historical critics more closely to limn in the manners and times of Emerson. Cabot, he thought, missed his opportunity. "We know a man imperfectly until we know his society, and we but half know a society until we know its manners."[31]

This approach to literature led James into habits of mind he scarcely abandoned the rest of his writing career. Always concerned to specify the attributes of the good artist—a knack for organizing experience, an "extraordinary sensibility," a knowledge of pleasure and pain, a "quick . . . yet reflective imagination," and a "faculty for language"[32]—James placed this concern within the broad context of national character (in which he commonly contrasted French and English temperament) and of different ways of thinking, behaving, and reacting as these are found in males and females. The latter view does not seem to have had an appreciable effect on his criticism, since on the whole his judgments are just though his reasons are suspect; but his absorption in the complexities of French and English national character had consequences for both critical theory and literary practice. His expressed intention was to blend the French capacity for grace, symmetry, and system with the English attempt to deal with life, perhaps not always satisfactorily, in the fullest terms. James had certain preferences for the English side. While an English propensity for "an immense amount of conventional blinking" could be admitted, he liked the English character as expressed in its behavior: civil and domestic piety and good humor, a sense of decorum combined with a need for action, a love of sport, an absence of irony and a pervasive respect for childhood, and a generally expansive tendency.[33]

A. *Hawthorne*

James' book on Hawthorne, the only full-length critical study he devoted to a single writer, was prepared in response to a request from John Morley, general editor of the English Men of Letters Series, for a work on the American author. Though the series ultimately went to thirty-nine volumes, Hawthorne remained the only American writer represented and James the only American critic.

For his information, James relied on George Parsons Lathrop's *A Study of Hawthorne* (1876), but the structure and interpretation are his alone. The book is one of James' least successful efforts, though it abounds in individual insights and generally comes out on the side of an appreciation of Hawthorne.[34] The influence of Taine informs much of the book, and is partly James' undoing. Having moved permanently to England in 1876, James was deeply immersed in and affected by the cultural life of London, and he persistently silhouettes Hawthorne against the blank provincialism of mid-century America.[35] The result is a certain falsity of tone that verges on condescension. And the dimensions of his cultural scene were too broadly drawn. He attributed an organic sameness and coherence to American life that were simply not true. Consequently, he was unable to reconcile his two major points, that the lack of American history and custom undercut Hawthorne's genius, and that Hawthorne's achievement lay in his "vivid reflection of New England life."

Hawthorne's fancy, small ingenuity, and taste for conceits all troubled James. Yet, as William M. Sale, Jr., suggests, James was sufficiently impressed with the quality of Hawthorne's mind to see him as a more suitable model than, say, Howells or Balzac.[36] He liked the penetrating imagination of Hawthorne, for it worked in an area that attracted James himself: "The shadows and substructions, the dark-based pillars and supports of our moral nature."[37] Hawthorne's "dusky, overshadowed conscience" invariably phrased itself in moral analogies, to James one of his most attractive points, for it showed that Hawthorne "cared for the deeper psychology, and . . . tried to become familiar with it."[38] James suggests that Hawthorne did not wholly succeed in penetrating to the floor of the human unconscious. But the attempt itself revealed Hawthorne as a "realist" who had a "cat-like faculty of seeing in the dark."[39]

James' attempt to allay the impression of Hawthorne as a somber, withdrawn man also constitutes a plus for his book. Admitting that Hawthorne temperamentally liked solitude, he went on to deny that Hawthorne was simply a heavy-pedaling moralist shrouded in a continual pall of psychological gloom. Since Hawthorne wished to be a writer, James assumed that he sought enjoyment. The artist "proposes to give pleasure, and to give it he must first get it."[40] The statement is good in testifying to the essential sanity of the writer. And James reads Hawthorne very well when he describes his imagination as a "heavy moral burden" imported and then transmuted "in the light and charming fumes of artistic production." The presence of sin thus had an intellectual rather than a moral or theological intent, and served Hawthorne "merely for an artistic or literary purpose."[41]

James had reservations about all the novels. *The Scarlet Letter* suffered from "a want of reality and an abuse of the fanciful element," a criticism that others have offered, so that the novel was curiously lacking in the "solidity of specification" which so absorbed James at this time. Nor did he think well of *The Marble Faun*. It ailed from a too conscious complexity of incident and detail, even though the subject matter itself was "admirable." Yet James' final verdict was appreciative. Hawthorne's "charming art" was "too original and exquisite" not to enjoy a continuous readership. "He was a beautiful, natural, original genius, and his life had been singularly exempt from worldly preoccupations and vulgar efforts."[42]

B. *The Artist's Perception of Life*

In theory James would open art to all of life, in order to filter that life through the "powerful and original" minds of the writers. Reflection was part of "disciplined manhood." One tried to be cheerful, but at the same time life is frustrating—a view that culminated in this fine statement:

Evil is insolent and strong; beauty enchanting but rare; goodness very apt to
be weak; folly very apt to be defiant; wickedness to carry the day; embeciles
[*sic*] to be in great places, people of sense in small, and mankind generally,
unhappy. But the world as it stands is no illusion, no phantasm, no evil dream
in the night; we wake up to it again ever and ever; we can neither forget it nor
deny it nor dispense with it. We can welcome experience as it comes, and
give it what it demands, in exchange for something which it is idle to pause to
call much or little so long as it contributes to swell the volume of consciousness. In this there is mingled pain and delight, but over the mysterious
mixture there hovers a visible rule, that bids us learn to will and seek to
understand. [43]

The passage stands as almost an index to James' intellectual and
emotional career. He was naturally attracted to the large view of life
filtered through an exquisitely tuned consciousness. Because
Turgenev was so congenial to James' own views at this time, what he
has to say about the Russian author illustrates his own interest in "life
itself." Turgenev sought to cultivate "comprehension." He seemed to
instinctively realize that grasping for happiness, or for some closely
refined "moral" view of life, lessened the insights which otherwise
might accrue to the writer. People who pursued happiness acted as if
they could control life, could plot for happiness. As the "searching
realist," Turgenev's temper was that of "an earnestly attentive
observer," which resulted in a deep, impartial, and "unreservedly
intelligent" view of life that most writers and most people lacked.
Consequently, in the way of "substance" there was almost literally
nothing about which Turgenev did not care. [44]

At the same time, James felt that Turgenev's "sombre portrayal" of
things sometimes verged toward the "pathetic," not a wholesome
tendency since it could easily lead to a "superficial morality."
Turgenev's sadness had an "element of error," then, but James
concluded it also contained some wisdom, for "Life *is*, in fact, a
battle."[45] Trollope fared no better than in the earlier criticism, for
James continued to think that his talents were uneven, though he did
possess a "happy, instinctive perception of human varieties."[46]
Impatient with minds incapable of reacting to the moral complica-
tions of human existence, James indicted Gautier for spending his
"visual discrimination" and unerring "descriptive instinct" on relatively trivial matters.[47] Charles de Bernard's cleverness was second-
rate because "he had no morality."[48] Emerson's "ripe unconscious-
ness of evil," to James one of the "most beautiful signs by which we
know him," was attributed to the fact that "practical" society simply

had not offered him much in the way of temptation, so that his reading of life was essentially incomplete.[49] And the esteem previously extended George Sand was now partially withdrawn on the grounds that "She never allows facts to make her uncomfortable."[50]

C. *Literature and the Moral Element*

James was far from saying that experience could explain everything. Too limited an experience, on the other hand, was scarcely better. The artist's intent should be to produce a transcript of life, but one informed with the moral dimension that we commonly encounter in real experience. In 1875 James attended a meeting at which Turgenev and Zola were present, and was mystified to find that at no time in the discussions did the question of the relation of art to moral concerns arise. The matter seemed to have been settled long before in terms of a complete separation of the two issues, as if they were "completely different things." James could not agree. To him it was "very childish" to remove the "moral quality" from considerations of technical skill and literary form. Great artists, he said, "feel that the whole thinking man is one, and that to count out the moral element in one's appreciation of an artistic total is exactly as sane as it would be . . . to eliminate all the words in three syllables."[51]

He found precious little evidence that anyone before him had succeeded in solving the problem. Sex, for example, was usually handled badly. The work of Scott, Austen, and Dickens appeared "strangely loveless," "like vast, cold, commodious, respectable rooms."[52] Maupassant dealt with sex as if it were part of the "monkey's cage," and George Sand, in her failure to distinguish between "virtuous and vicious love," seemed unduly romantic in picturing sex as "always divine in its essence and ennobling in its operation."[53] Even when writers attempted to inform their work with the moral element, they usually failed. The vaguely didactic purpose of George Eliot now proved troubling to James as a self-imposed artistic limitation which prevented her from fully realizing "the game of art."[54] Of the various writers that James examined, only Turgenev and—strangely enough considering his other reservations—Flaubert occasionally managed to hang the tale and the moral together, which to James consisted in the "excellence" of the matter. Most of Flaubert's work failed in various ways, but James thought that *Madame Bovary* successfully reconciled the demands of literary realism and the deeper demands for a full exposition of human nature. Turgenev, too, in his success in blending form and moral vision, offered a "capital example of moral meaning giving a sense to form and form giving relief to moral meaning."[55]

D. *Imagination and Form*

Absorbed as he was in working out the aesthetic implications of form, James neglected to define imagination, though the term appears often enough in this middle period of his criticism. He generally used the word in two different but complementary senses. On the one hand, imagination helped the writer to avoid the limited "hardness of consistent realism" by investing experience with a general illusory power that had in it a "tinge of the ideal, a touch of poetry."[56] It provided the "ideas" for fiction and at full employment could provide a world view. More commonly, however, James used imagination as a term to describe the artist's faith in and commitment to his discipline. In this sense, the imagination enhanced the literary work to make it as substantially "real" as the circumstances on which the work was based. The "incomparable vividness" that James detected in Balzac's work was due, he thought, to the "immense sweep" of Balzac's imagination, which clothed the work in such a density of texture that it became plausible and authentic in its own right. In contrast, the equally prolific George Sand, Dumas, and Trollope appeared to be basically distrustful of the literary process, so that their work was "loose" in texture and consequently artificial.[57]

In order for a literary work to imaginatively scan and even rival life, its parts needed to be harmonized in an "organic whole." Tone, mood, structure, language, character, and style were to be so intimately intermingled and balanced that one could almost say that the highest endowment of the writer was to make the illusory real.[58] By the time James published *Partial Portraits*, he was inclined to ask little else of the writer. The question of form, he said, was "the only canon we have a right to impose."[59]

E. *James' Distrust of Critical Formulas*

Even though James spoke of the "interest and value" that attached to a novel in providing a "direct impression of life," he had no notion of life as a seamless unity. The very diversity of novels suggested that there are many different kinds of reality. In fact, novels are as various as the writers who produce them. The variety itself implied that "everything is remunerative" in experience if one "only look at it closely." And this is true even of "certain vulgarly obvious things," for their close examination allows the opening of entire vistas previously closed to the reader.[60] Thus the critic should carry his expectations lightly. "All rigid critical formulas are more or less unjust."[61] They clog critical perception through the introduction of extraneous presumptions. They are vain and meaningless, since writers never recognize them anyhow. And they mislead critics into "some flight of metaphysics, hovering over bottomless gulfs of controversy," that have almost nothing to do with the literature at hand.[62]

F. *"The Art of Fiction"*

In 1884 the English critic Walter Besant presented a lecture at the Royal Institution entitled "The Art of Fiction," which was published several months later as a pamphlet. Late that same year James published his rejoinder, under an identical title, in *Longman's Magazine*. His essay in its turn provoked the response three months later of Robert Louis Stevenson, "A Humble Remonstrance." James' article was not a fully reasoned analysis of literary and critical processes. He himself wrote Stevenson that his main intention was to make "a plea for liberty."[63] So long as feeling, observation, and vision were contained within a formally satisfying design, James was content. His emphasis was thus on two criteria: artistic sensibility and formal pattern.

In his discussion of artistic sensibility, James embraces a position traditional in English criticism. No good work can be produced by a superficial mind. To the extent that the artist's "intelligence is fine," he believed that the artist's work would reveal "the substance of beauty and truth." This particular but important point crops up repeatedly in James' criticism. The "complete" writer is also the complete man. It could not be otherwise, since whatever we read is the distillate of the writer's sensitive interaction with his experience. That experience is of two kinds: "raw" experience as we encounter and partake in it during our everyday activities; and the more refined experience of social intercourse with other artists in which the writer is offered the opportunity to develop "upon discussion, upon experiment, upon curiosity, upon variety of attempt, upon the exchange of views and the comparison of standpoints."[64] If, however, the latter is too greatly indulged at the expense of the former, as was the case according to James for the French naturalists, the work is limited by too heavy a larding of theory. "Raw" experience resists theory, and is thus an effective counter to canons of literary faith. The observation prompted James to one of his finest statements on the nature of experience:

Experience is never limited, and it is never complete; it is an immense sensibility, a kind of huge spider-web of the finest silken threads suspended in the chamber of consciousness, and catching every air-borne particle in its tissue. It is the very atmosphere of the mind; and when the mind is imaginative—much more when it happens to be that of a man of genius—it takes to itself the faintest hint of life, it converts the very pulses of the air into revelations.[65]

Revelations, then, constitute the significance of good art, and we must thus grant the artist his subject and intention. But to James the writer is a painter as well as a philosopher, and it is the province of criticism to apply the "test of execution" to literary work—to James one of the "most charming of pleasures" for perceptive readers. The writer never admits that he is "making believe." In fact, he should be so preoccupied with making a direct *impression* on the reader that the question of make-believe should never suggest itself. In addition, since the novel is a "picture" of life, and since no picture is moral or immoral but simply exists, the whole issue of "morality" is moot. Consequently the critic may concentrate his full attention on the formal aspects of a work, on how the writer manages to create an "illusion of life." Partly the writer achieves his intention through a process of selection from experience that results in a "solidity of specification" which simulates an "air of reality" so cleverly that the reader is persuaded to accept the work itself as an experience of life.[66] Partly it is through the writer's ability to interrelate fictional elements in such a way that the work presents existence in an almost perfect and unqualified state. Here the illusion is complete, for the work itself has become a "living thing, all one and continuous, like any other organism, and in proportion as it lives will it be found, I think, that in each of the parts there is something of each of the other parts."[67]

III *Criticism, 1890–1916*

Between 1890 and 1916 James published *Essays in London* (1893), *The Lesson of Balzac* (1905), the essays that serve as prefaces to the New York edition of his *Works* (twenty-six volumes, 1907), and *Notes on Novelists* (1914). Unfortunately, the style is often prolix and indirect, and on occasion downright fussy. The views expressed in his earlier criticism have not changed in essential aspects. But they are now stated with greater strength, and the period as a whole embraces criticism of a consistently high quality.

A. *The Office of Criticism*

There is professional care and pride in the way that James approached criticism. The familiar stress on reflective intelligence as a means to develop sensibilities and awareness is encountered continually. Its purpose is the same, to hone the intelligence until we are free of necessity. In turn our interests are broadened, and mankind in general can wander farther afield in pursuit of those "certain things" which "refine" our minds the most. To James this activity was the "very education of our imaginative life," for we could then act upon knowledge and increase as human beings.[68]

This high view of criticism meant that the critic had to have the finest attributes: pliancy of intelligence, maturity of judgment, distinction of tone, quick perception of quality, a feeling for shading, a heightened sense of the moral value of the individual.[69] The critic offered himself as a "general touchstone" who felt to understand and understood in order to say. His office was "absolutely rare." "Just in proportion as he is sentient and restless, just in proportion as he reacts and reciprocates and penetrates, is the critic a valuable instrument." Because he dealt with life at both first- and secondhand, his experience was both actual and vicarious. The combination complicated the critical task. But it also broadened the range of experience of the critic and made him witness to a more complex reality than generally admitted by people who popularly reduce reality to first-hand encounters.

B. *Practical Criticism*

Always interested in individuality and insight, James habitually sought, in his practical criticism, to accommodate himself to a writer's "general range of vision." "It is not the sign of a free intelligence or a rich life to be hysterical because somebody's work whom you don't like affirms itself in opposition to that of somebody else whom you do."[70] Odd quirks of critical fashion nettled him. He had a deep dislike for the English and American taste for reviewing, in which books were indiscriminately accepted simply because they had been produced, even though they were "no aid to vision" and served only to darken counsel. Nor did James like capricious criticism—such as that practiced by the Goncourt brothers—which failed to appreciate the moral, personal, or psychological elements in writing, elements that James himself scrupulously observed. Indeed, to James the brothers seemed to react so perversely to practically all their encounters with writers that there was always, for them, the danger "that an impression will act as an emetic."[71]

In this period James himself inclined to scant individual works in order to concentrate on the "connections" to be discerned in a review of a writer's entire productive career. Less attention is paid to ideas as entities in themselves and more to *why* certain writers entertained particular ideas and not others. In the first flush of youth, James had populated his intellectual world with ideas and had defended them vigorously. That world is now populated with people who have ideas. His defense was that any critic "worth his salt is indiscreetly curious and wants ever to know how and why." Thus he examined Stevenson in terms of "his views, sympathies, antipathies, *obiter dicta* as an artist," Balzac "in his magnificence totally as an artist," and Flaubert "with complete attention and even excitement of wonder at Flaubert's achievement."[72] And in the prefaces to the New York edition of his work, this sort of interest was even turned inwardly upon himself, as he reconnoitered the generation and gradual evolution of his novels and sought to communicate the excitement of literary composition.

C. *Response to Literary Movements*

In his preface to *The Golden Bowl*, James observed that the writer is a "seer and speaker" who remains under the auspices of the god of fiction so long as his form stays pure. Once form is lost, the writer is lost. Form itself defines human experience by identifying its general and comprehensive characteristics, especially in relation to human impulses and passions. If the writer's experience is too narrow, or too personal, or if he fails to find any correspondence in the experience of the reader, his form will inevitably be ineffective and inadequate.[73]

For these reasons, James was generally out of sorts with the popular literary movements of his day: art for art's sake, naturalism, and the master-movement from which the two were apparently

descended, romanticism. He read Sir Walter Scott and other romantics with pleasure. He thought romanticism was "by no means
necessarily expensive." Yet it seldom worked in practice. Romantics
were impractical. They lacked a "nose for the ridiculous," which
confers objectivity. Serious to a fault, their work revealed such an
"excess of indulgence," such a pervasive sentimentality, that these
weaknesses must finally be attributed to a particular constitutional
inability of Romanticism to cope with human life. [74]

As if in recognition of this inability, the art for art's sake movement
radically separated art and life to concentrate on the former. Uncomfortable with a bourgeois world that seemed tawdry, lacking in
nobility, advocates of art for art's sake stressed style so that it became
a "certain exercise in pride." For its part, naturalism chose to
concentrate on life at the expense of art; but in James' view life was as
rigidly defined as in any romantic scheme. The transitive relation of
circumstance to life was supposed to explain the nature of life totally.
Consequently the emphasis was on quantity rather than quality,
upon a lusty embrace of the common in which the cultivated and
discriminating consciousness played no role. The naturalist school
gave slices of life, which could momentarily ease one's hunger, but
the slices never added up to a whole, for they did not minister to
comprehensive knowledge. What Balzac and Zola, and the new
English school of Arnold Bennett, Gilbert Cannon, D. H. Lawrence,
Hugh Walpole, and Compton Mackenzie, seemed to do was to
endlessly repeat unrefined experience over and over, as if through
this form of incantation they might ultimately find something meaningful. [75]

Yet James did not reject the naturalists out of hand. He consistently
admired Balzac's "sustained fury of perception" of the provincial life
of France even while he acknowledged that a comparable "fierceness
of judgment" was lacking. Balzac was "the first and foremost member
of his craft," so compelling in the mass of his historical data that the
reader found himself helplessly immersed in a fictionally created
world. [76] Generally affirmative toward Zola, James nevertheless
viewed him as a romantic turned sour, so bound up in theory that he
actually failed to meet life head on. The new school of English
naturalists, of whom James thought Arnold Bennett the most forceful
in intellectual power and vigor, at least had broadened English
apprehension of the human scene and of human beings, so that its
adherents could successfully challenge the prevailing timidity about

sex and the general reliance on convention as a means for skirting the
more painful truths of human existence.[77]

D. *The Principles of Art*

These movements suggested that by the end of the century cultural
standards and discriminations were either declining or disappearing
altogether. In their uncertainty, people were turning to history and
philosophy rather than literature to examine the national life. James
admitted that the period was certainly bewildering. But the national
predicament was not essentially different from other periods of
human history. Our error lay in thinking that life testified to an order
somehow lost to view in the present, whereas life really made "no
direct sense whatever for any subject" at any time. It revealed
"nothing but splendid waste," and was at bottom "all inclusion and
confusion."[78] History and philosophy, essentially descriptive disciplines, could only describe the basic disorder of our world. Literature, however, was an evaluative instrument in the sense that it was
concerned with the "hard latent *values*" to be abstracted from the
disorder of primary experience.

Conscious of this purpose of literature, James found it, as Diderot
wrote, "so easy to detect mediocrity." When the naturalists persisted
in giving facts, James as the attentive reader was inclined to ask for
more, and was unsettled when the implied response said that it was
quite sufficient to have danced the "imaginative dance" without
measuring its performance. In most writing, James concluded, the
reader would look in vain for "some projected mass of truth, some
solidity of substance." Floods of dialogue and reams of "illustrational"
material were insufficient, for art also needed to attend the "structural
and compositional office." In his preface to *The Spoils of Poynton*, he
observed that art is economical in contrast to the wastefulness of raw
experience, and thus clarity and purpose are primary to art. To break
unity of tone was the "one unpardonable sin." But he wanted, too,
unity of effect, purpose, character, and situation.[79] Then the snippets
and snatches of experience were caught up in the totality of form,
meaning and value were laid bare, and our commonplace lives
enriched.

To deny that meaning was *within* art struck James as a downgrading
of the role that art can play in human knowledge. On the other hand,
to praise *The Newcomes, The Three Musketeers,* and *War and Peace*

as somehow transcendentally superior to art did much the same thing. Art does not transcribe experience, nor does it transcend it; art transforms the character of experience to make it legible. Thus to James the idea—that which ultimately provides us our "revelations and notes"—was the "determinant thing" in the writer's approach to his craft, varying in obliqueness or directness, moral simplicity or complexity, according to the writer's temperament.

E. *Writing as an Art*

The basic problem for James was to recover the novel from the plight into which it had been driven by the new movements. The radical inanities of the sexual novel and the hard-line ideological bias of naturalism which had been eagerly received by many when they were first thrust up by the momentous changes in thought and attitudes in the latter part of the nineteenth century were subjected to a thorough critical review, and found thin. He was inclined to think that the fault lay in the older romanticism, whose impractical aims James saw as having brought about its disintegration into marginal wayward sects. Flaubert's aestheticism and Balzac's naturalism were both examples of the fatal erosion of the romantic tradition into movements which effectively isolated art from life because their interconnection could no longer be sustained. Romanticism, along with its natural heir, naturalism, chose life against art, and denied to art any field or standard of its own. Aestheticism chose art against life. In either case the isolation of art was complete, and human life was emptied of cultural meaning and moral content.

James' proposed solution was that writers abandon, for practical purposes, commitment to ideological views, which amounted to little more than a neurotic tic anyway, and redirect their attention to the aims of art as these are subsumed in convention, language, imagination, artistic sensibility, and artistic intelligence. This tack, he thought, had certain advantages. The writer was steadied, and at least to some extent his way was pointed out. The purposes of his craft were clearer. "There may be a cool virtue therefore even for 'art,' and an appreciable distinction for truth, in the grace of hanging back and the choice of standing off . . . which we best defend by simply practising it in season."[80] Overwhelmed by the "sexual," for instance, we turn away in quest of hardier fare, and encounter, unexpectedly, the "clinging hand of dear old Jane Austen." And so in this last period James restated with concision and sometimes with impatient directness the essential conservatism of his enterprise, the rich solid ground of art, and sought to recall writers to those classic principles of art which he himself had observed for so many years.

Recognizing that reality is one but that perception varies, James complicated the writer's task by suggesting that artistic "intensity" was best gotten through the use of a registering consciousness. A writer necessarily draws his incidents from experience. But the incidents gain in art, and at the same time concede the ambiguous nature of experience, by being filtered through various "reflectors and registers," people of such keen sensibility and intelligence that we accept their competence to successfully unriddle the experiences they are undergoing. "We want it clear, goodness knows, but we also want it thick, and we get the thickness in the human consciousness that entertains and records, that amplifies and interprets it."[81]

Finally, of course, all such matters are filtered through the consciousness of the writer himself, on whose perception art either lives or flounders. All relations, James said, "stop nowhere, and the exquisite problem of the artist is eternally but to draw, by a geometry of his own, the circle within which they shall happily *appear* to do so."[82] Writers helped to muffle the "ache of the actual" by putting bounds to the actual in order to restrict its sometimes devastating effect on the human spirit, a point Robert Frost later confirmed in his remark that a poem is really a defensive maneuver to arrest the flood of uncomprehended experience. "Such recording and illuminating agents are precious," James said. "They tell us where we are in the thickening fog of life. . . ."[83] Reality lay as one vast inert lump of unconsumed experience. But just as the use of reflectors and registers illustrated the complicated equ   al nature of human perception, so writers framed reality from a ultitude of angles and strategms. In this light, literature should be viewed as a series of dramatic disclosures of things not previously known or realized, though writers sometimes mistakenly took their special insights to be the equivalent of truth. The "house of fiction," James wrote in his prefaces to *The Princess Casamassima*   *Portrait of a Lady,* has many apertures or windows. Each window—of which there could literally be millions—met the "need of the individual vision and the sure of the individual will." Writers, then, had their own vantage , but the reality they viewed was one. Thus the "power" of the James, lay in its vast range of observation while remaining sense of "what is."

CHAPTER 4

Historical and Evolutionary Criticism

T HE prestige of history in the nineteenth century and of the great
philosophies fashioned in its name was such that few men were
prepared to forego its authority, so that almost everyone who wrote
literary criticism sooner or later paid tribute to its value for understanding the complex nature of cultural life.[1] Historical criticism rose
to a prominence of sorts in the antebellum America of 1830 and
following, partly in response to a prevailing nationalistic spirit
anxious to know and to understand origins, and partly in response to
European formulations, principally German, of critical principles
and procedures which had their basis in an historical point of view.
The new techniques encouraged a lot of nonsense about national
character, folk spirit, racial traits, and the like. But they were
nevertheless instrumental in moving American critics away from a
narrowly moral and judicial evaluation of literature and toward a
more dispassionate analysis of literary continuity and cultural context.[2]

In the post–Civil War period, the romantic emphasis on vast,
sweeping divisions of human experience, such as national psychology, Anglo-Saxonism, historical milieu, and time spans continued to
inform theories of historical criticism. Even in antebellum America
these divisions oversimplified social experience; in the post–Civil
War period their use was complicated even more by the emergence
of new situations, movements, and leaders in which the old hand-
books did not seem to be of much use. Explanation and validation of
evolutionary and historical theory amounted virtually to an industry,
yet persistent problems endemic in the culture were largely ignored:
the need to adjust to the sheer size of the American environment; the
obligation of literature and scholarship to meet the demands of an
ever-growing public, including immigrants increasingly alive to the
actual realities of their work-a-day world; the exploitation of the

country's resources through scientific inventions and industrialism, which brought to a focus many of the problems inherent in our professed ideal of democratic equality and the welfare of all.

At least four movements rose that ran counter to the historicism encouraged by evolutionary views. First, the evolutionists' emphasis on the ruthlessness of the struggle for existence, and their corollary emphasis on supermanism, led some writers, such as the later Howells, to safeguard democratic equality of opportunity through a "planned economy." There thus developed through this reaction to evolution a considerable demand for a literature of propaganda and social reconstruction.[3] Next, the end of the century was witness to a revival of Waverleyism as well as of attempts to justify a literature of entertainment and escapism. A spate of essays in support of these views was published, typified in Marion Crawford's "The Novel— What is It?" (1893), James Lane Allen's "Two Principles in Recent American Fiction" (1897), and Richard Burton's "The Healthful Tone for American Literature" (1895). Third, there was an aesthetic reaction to the "bleak and terrifying" vision of evolution which led some persons to seek psychological compensation for the thralldom to blind forces seemingly supported by evolution. The result, for such men as James Gibbons Huneker, was a turn to bohemian iconoclasm, egotism, and aesthetic anarchism. Finally, a small group of judicial critics took high ground among the ancient Greeks. In *Interpretations of Poetry and Religion* (1900), George Santayana paid homage to "that pursuit of something permanent in a world of change, of something absolute in a world of relativity, which was the essence of the Platonic philosophy."

These reactions were in most cases healthy, for they encouraged attention to matters of literary technique and form and craftsmanship largely ignored in historical criticism. But if historical criticism evaded the ultimate problem of yardsticks and evaluation, it did some good in correlating literature with other forms of expression and in relating literature to social history, which subsequently aroused interest in literature as a part of what Vernon Parrington called "The Main Currents of American Thought." Here the combination of Spencer and Taine, which Donald Pizer says served as "the basic pattern in most evolutionary critical systems of the 1880's and 1890's,"[4] helped people to connect all the individual pieces of an author's work in genetic relation to his life and the civilization which produced him. In some measure, then, the author could be taken as the illuminating spokesman for that civilization.

I   *Herbert Spencer and Historical Criticism*

Spencer was trained as an engineer, which may partly account for the mechanistic orientation of his philosophy, but by 1855 he had turned his attention to political economy, sociology, psychology, and metaphysics. He was so heavy-handed in expressing his philosophical views that one can only marvel that Mark Twain chose to remark on the clean, crisp nature of his English. And he was not particularly logical, as many Americans of the time saw. But it was the broad outlines of his Synthetic Philosophy in which they were interested. Its main tenents were clear enough. The universal process of life and matter was evolutionary, occurring within a closed universal system, and was marked by a change from simple homogeneity to increasingly complex but integrated heterogeneity. The process could be observed in the physical evolution of the universe, in organic life, human knowledge, and social organization. Energy and matter were interchangeable, so that the rhythmic pulse of the universe testified to economy, conservation, and the persistence of force. All societies were organic entities responsive to the physical laws of nature, and proceeded from the relative simplicity of primitive societies through increasingly complex growth, marked in mid-passage by industrialism and differentiation of social functions, to an ultimate equilibrium in which all citizens were happy and the state, never more than a police agent anyhow, simply withered away. Spencer brooked no interference with the functioning of these cosmic processes. Hence his social quietism, his laissez-faire, his suspicion of state-supported education, welfare, even sanitation projects. He recognized the fact that certain "evils" attended the evolutionary process. But these were temporary manifestations of the survival of the fittest which in the long run were erased by the achievement of human perfection. Almost as a concession to more timid thinkers, he allowed for an "Unknowable," basically the substantial ground for those observable natural laws which directed evolutionary change, but variously interpreted as God or some kind of Force according to interpreters' predilections.

Periodicals of the time were crammed with criticism, interpretations, and defenses of Spencer. Evolution was "in the air," and the miracle would have been that anyone was unaware of it. He was very nearly an instant classic, though he failed to survive his historical period. In the United States, his fortunes were at best ambiguous, as commentators put strange constructions upon his work. Literary reaction took one tack, social philosophy another. The latter moved over the three-decade period of his influence from the stringent impersonal quietism of E. L. Youmans and William Graham Sumner, whose views most nearly correspond to those of Spencer, to the humanitarian social theories and celebration of the state of Richard T. Ely and Lester Ward, rebellious young men who nevertheless also invoked the name of Spencer. The trend in literature, on the other hand, was almost the reverse. Howells, Garland, and numerous other writers early in the period were optimistic, sanguine about the role of the individual in the evolutionary process, and disposed to accept conscious decision in human affairs. Then, perhaps as the result of an increasing tendency to interpret Spencer's "Unknowable" as a physical rather than spiritual force, a gloomier view began to prevail. Writers equipped with new theories, new practices, and new social outlooks moved to establish the rival school of literary naturalism. Stephen Crane spoke bleakly of men covering this ice-locked planet like so many lice; Theodore Dreiser attributed man's predicament to the tyranny of preemptive "chemisms" in his blood (almost a parody of the medieval notion of humors); and Frank Norris, like his character Mrs. Derrick in *The Octopus,* "recognized the colossal indifference of nature, not hostile, even kindly and friendly, so long as the human ant-swarm was submissive, working with it, hurrying along at its side in the mysterious march of the centuries."

In addition, the rise of the sciences of aesthetics and psychology and the quest for "laws" in these fields led to a revolt from traditional intellectual theories and a turning toward new horizons of psychology, animal physiology, and comparative and genetic behavior. In "A Note on Modern Criticism," Richard Burton stressed the significance of science in the turn from absolutes to relativism in literary criticism, and then went on to state what he thought that Spencer had accomplished:

In the domain of ethics a similar substitution of relative for absolute has been brought about. The conscience is still regarded as innate by conservative thinkers who accept the sense of right and wrong as directly God-given; but in the Spencerian view it is explained as a matter of racial experience, utilitarian in its origins. Latter-day psychology inclines to this theory; and, as a result, it may be found working in the philosophy of literature and of aesthetics. This thought tendency when transferred to literary criticism irresistibly leads towards a more personal and less hide-bound interpretation of the phenomena of literature.[5]

Under the dispensation of evolutionary monism—the idea that everything comes out of matter—writers felt free to deal with all phenomena as worthy of treatment if not of equal significance. There thus came into American literature an unaccustomed frankness regarding sex and the lives of everyday working people. But Spencer's evolutionary system, with its dialectical progression from homogeneity, its various homologies, and its promise of filling out the system through the cumulative increase of knowledge so governed men's understanding that the real trend was to apply theory to experience in order to demonstrate the structure of reality. Critics like H. H. Boyesen urged novelists to minimize individual heroes and to expand their horizons to deal with the variety of influences conceived as molding the characters and actions of men. Others, however, also influenced by evolution, sharply restricted their work to the physical setting of a story in order to show the adaptation of the organism to its environment. Even the presumed scientific proof of the "rhythm of the Universe" prompted men to subject literary forms and techniques to rhythmical analysis, which helps to explain the more abstruse passages in Oliver Wendell Holmes' "Physiology of Versification," Sidney Lanier's *The Science of English Verse*, E. R. Sill's study of Spencer and music, and John Fiske's chapter on rhythm in *Outlines of Cosmic Philosophy*.

A. *The "Soft" Spencerians*

Though Spencer's philosophy postulated a closed system, it yet gave rise to a great deal of controversy and varying interpretations. Chiefly at issue were how and why natural law functioned teleologically, and how his metaphysics provided a ground for his psychology and sociology. Debate frequently devolved into arguments about the respective roles of religion and science, in which moderates tried to effect some sort of reconciliation between the two, so that at last, as E. C. Stedman said, "a clearer vision and a riper faith will come to us, and with them a fresh inspiration, expressing itself in new symbols, new imagery, and beauty, suggested by the fuller truth."[6]

The soft Spencerians recognized the iconoclastic effect of science on tradition. But so long as science did not arrogate the entire field of human inquiry to itself, and so long as provision was made for something like moral or spiritual truth, they were disposed to accept science as adding another dimension to human knowledge. Stedman was proud that *Victorian Poets* (1875) was "almost the first extended consideration" of the impact of science on poetry, which he thought of "an importance equal to that of all other forces combined." And Hamilton Wright Mabie commented in "The Significance of Modern Criticism" (1892) that the scientific spirit "could not rest in any isolated study of literary works; it must study literature as a whole, determine its rank and place, and interpret its significance in the totality of human development."

Moderates were often ambivalent toward the new science and hesitant to fully embrace its views. Both G. W. Cooke and Vida Scudder thought that evolution limited artists in their work, encouraged despondency, and was easily perverted into fatalism, materialism, and a general stupidity. Yet properly assessed and used the new science could be a basis for hope. In "The Effect of the Scientific Temper in Modern Poetry" (1887), Vida Scudder emphasized the salutary effect that evolution had had in inculcating a faith in progress, in promoting the interdependence of man and nature and God, and in fostering a new realism based on facts and the laws which govern them. These ideas were later expanded in her book, *The Life of the Spirit in the English Poets* (1895). Cooke, who professed himself a disciple of the antiscience Ruskin in *Poets and Problems* (1886), admitted in his book on George Eliot, published three years earlier, that the new science had "justified itself, and opened up new and valuable results giving the world an enriched conception of the life of man." Both Cooke and Scudder, as a matter of fact, took George Eliot as the exemplar of the new thought, commending her humanitarianism, the complexity of her psychological analyses, and her attention in her fiction to the "interplay of two great natural forces, heredity and environment."

B. *The Naturalist Response*

The naturalists held that writers should limit themselves to the factual or realistic representation of personal and social experience. This relatively simple objective, however, was considerably modified in their belief that all phenomena can be explained in terms of natural causes and laws without attributing moral, spiritual, or supernatural significance to them. According to Donald Pizer, Hamlin Garland made use of Spencer's views as early as 1885 in a manuscript version of "The Evolution of American Thought,"[7] which sought to depict the orderly development of American social life and literature through the application of Spencer's theory that social and cultural change is from homogeneity to heterogeneity. Through Spencer, Garland was able to discount the objective order and value of literature and to take an antitraditional view of the past. This in turn led him to abandon the criterion of beauty and to substitute two other literary and critical objectives: the pursuit of truth and the spread of justice.[8]

Garland attacked Frank Norris' *McTeague* because it did not lead to "a notion of social betterment." But the fact is that Norris, Jack London, and Theodore Dreiser all developed a critical position which focused on the "sharp contrast" between current idealist literature and their own observations of how people really lived. In *The Responsibilities of the Novelist* (1903), Norris defended writing for a "purpose." "The survival of the fittest is as good in the evolution of our literature as of our bodies, and the best 'academy' for the writers of the United States is, after all . . . to be found in the judgment of the people, exercised throughout the lapse of a considerable time." London, adopting the overall drift of Spencer's philosophy, wrote critical essays like "The Phenomena of Literary Evolution" and "The Terrible and Tragic in Fiction" in order to encourage writers to put the economically repressed in the mainstream of evolutionary change so that their dogged, embattled progress to the perfect society might be charted. And Dreiser, finding his own observations as a night police court reporter corroborated in Spencer's philosophy, called on critics and writers to support social struggle and social justice: "[then] all mankind will conform to the laws which he has written down, as they were given to him by the One whose work is creation, and whose all-covering generosity has given the world a mind so philosophic as that of Herbert Spencer."[9]

C. *Academic Response*

Historical criticism and the scholarship on which it is based were fully established in the universities by the end of the period. Even Irving Babbitt, a humanist who disparaged the positivist inclination of historical criticism, produced some of his most stimulating critical work in examining the cross-fertilization of ideas—religious, political, humanitarian, and literary—in a series of volumes and essays on the history of ideas. Increasingly hostile to the flux and miscellaneousness of literary activity, scholars were influenced by the general theories of evolution and organicism to put a new emphasis on the amassing of objective facts while remaining relatively indifferent to meaning and value. The primary objectives were two: to establish the relation between literature and the "national spirit," and to discover the "laws of development" of literary genres within their historical milieux.

It was Spencer and the pervasive dissemination of his views which helped to codify and accelerate such critical procedures. In a series of essays,[10] John P. Hoskins developed the focus that most scholars took to be the model for historical criticism: "In order to survive, a literary form must be assimilated by society, must demonstrate its utility by expressing better society's view of what is real and true in life." Harry Thurston Peck of Columbia, a professor of Latin who combined a dual interest in historical and impressionistic criticism, made the same point in *The Personal Equation* (1897) and *Studies in Several Literatures* (1909). Kuno Francke, chairman of the German Department at Harvard, noted in *Social Forces in German Literature* (1896) the "steadily widening influence exercised by the idea of organic evolution, whether this idea be applied by a Grimm, Hegel, Ranke, Alexander von Humboldt, Comte, Marx, Darwin, or Spencer."[11] And in *Essays on German Literature* (1892), a book which in six years ran through four editions, H. H. Boyesen, after citing Spencer's definition of evolution, concluded that "if the novel is to keep pace with life, it must in its highest form convey an impression of the whole complex machinery of the modern state and society, and by implication, at least, make clear the influences and surroundings which fashioned the hero's character and thus determined his career."

1. John Fiske (1842–1901)

The American popularizer of Spencer in *Outlines of Cosmic Philosophy* (1874), John Fiske contributed his considerable prestige to the cause of historical criticism. A professor at Harvard who enjoyed a wide range of intellectual friends, Fiske became best known for his work in history, though he was not the equal to the new school of scientific historians, among them Hubert Howe Bancroft, John B. McMaster, Frederick Jackson Turner, H. B. Adams, and James Ford Rhodes. But he was better known and popularly viewed as a scholar in a variety of fields. His interest in origins led Fiske under the influence of Spencer and others to explore earlier literatures, though he did some work on relatively modern writing. The essay "Juventus Mundi" (1870) is typical of the eclectic way in which Fiske worked. In this rather severe criticism of Gladstone's studies of the Homeric poems, Fiske professed to use "the science of comparative mythology" and the "science of philology, as based upon established laws of phonetic change" to counter Wolf's theory that the poems had many authors. The result is an impressive display of what seems prodigious knowledge of early literary history. But his dependence upon "laws" of historical investigation is considerably dampened when one reads the preface to *Myths and Myth-Makers* (1872), in which "Juventus Mundi" ultimately appeared. For there Fiske admits that he had drawn on the researches of philologists such as Grimm, Muller, Dasent, and Tylor, and had himself added nothing of consequence.

According to this student of man's historical and biological origins, the critical spirit in previous literary periods had been indifferent to its artistic legacy and had even treated it with contempt. But the critical spirit of his time, Fiske thought, promoted tolerance for and interest in the literature of the past. Accordingly he devoted "Sociology and Hero-Worship" to the Spencerian idea that great men are a "product of the age," an idea he partly illustrated in his essay on Milton. And in "Forty Years of Bacon-Shakespeare Folly" (1897), he devoted a great deal of attention to how conditions in an era foster literary productivity. He used the same point elsewhere to explain the slowness with which literature appeared in the United States. The critical but tactful essay on Longfellow's translation of Dante clearly illustrates his evolutionary assumptions. The essay is based on three points: that different periods in the past are distinct and unique, to be studied in their own terms; that words of Anglo-Saxon and Romance origin have different emotional and intellectual appeals (a theory once held by De Quincey but now outmoded among philologists); and that a "truly realistic" translation must transcend line-by-line literalism to reproduce the inner meaning and power of the original. Throughout these essays, Fiske's primary aim was to demonstrate how historical criticism advanced critical tolerance and objectivity: "men of all shades of opinion were but the representatives and exponents of different phases in the general evolution of human intelligence, not necessarily to be disliked or despised if they did not happen to represent the maturest 'phase' which will undoubtedly itself 'in due course of time be essentially modified or finally supplanted.' "[12]

2. *Thomas Sargeant Perry (1845–1928)*

T. S. Perry was an intimate of Fiske and Howells and of both the Jameses, and though comparatively quiet seems to have been one of the pivotal figures in the whole scientific-realistic movement. Indeed, in *Realism and Naturalism in Nineteenth-Century American Literature,* Donald Pizer devotes a whole chapter to Perry to illustrate the principles and impact of evolutionary criticism. An assistant editor for several years under Henry Adams on the *North American Review,* Perry was later in charge of the reviews of fiction for the *Nation,* taught for a decade at Harvard University, and played the part of squire in arming the St. George of realism, William Dean Howells. So close was he to Fiske that each affectionately and with deep respect dedicated a book to the other, and upon Fiske's death Perry published his biography (1906).

Perry's own many reviews and essays for the *Atlantic,* the *North American Review,* and in particular for the *Nation,* together with his few but scholarly books, not only served as the first strong introduction of Turgenev and other Russian authors to the American public, but constituted important realist manifestoes in themselves. When Hutcheson Macaulay Posnett published *Comparative Literature* in 1886, Howells praised it for its interpretation of all literature in the light of evolution, but, he insisted, Perry's *English Literature in the Eighteenth Century* (1883) and *From Opitz to Lessing* (1884) had effectively anticipated Posnett, though they were finally inferior in scope.

Perry was a moderate who believed that human nature was legitimately the province of literature. "The idealizing novelist will be the real novelist," he declared.[13] Even so, he felt that evolution had "brought order where had been confusion."[14] In regard to literature, science had been particularly salutary. It had shown literature to be subject to law, more specifically the law of development. It had proved that both books and their authors are in large part the products of their environment and genetic heritage. And it had opened the way for literature to abandon all the impediments of convention and usage in order to realize the Emersonian dream of a literature based freshly upon a sincere reading of the facts of contemporary existence. Thus the avowed aim of his well-documented studies of the eighteenth century was "to supplement the histories by pointing out . . . the more evident laws that govern literature."[15] Something must be left to genius. How could one possibly trace the "progress" of literature from Shakespeare through Dryden to Dean Milman? But science had demonstrated a general though not uniform line of progress in which even genius had to build on "the foundations that society is laying every day."[16]

Perry admired realism, and he took his straight, the Russian way. Evolutionary theory demanded a realism which accounted for the actions of characters and situations. Hence realism meant "patient observation," "life-like description," and absolute precision in focus, which Perry professed to find in such Russian writers as Turgenev, Chekov, and Artsibashev. We are too prone, he said, to insist that the writer be "a political economist, a patriot, or certainly a moralist in disguise," and overlook the primary fact that the writer is "an artist, writing for his own delection as well as ours."[17] No matter how "scientific" a writer may be in accumulating his incidents, that fact alone does not make a novel: "the informing spirit must control the selection and arrangement which go into every work of art."[18] The essential conservatism in these remarks is obvious, as well, perhaps, as the good sense. What means so much in Perry is his calling attention to a national literature not really known before in this country, the Russian, as well as his insistence that literature reveal the same thin thread of causality in art that runs through life.[19]

II   Hippolyte Taine and Historical Criticism

Hippolyte Taine (1828–1893) was the acknowledged leader of a group of intellectuals who emerged in postromantic France as advocates of the use of science in human affairs, the superior value of truth to beauty, and of freedom as the natural objective of man. A positivist of extraordinary logical ability, Taine elaborated a philosophy of strict determinism. His first book to earn wide attention in France, *Les Philosophes Francais* (1857), supported the use of science to vivify psychology and metaphysics, and was favorably reviewed by Scherer and Sainte-Beuve. Subsequent publications, devoted to various subjects, were organized on the same theme: *La Philosophie de l'Art* (1865), *L'Idéal dans l'Art* (1867), *Théorie de l'Intelligence* (1870), *Histoire de la Littérature Anglaise* (1863), *Notes sur L'Angleterre* (1872, based on trips to England in 1858 and 1871), and *Les Origines de la France Contemporaine* (1871), left incomplete at his death.

Taine viewed the arts as the effects of conditions obtaining in the society. Thus the arts should not be regarded as separate and distinct phenomena. They were intimately related to manners, general culture, religion, and race and climate, so that it was possible on the basis of knowledge of these subjects to predict the kinds of art that would flourish in different cultures, just as the botanist knowing the condition of the soil, the temperature, and the like can predict the types of vegetation to be found. In addition, Taine embraced the questionable belief that all men possess one dominant distinctive feature that serves as an index to character by thoroughly controlling motive and action. He was not delighted with the prospect. Man, he thought, was *bête humaine,* the stupid creature who introduced terror into the world and before whom intellectuals stand in mute resignation.

Taine's technique concealed a certain instability. It encouraged attention to those easily perceived phenomena in society that can be used to account for and to describe art. But at the same time it discouraged attention to those aspects of the arts for which no corresponding data can be found in the society, or which can only be uncovered through drudging effort. Conditions as they exist in a culture are enormously complex, existing as they do in a kind of social solution that is very hard to "read." Taine's attempt to dissect art in terms of race, environment, and occasion can thus seem an overly simple solution. But for that very reason, perhaps, his American followers thought that they had the "key" for fathoming the relation of art to life.

In the matter of race, Taine accepted the doctrine of "progressive heredity" or acquired characteristics, a position which corresponds to Lamarck and Spencer and in part Darwin, as opposed to Weismann and DeVries.[20] To Taine, "temperament and character" were determined by both environmental and hereditary transmission. In *The History of English Literature* he wrote:

Different climate, and situation bring it [the human mind] various needs, and consequently a different course of activity; and still again, a different set of aptitudes and instincts. Man, forced to accommodate himself to circumstances, contracts a temperament and a character, corresponding to them; and his character, like his temperament, is so much more stable, as the external impression is made upon him by more numerous repetitions, and is transmitted to his progeny by a more ancient descent.[21]

As Sholom Jacob Kahn points out, Taine worked out his method, but not his theory, before Darwin.[22] Once Darwin published *The Origin of Species,* Taine had scientific ground for examining the environment to discover the persistence of traits. "The theory of the great English naturalist," Taine wrote, "is nowhere more precisely applicable than in psychology."[23] Adapting Darwin along the lines of the Englishman's followers, Taine used race not merely as an instrument in biography but to show how a particular environment conferred a superior quality on literature by moving it in a particular direction. This tactic took his criticism out of the area of scientific neutrality, as Martha Wolfenstein has demonstrated, since it implicitly supported a theory of value in terms of survival.[24]

In general, however, Taine's intention was to describe and classify rather than to evalute. Literature was a social document which told us how previous generations had lived. "It resembles," he said, "those admirable apparatuses with their extraordinary sensitivity which physicians use to detect the intimate and delicate changes which take place in our bodies."[25] And elsewhere he wrote, "whether facts are physical or moral matters not, they have always causes. There are causes for ambition, for courage, for truth, as for digestion, muscular movement, animal heat. Vice and virtue are products like vitriol and sugar."[26] Thus mind and the productions of mind could be subjected to the same kinds of measurement developed for the natural sciences.

A. *Criticism of Taine*

American critics of Taine tended to focus on his positivism and determinism. David Wasson ridiculed him as a "one-eyed seer of modern France" who preached the "gospel of no-belief,"[27] while Alfred Fouillée condemned his philosophy as "Spinozism superposed upon positivism," and reproached Taine for defining man as "diseased and demented by nature."[28] The liberal Unitarian, James T. Bixby, also opposed the "scientism" of Taine for uncritically assuming the physical basis of mind, since it eliminated any suggestion that evolution could be oriented toward spiritual and moral ends.[29] William Kingsley, a Christian Transcendentalist, deprecated Taine's "molecular theory" of mind as useless in forming a theory of value in literary criticism.[30] Others argued that Taine's determinism forced him to focus on secondary physical causes at the expense of a broader perspective. Thus the Reverend John Bascom insisted as a professed liberal that morality in art should "not curdle on the surface . . . not separate as a thin cream to be skimmed off," but should be unobtrusively organic with the whole work. Like Kingsley, then, Bascom presupposed a mind of intuitions and beliefs which could move beyond mere historical description to capture and describe the moral dimensions of a literary work.[31]

American critics frequently acknowledged Taine's learning, professional devotion, and the grandeur of his undertaking. But again they often had reservations. Both H. W. Boynton and Percy Bicknell noted Taine's "inexorable" determinism and his position as a "spokesman of positivism."[32] Lowell repeatedly said that Taine assumed his "ethnological postulates" and seemed "to shape the character of the literature to the race rather than to illustrate race through literature," a point confirmed by H. W. Mabie, E. C. Stedman, and the Christian socialist, Tourgee.[33] Partly they attributed these failings to Taine's mania for classification, partly to a lack of profundity in dealing with complex social issues. T. S. Perry, for example, could pay tribute to Taine's observation. But he was put off by Taine's "tendency" to arrange "all the world in labelled compartments."[34] And Harvard's Lewis Gates, an impressionist critic who trained writers such as Frank Norris, was ambivalent about Taine's method, though finally, he thought, Taine's views were "as healthy as sea air" in a day when literature had become counterproductive.[35]

B. *Taine and American Writers*

A few American writers knew Taine personally. After his tour of Egypt, Emerson had dinner with Taine and Turgenev in Paris, and the next day Taine sent him an inscribed copy of *History of English Literature*.[36] Henry James, following a dinner with Taine, found that he had to revise his previously held views, which were reserved at best, and to credit Taine with scholarly intensity and an immense erudition. Whitman referred to Taine's "fine ensemble of the letter and spirit of English literature," and according to R. M. Bucke once said that Taine's theory had conclusively demonstrated the tie between a writer's work and "his origin, times, surroundings, and his actual fortunes, life, and ways."[37]

Taine's emphasis on environment encouraged such American writers as Hamlin Garland, Edward Eggleston, and Edward Bellamy to direct their work toward American regional life. On his first trip to Boston, Garland procured an expurgated volume of Taine and found there all his incipient speculations confirmed. "The American artist must grow out of American conditions and reflect them without deprecatory shrug or spoken apology," he wrote later.[38] In 1886 Garland wrote Whitman that he had begun writing an outline study of the "evolution of American Thought," in which he referred to Spencer, Taine, and Whitman as main inspirations.[39] And in *A Son of the Middle Border*, Garland told how he had derived "the principles which govern a nation's self-expression" from Taine, "pondering all the great Frenchman had to say of race, environment, and moment," for as Taine had said, "every living thing is held in the iron grasp of necessity."[40]

In view of Garland's statement that Edward Eggleston was "the father of us all," it is instructive to note that Eggleston's intellectual odyssey was from Methodist circuit rider to Darwin and Taine and the presidency of the American Historical Association. In his preface to *The Hoosier Schoolmaster* (1871) this pioneer of midwest regionalism confessed that he had read Taine's *Art of the Netherlands* as "little else than an elucidation of the thesis that the artist of originality will work courageously with the materials he finds in his own environment. In Taine's view, all life has matter for the artist, if only he has eyes to see."[41]

Bellamy is known today as the author of *Looking Backward: 2000–1887* (1888) and its sequel, *Equality* (1897). But he was also the author of such books as *Ludington's Sister: A Romance of Immortality* (1884) and *The Duke of Stockbridge: A Romance of Shay's Rebellion* (1900), as well as of numerous magazine articles. The social orientation of Taine's writing especially attracted Bellamy, who thought that the French philosopher brought clarity, vigor, and picturesqueness to his portraits of manners and morals. Taine's "broad philosophical grasp" and the way in which he was able to adapt the broad outlines of his theory to a complete analysis of complex historical incidents made him in Bellamy's mind one of the leading historians in Western civilization. In reviewing *Ancien Régime*, Bellamy felt that Taine had exquisitely achieved in his portrait of monarchical France a "methodical arrangement" and "sustained vigor," and a "vivid and complete tableau" of the period.[42]

C. *Howells and James on Taine*

As early as 1871 William Dean Howells read and reviewed for the *Atlantic* J. Durand's translation of Taine's *Art in the Netherlands.* His reaction was unfavorable. There was a "cheapness" and "love of generalization" in the book which appalled Howells. Less than a year later his rejection of Taine was still apparent. Although he admitted to not having read all *The History of English Literature*, he alluded to

Taine's "jack-a-lantern" approach to literary history and to the "sparkling errors of that ingenious gentleman." "m. Taine's method," Howells wrote, "does not take into sufficient account the element of individuality in the artist."[43] In reviewing *Notes on England*, Howells admitted to being deeply moved by Taine's style, and he thought that Taine through his "facts," "guesses," and "lucky thrusts in the dark" had managed to bring out some of the complexities of English social and literary life. Finally, however, Taine's "distorted philosophy" eroded his ability to "judge profoundly." "We read him with the greatest delight; and we leave him with penitential distrust."[44]

As a man who entered deeply into the study of French writing, Henry James recognized and valued Taine's philosophy as well as his artistic ability, though finally he too confessed to deep reservations. James' book on Hawthorne, which endeavors to explain the fragile flowering of Hawthorne's great native gifts despite the artistic poverty of the American environment, was in the main an unsuccessful attempt to apply Taine's theory to American experience. And the controversy with Howells, in which James defended the right of an American-born novelist to work abroad in an environment rich in tradition and "color," suggests the general influence of the "great and admirable Taine."

In four essays at various periods in his critical career, James' opinion stayed fairly constant. He saw Taine as a philosopher rather than a critic, an empirically minded man who at least chose to emphasize the accumulation of facts rather than concentrate on petty "moralizing and sentimentalizing." However much the question might arise whether "the description covers all the facts," James was sure that "the theory makes incomparable observers, and that in choosing a travelling companion he cannot do better than take him from the school of M. Taine."[45] Taine's historical position was often insecure. He passed too quickly from general conditions to the particular case. And he was guilty of "imperfect science." However, Taine made the "constant demand" for facts. He talked, observed, listened, and analyzed constantly; "as to the value of some of M. Taine's inferences there will be various opinions, but his manner is the right manner, and his temper is excellent."[46] Thus James admired the energy and power of his intellect, his masterful pictorial style, and the range and intelligence of his observations. In actual practice, James concluded, Taine played "fast and loose with his theory, and is mainly successful in so far as he is inconsequent to it

. . . . his best strokes are prompted by the independent personal impression."[47]

D. *Henry Adams*

As Max Baym has demonstrated, Taine was a large factor in Adams' speculations.[48] Intellectually committed to the search for unity, his sense of irony warned him constantly of the potential error in generalization. For that reason Adams wavered in regard to Taine's simplified, all-encompassing theory. But like Taine, Adams sought for unity through mind. Thus his interest centered on psychology, and especially on the idea of race consciousness in the manner of Taine, Spencer, and the later Jung, in which attention was devoted to relationships rather than to things alone. The speculations in *The Education of Henry Adams* (1907) and *Mont-Saint-Michel and Chartes* (1904) were efforts to substitute psychological unity for a metaphysical unity which had simply ceased to exist. Hence the need for a philosophy of history in terms of psychology, which was about the only means for imposing pattern and order on an otherwise confusing world.

Adams' greatest debt to Taine is in *Mont-Saint-Michel and Chartres*. There Adams sought to apprehend the subliminal psychological unity of a race, expressed in its architecture, its religion, its whole mode of living, even its philosophical systems. The focus of attention, then, was on the unexpressed, even unconscious aspirations and habitual modes of conduct of the French medieval period. Adams has been criticized for misrepresenting or misunderstanding church doctrines and medieval social organization; but he was simply not concerned with these features in and of themselves, and frequently in the book he said so. He was concerned instead with pinpointing for a moment in time the race, milieu, and circumstances, and to this extent he owed much of his approach to Taine.

E. *Literary Scholarship*

Taine's methodology and evolutionary theory are unquestionably behind the stream of literary histories published toward the end of the period. Moreover, the method followed has on the whole served subsequent historians of literature, though there has of course been increasing sophistication in the use of sources. Interest in cultural history, with an emphasis on literature, was intense around 1890, leading to ambitious attempts to fully get in hand the country's social and cultural heritage. Chief among these early undertakings are E. C. Stedman and Ellen M. Hutchinson's edition of *A Library of American Literature from the Earliest Settlement to the Present Time* (1888–1890); Charles W. Moulton's *The Library of Literary Criticism of English and American Authors* (1901–1905); the standard index to nineteenth-century magazines, *Poole's Index to Periodical Literature*, established in 1891, which with various supplements covers the period 1802–1907; and the founding of various scholarly journals, for example the *Sewanee Review* and *Yale Review* in 1892.

Among literary historians, Moses Coit Tyler is the most prominent, and still worthwhile consulting. In a series of books, most notably *A History of American Literature, 1607–1765* (1878, revised 1897) and *The Literary History of the American Revolution 1763–1765* (1897), Tyler fully developed a social and cultural context for American writing. An occupant of a chair in history at Cornell and later at the University of Michigan, and one of the founders of the American Historical Association, Tyler owed his critical theory to both Sainte-Beuve and Taine, so that he was able to deal with both the individual and the social patterns of historical development without reference to any theory of social determinism. Among other historians of the period are Lorenzo Sears, who published *American Literature in the Colonial and National Periods* (1902), and William B. Cairns, who published *Selections from Early American Writers, 1607–1800* (1909).

The materials uncovered by these early researchers quickly led to a spate of literary histories in which primary attention was given to the relation between literature and life. Though he professed objective comparative criticism, Montrose J. Moses in *Literature of the South* (1910) actually was environmental in dealing with Southern literature and began most of his chapters with sections on "Social Forces." Frederick Lewis Pattee's *History of American Literature, With a View to the Fundamental Principles Underlying its Development* (1896) and *Foundations of English Literature* (1899) were both based on Taine's theories of race, milieu, and moment, though Pattee was uneven in handling the technique. The former was a school text which announced an ambitious program strongly influenced by Taine. The preface to the latter observed that literature was the "merely natural results of previous conditions," so that it should be connected to political history. In its first chapter, "Physical Geography," Pattee made an effort, largely unsuccessful, to trace the complementary relationship between England's island position and its literature. Similarly, C. F. Richardson, in his two-volume *American Literature, 1607–1885* (1887–1888), sought to place literature in the context of the evolution of American thought, though as Howard Mumford Jones points out he was also affected by Matthew Arnold in his critical principles.[49] And E. C. Stedman, despite his belief that genius was superior to environment, used Taine's general propositions in writing *Victorian Poets* (1875). "The most important art of any period is that which most nearly illustrates its manners, thoughts, and emotions in imaginative language or form," he said, adding that the critic "must recognize and broadly observe the local, temporal, and generic conditions under which poetry is composed, or fail to render adequate judgment upon the genius of the composer."[50]

Among other literary historians of the period, mention should be made of Brander Matthews, author of *An Introduction to the Study of American Literature* (1896); and of William P. Trent, a Southern professor who founded the *Sewanee Review*, published *A History of American Literature, 1607–1865* (1903), and served with John Erskine, Stuart P. Sherman, and Carl Van Doren on the editorial staff of the monumental *The Cambridge History of American Literature* (1917–1921), a four-volume study that is still useful. In addition to Moses Coit Tyler, Barrett Wendell is in many ways our most impressive example of Taine's method before Parrington, though *Literary History of America* (1900) falls short of its title, concentrating as it does on the New England scene. In *France Today* (1908) Wendell praised Taine as the most conscientious French writer of the nineteenth century. And he organized the whole of *The Temper of the Seventeenth Century* (1904) around grandiloquent concepts of how the Elizabethan age, like "any school of art . . . rises, flourishes, and decays." Human expression, Wendell said, should be viewed "much as one thinks of physical phenomena throughout the living world. Wildly various and strong and individual as these may seem, they prove, in truth, nothing more various or individual than cumulative examples of how those great forces work which we begin to recognize as natural."

CHAPTER 5

Aesthetic Criticism

I DEALISM, realism, naturalism, and humanism were all in their ways true movements. Each possessed an identifiable silhouette, a cluster of writers and critics known to one another and sympathetic to one another's aims, a stock of opinions grown into conviction about the function of literature and the nature of man. Aestheticism possessed no such unity. Its advocates could not pose as a band of believers struggling with a wayward world. They simply shared a critical mood inclined toward problems of artistic technique and artistic effect. Like most poets, they believed that our joy and our aesthetic pleasure derive from a common source, so that lives can be measured in terms of the intensity of sensuous response.

The dominant movements, on the other hand, regarded man as a political and social creature, and they measured all things by a standard of judgment that was essentially nonaesthetic. To the aesthetes, this notion subordinated the arts to the same institutional level of performance that generally made life grim and unpromising for those human beings who trim their lives to social considerations of reputation, work, and codes of behavior. Such people ransacked the arts for models of social conduct and historical knowledge. They valued truth rather than beauty, and they subjected the arts to ethical rather than aesthetic evaluation. The main objective of the asthetes was to rescue the arts from this bondage to social policy. Their second objective was to celebrate the sacramental character of the arts as they minister to our senses and imagination.

The aesthetes emerged too late in the period to coalesce into a movement, and can best be viewed as a kind of nuclear emulsion which suggests the paths aestheticism took in the twentieth century. One such path was basically journalistic, in which Ambrose Bierce, Vance Thompson, Percival Pollard, and particularly James Gibbon Huneker prepared the way for the brash, sophisticated work of Gelett Burgess and H. L. Mencken. Another path was taken by speculative academics like Lewis E. Gates, Joel Spingarn, and George Santayana. They did not themselves engage in much practical criticism, but they set the stage for the later emergence of Ezra Pound and his colleagues in the 1920s and of the New Criticism in the 1940s.

I   Sidney Lanier (1842–1881)

The Southern poet Sidney Lanier was an early writer on aesthetic matters. Author of our first book-length study of *The Science of English Verse* (1880), Lanier was a spokesman for some of the distinctive humors of his region: a refined hedonistic delight in all the higher phases of the beautiful to which form, technique, and music are the pathways; devotion to the paternalistic features of feudal chivalry; an appreciation of "wholesome" personality drawn by writers like George Eliot, whom Lanier preferred to the "naked" Zola; and the celebration of all that is meant by the "heart" and the "warmth of love" as opposed to cold-blooded technology, the scurrying for profit, and uncontrolled competitive social conflict.

Like Jonathan Edwards, Emerson, James, and Willa Cather, Lanier's thought centered on "the holiness of beauty." Art was the highest in the hierarchy of forms. With the triumph of art, religion would disappear into the arts and conscience into "the love of the Beautiful." Through form the artist's pursuit of beauty gained in control and focus, and for this reason the artist was always on the alert for new forms: "The genius, the great artist, is forever ravenous after new forms, after techniques; he will follow you to the ends of the earth if you will enlarge his artistic science, if you will give him a fresh form."[1] The transformation of the reports of sense into "the dignity of spiritual things" was effected through the fine imposition of form upon matter. In themselves, touch, taste, smell, hearing, and sight were "forever engaged principally as scullions and waiters for humanity." Part of this dross of sense never really disappeared in using the objects of sense to suggest universal implications, for in this world even the ideal needs a fleshly dressing out. But the true poet uses the senses to perform the offices of genii and angels: "the eye and ear are ever willing, either as swineherd or as Apollo, to serve and befriend the kings who paint and sing."[2] The reports and limitations of the senses, then, provide the artist with his imagery, his point of view, the elements of his form. The artist's reading of these reports frees his imagination, and ultimately, at the highest level of art, he comes to understand the holiness of matter.

The idealistic bent of Lanier's mind prompted him to view Spencer's mechanical theory of evolution as a process in which matter becomes increasingly "etherealized." That is, over the long evolutionary time-span the "sense-kingdom" gradually decreases while the "soul-kingdom," which Lanier associated with the beautiful, concomitantly increases. In the essay "Retrospects and Prospects," which presents about as systematic an exposition of evolution as he ever managed, Lanier argued that since art is a force that can effect change or motion, and since science is the study of motion, then science properly studies that which art has caused to come into being. Lanier's dream that the professor of music would ultimately be a master spirit of his age, equal in station to the professor of chemistry, followed as a necessary if poignant conclusion.

Lanier began his scholarly work at Johns Hopkins as a lecturer in English, and soon became interested in broadening his understanding of the basic principles of poetry. The eventual result was *The Science of English Verse,* a pioneering prosodic study for which Lanier used the facilities of the Johns Hopkins acoustical laboratory. Here, too, in his discussion of periodicities of rhythm, he relied on Spencer's authority in affirming the universality of rhythm in nature.[3] His major thesis, however, was that the laws governing versification and music are precisely the same, and so he divided the physics of poetic sound into the same divisions as found in music: duration, intensity, pitch, and tone-color. The errors of the accentualists, Lanier thought, lay in their confusion of "primary rhythm" (quantity) with "secondary rhythm," the arrangement of pitch and stress: "All secondary rhythm necessarily presupposes a primary rhythm which depends upon considerations of time or duration: in other words, rhythm of any sort is impossible except through the coordination of time."[4] Time itself appeared in two guises within the poetic line. Intervals of time roughly equal to one another appear in the line and are divided from one another by stresses. Then within the time intervals one encounters subdivisions based upon syllabic count. Together they serve to provide the reader a sense of primary time. Lanier cleverly develops these points in part 1 of the book, an extremely long section having to do with "The Rhythms of English Verse" and the most important in terms of his prosodic theory.

For the general reader who will discount minute technicalities, Lanier can be helpful in increasing enjoyment through mastery of prosodic techniques. His book has been a controversial one. Gay Wilson Allen, who provides a thorough, detached, and expert analysis in *American Prosody* (1935), concludes that Lanier's "own musical talent and predilections cause him to set up an untenable major hypothesis, but a great part of his treatise is scientifically correct, and all of it is challenging and suggestive." Unquestionably Lanier helped to break up the old jog trot of versification in sanctioning new experiments in the direction of sound effects, though his influence on such "quantitative" poets as T. S. Eliot and William Carlos Williams is problematic. Joseph Hendren's pamphlet on Lanier's prosodic theory is the most thoroughgoing scholarly defense of Lanier's principles, and presents a persuasive argument for the use of mathematical ratios in poetic scansion.[5] "Nowadays when linguistic phonologists are arousing so much interest with their investigations of juncture and intonation (including pitch and stress), few among us are aware that Lanier was studying pitch, stress, timbre, and duration half a century before linguistic science, as we now understand it, was even in its infancy."[6]

Though flawed, Lanier's *The Science of English Verse* constitutes his most important contribution to literary theory, and the only book of criticism published during his lifetime. *Shakespere and His Forerunners* (1902) and *The English Novel and the Principle of Its Development* (1883) were posthumous publications. The book on Shakespeare, subtitled "Studies in Elizabethan Poetry and Its Development from Early English," is a collection of lectures intended for an "extension" audience. Lanier's semievolutionary theme of the gradual "etherealization" of matter from sense to ideality, the theory of Spencerian opposition, and his doctrine of the interpenetration of beauty, truth, and goodness are all central to the book.

Lanier's approach subordinates analysis of individual plays to an idea. He was interested in the "wholeness of growth" of Shakespeare as a personality. In establishing the chronology of the plays he did, however, make use of academic scholarship, principally German, in citing such technical matters as Shakespeare's shift from end-stopped to run-on lines. He also used, not always effectively, his favorite method of citing earlier works, including Anglo-Saxon poetry and Chaucer, to illustrate shifts in attitudes toward various motifs like revenge and forgiveness.

Lanier's emphasis on "cordinate development," supported by a fairly close discussion of *A Midsummer Night's Dream, Hamlet,* and *The Tempest* to illustrate each of three periods in Shakespeare's development, constitutes his central contribution. The strategy was to trace Shakespeare's growth from an early concern with chaotic oppositions to a point where opposites are reconciled in acceptance of life's benign harmonies. This strategy was then complicated by what Lanier called, in *The English Novel*, his "organic" approach. The verse-structure was analyzed in terms of its "necessary oppositions." These were then balanced against oppositions in Shakespeare's life and moral development. Finally Lanier triumphantly declared that Shakespeare's "advance in art and his advance in morals is one and the same growth."[7]

To support this thesis Lanier subjects each of the three plays to an analysis of man's relationship to God, his fellowmen, and nature as Shakespeare conceived these relationships at various stages of his career. In the process he dwells on the structural-thematic function of the plays-within-plays: the Pyramus and Thisbe antimasque, the "mouse-trap" scene in *Hamlet*, and the masque of the gods which Prospero conjures for Ferdinand and Miranda. The succession of motives, Lanier argued, is from ridicule to revenge to blessing, the last serving to prove Shakespeare's final emergence from "the pit into a large blue heaven of moral width and delight."[8]

If *Shakespere and His Forerunners* gets sticky at times, *The English Novel* is a positive disaster as a piece of objective criticism. It is best approached as a specimen of the peculiar twists and turns of Lanier's mind. The book is pervaded by the belief that the best writers transcend realism to make a kind of moral music. George Eliot is awarded the halo. Her faith in "the possibility of moral greatness on the part of every most commonplace man and woman" redeemed her novels, and served to support Lanier's thesis that the process of etheralization should be construed as moral growth: "unless you are suffused with beauty, truth, widsom, goodness, and love abandon the hope that the ages will accept you as an artist."[9]

Ordinarily, when one encounters eccentric or capricious criticism, at least some flashing insights can alert us to look at writers from a fresh point of view. Lanier's insights are usually doubtful, unluckily occasioned by a soft idealism or prudish moralism. In addition, there is a finicky lack of clarity in his ideas, and a dreadful lack of common sense in dealing with earlier literature. He disliked Fielding, Richardson, and Sterne because they were "brutish" and "earthy." Scott was acceptable, though he was never "moral" in the sense that Lanier would most appreciate. Dickens, Thackeray, and the Brontë sisters were imaginatively stultified by the social order within which they chose to work. Only George Eliot, cool and analytical and morally correct, was legitimately in the line of Shakespeare. These views do not inspire confidence in Lanier's critical judgments. Of his various critics, Edd Winfield Parks in *Sidney Lanier: The Man, The Poet, The Critic* (1968) is the most charitably disposed, though even Parks concludes that his works "express his convictions with more violence and less balance than finished works might do." Both Gay Wilson Allen and Elmer A. Havens, who have provided objective and essentially negative evaluations of Lanier's criticism, are inclined to think that *The Science of English Verse* is superior to his other work, which suffers from a hapless philosophical point of view and a highly fastidious morality—a judgment with which most scholars doubtless agree.[10] Yet his evangelical fervor, his twin interest in music and poetry, and his absorption in metrics are reasons why he serves, in his own way, as a transitional figure in the aesthetic tradition begun by Poe.

II *Lewis E. Gates (1860–1924)*

Lewis E. Gates joined the Harvard faculty in 1885 as an instructor in forensics, moved to the English Department, and in 1901 moved once again to become an assistant professor in comparative literature.[11] His productivity was limited, and consists of three anthologies of the work of Jeffrey, Newman, and Arnold; *Three Studies in Literature* (1899), based on his critical introductions to the anthologies; and *Studies and Appreciations* (1900), which was a loose attempt to adapt the impressionism of Walter Pater and Anatole France to some other preoccupations that Gates felt important. Among these latter, he tried to blend the biographical-psychological theories of Sainte-Beuve and the social theories of Taine with the new work being done in aesthetics. Most Americans, he felt, were undernourished in the *process* of art, and it was in this area that he sought to make his contribution. Thus the impressionism of Gates, if that is what it is to be called, was far removed from the single, momentary delight of response which Pater and France understood to be the final aim of literary criticism.

To Gates, impressionism was the final step in a long process of critical maturation that had its origins in the eighteenth century. As he pictured the process, the English essayist and poet Joseph Addison, in his reflections on the imagination, had initiated an inquiry into mental and artistic phenomena which culminated in the finely honed critical sensibility of Gates' own day. In the eighteenth century, the poem had existed as an object in an abstract world to which men turned only on occasion, and then deliberately and on the whole dispassionately. The poem as object and the reader as subject in effect occupied different worlds. In the modern world, however, the artificial world of the poem for a variety of reasons had ceased to exist and the old distinction between poem and reader was abandoned. The poem entered the functional everyday world of common experience, and people in turn cultivated their sensibilities to apprehend the poem and to make it "an intimate part" of their personalities.[12] Before, the reader had to enter the world of the poem. Now the poem existed within the subject as a more or less continuous "series of thought-waves and nerve-vibrations" which brought the poem as object and the reader as subject into one whole.

To this point Gates' procedure is largely historical, devoted to tracing the swelling sensibility of man over the past two centuries. But he also had a personal or philosophical objective. He wished to universalize the poetic experience, to make poetry more accessible to people and to convince them that they had the resources to appreciate art. Art was a native possession, and needed to be fostered. Without art, people were cut off from those forms of beauty that ennoble and complete life. Living in a world of objects, even considering themselves objects, people neglected that portion of their selves that results in spontaneity, creativity, openness, a sense of the complete life.

Even while Gates focused attention on the affective side of poetic experience, he still believed that the creative act resulted in a product beyond its creator. Anatole France's summation of criticism as one's adventures with a book ignored the fact that the book, too, existed and had its own demands to make. The solipsistic approach of France, Gates thought, concentrated attention upon one's own needs, and in its own way converted the poem or book into an object to be manipulated according to one's private urgencies. In Gates' mind, both reader and book have their privileges and should be given their due.

Just as we have an infinite curiosity about people whom we like, a book, if we like it, moves us to examine its origins and its nature in order to understand its reality. A work of art betrays its origin just as an accent betrays the origin of a person. It was thus to some purpose, Gates thought, to study the milieu of a work, for it typified and in a sense coalesced whole groups of forces, moral, physical, and social, that impinged upon the writer's unconscious.[13] The work of art really had two attributes to which the reader should respond: the modes of expression prevailing in the period in which the writer lived, for the period sets the intellectual tone and distinctive coloring of a work; and the expression of the writer himself, what he wished to say, how he said it, his "approach" for making human contact with the reader. To ignore this aspect of literature was, Gates thought, to ignore one of the really important elements in human relations, the intimacy that can exist between two human beings.

Unlike the historical critics, who dwelt on literary relations in examining processes of change and who consequently ran the risk of losing the work altogether in their concern for its setting, Gates was interested in fixing the precise nature of the work in as sophisticated a reconstruction of its time as possible in order to see it whole. In this respect, he is analogous in his goal to an impressionist painter like Claude Monet, so concerned with the "real" that he must arrest time and change to focus on the object itself as precisely as humanly possible. Monet, of course, was concerned with color and shifts of light and with the changing context within which one observed. For his part, Gates too wished to arrest the processes of change by locating the work of art in a timeless contextual situation, so that it is "fixed" in the same way a print is fixed in photography.

At the same time, Gates was conscious that a great deal more impinged upon the contemporaneous reading of a literary work than had prevailed at the time of its creation, especially in terms of the reader's own set of intellectual and affective impulses. All that had transpired between publication and the moment of reading bore inexorably upon the reading situation. A contemporary of Pope read his poetry with quite different assumptions and "sets" of responses than a late nineteenth-century reader, who looked at Pope's pages through eyes conditioned by the intervening romantic and realistic periods. This complicating factor could not simply be held in suspension, much as historical critics might hope. It had its effect too, and it could be a positive effect, according to Gates, for it enlarged the possible insights to be gotten from a literary work far beyond what the author would have thought possible.

In practically all of this argument, the continual thrust of Gates is toward the sensory enrichment that can result from such critical undertakings. While it is necessary that the reader "understand" the literary work, it is more important that he "appreciate," "delight in," and "feel" the "primal vital" excitement that originally moved the writer and which he incorporated into his work. Gates' address, in other words, is to those emotions or feelings which accompany literary experience. Various "rhythms of delight" continually stir within a poem. Often, however, they are lost to view for various reasons, and it is the province of criticism to bring them once more before the reader. Further, Gates wanted to feel "those swift counter-changes of feeling" which prompt the writer to invest his images with "spiritual power" and "rhythmical . . . sound-symbols." Finally, the experience of reading from the vantage of a different milieu than that of the poem was also rendered by Gates in affective terms: there is, he said, "a reinforcement of the original effect by the delicate interfusion of new tones and strains of feeling."[14]

Gates' impressionism here verges close to critical expressionism. There is precedent in the history of American criticism. Both George Allen and E. P. Whipple, for example, were influenced by Coleridge around mid-century to develop a theory of "reproductive" criticism intended to separate the work from its author in order to track the creative process. Whipple especially was a well-known critic, whose *Essays and Reviews* (1878) could have been read by Gates. At any rate, Gates' ideal critic is not only historical and impressionistic in his responses but engaged in a bit of aesthetic analysis. Psychological methods of investigation, he thought, had done much to remove aesthetics from the realm of metaphysics into a closer contact with the facts of reality, so that the "appreciative" critic could avail himself of *a priori* modes of criticism to form wiser and more meaningful critical judgments: "The relations between . . . impressions and effects and the form and content of a work of art have been tabulated. And so the science of aesthetics has become a really vital record of what may be called the mind's moral behavior both in the creation and the enjoyment of art."[15] Gates had perhaps more faith in statisticians than was warranted for his time, maybe even for ours. Unfortunately, he did not develop this statistical aspect of his theory. One suspects that he really relied upon a kind of empirical horse sense when dealing with the relations between impressions and psychological effects and their formal appearance in literature.

Gates' "appreciative" critic is mainly the sensitive, detached type of human being interested in all things intellectual but possessed by none. His main interest was in "revitalizing" art, and for this purpose he tried to limn in a "specialized temperament" capable of doing so. The whole picture is a bit vague about the edges, though the emphasis is clear. The critic should be sensitively tuned, wide-ranging in intelligence, and prone to center on the affective side of literature. To properly exercise his talents, he nurtures his own

impressionistic resources, explores the influence of artistic temperament and historical milieu on the work of art, and utilizes the results
of psychological investigation into how the constituent elements of
literature "work."[16]

III   *James Gibbons Huneker (1857–1921)*

Like a good impressionist, Huneker managed to convey as much
about himself as about the literary figures under discussion. The
picture that emerges is of a witty, mischievous man of wide taste so
entranced by his own iconoclasm that he wrote books about it. Here
one encounters the riches of the familiar essay: boundless curiosity,
latitude of view, enthusiasm, casualness, the revelation of an engross-
ing personality, attractive style.[17] He was economical of judgments,
for his values and fundamental concepts did not go very deep. He was
gossipy, overly fascinated by the alcoholic capacities of great men,
curious about intimations of scandal and reverential toward them.
Inside his mind various facts, scraps of knowledge, and ideas tumbled
about freely, like clothes in a dryer. His studies of Whitman and
Ibsen are commendable, as also those on Shaw, Baudelaire, and
Strindberg. His criticism centered on exposition, what to look for.
The reader was left to make his own judgments.

In spite of Huneker's occasional statements that writing may have
lasting significance or recognized worth ("a classic is always a
classic"), the formulation of a systematic set of critical principles to
examine those elements of a work that allow it to survive time did not
interest him. A critical agnostic, he did not think that criticism was a
demonstrative tool, so compelling in its method that everyone must
abide by its judgments. "As art is art and not nature, criticism is
criticism and not art. It professes to interpret the artistic work, and at
best it mirrors this art mingled with the professional temperament of
the critic."[18] Huneker admired Walter Pater for never trying to
"prove anything." The critic simply suffered the "slightly melancholy
happiness of the disinterested looker-on," and assayed literature
mainly to "spill his own soul."[19]

Like the realists, Huneker was almost totally uninterested in
literature other than that of his own period. But unlike them he did
not spend nearly all his resources on the novel. He spread his net
widely to bring to the attention of American readers European critics
like Remy de Gourmont, dramatists like Ibsen and Hauptman, the
philosopher Nietzsche (whose views he professed to have adopted),

and poets like Baudelaire. While his bohemianism emulated the American notion of the off-kilter lives of French artists and models, his literary sympathies knew no nation. He appreciated Howells' fiction, and urged his readers to look upon Howells as an accurate transcriber of American experience. He came to James as the American writer *par excellence,* an exquisitely modulated and perceptive writer equal to the finest anywhere. He was slightly ambiguous on Whitman, which Arnold Schwab ascribes to Swinburne's retraction of favor and to some remarks about Whitman that Havelock Ellis made in his book *Sexual Inversion.* [20] Poe was celebrated as the first American aesthete, and he pointed with some impatience to the fact that more sophisticated continental readers had long ago recognized Poe as an important writer and theorist in Western literature.

Certain in his politics and conservative in their practice, Huneker's skepticism undercut practically all other forms of belief. In criticism, he especially disliked Brunetiére, who spoke with such certitude and passed judgment with such grand authority. Academic criticism made the accepted the rule. The practice of moral criticism of dealing out bad marks for misbehaving struck him as absurd. He especially disliked abstractions, words such as "beauty," which led men astray in their pursuit of an evanescent universal. Openness, experiment, vivacity, geniality, all applauded in a slightly hothouse tone, were the assets that he opposed to the deliberation and fussiness of such conventional criticism.

Heavily influenced by the aesthetic bias against didacticism and soupy moralizing, Huneker explicitly took issue with the idealists' faith in the "idea" as a form of genetic control which guided the literary work through its development and full flowering. Such attention to a "subject" tended to encourage the rise of cults, which in turn curtailed artistic freedom. It also seemed to work adversely to the acquisition of taste. People were pushed into the side issues of moral impact and narrative continuity, and when these proved attractive were disposed to accept the trite and meretricious statements and the false, boozy sentimentality that informed all too much popular writing. In the process, people lost sight of what was most important in literature: its solemn commitment to technique as the means for realizing that "architectural" quality which informs all great art.

The most beguiling aspect of Huneker is the wide range of his artistic interests. *Chopin: The Man and His Music* (1900) was an early book that dealt with one of his continuing enthusiasms. *Melomaniacs*

(1902) was a collection of short stories dealing usually with artists. Not until *Iconoclasts: A Book of Dramatists,* published in 1905 as his fifth book, did Huneker deal specifically with a form of literature. Containing essays on Maeterlinck, Strindberg, Ibsen, Shaw, Sudermann, and Hauptman, the book was a milestone in acquainting American readers with continental playwrights. In 1909 he published *Egoists: A Book of Supermen,* which served to express his impressionist sentiments before *Promenades of an Impressionist* (1910), *The Pathos of Distance* (1913), and *Ivory Apes and Peacocks* (1915) did it better.[21] The book included essays on Stendhal, Baudelaire, Ibsen, and Nietzsche, all of whom Huneker regarded as strong individualists who ran counter to the prevailing spirit of their times. As he did elsewhere, Huneker disclaimed any "finality" for his opinions. Yet he put a great deal of faith in his book, and regarded it as one of his most important contributions. According to Arnold Schwab, he was annoyed when people failed to see the sweep of his intentions, writing his brother that "the damn ignoramuses speak of me as digging up queer birds &c. When as a matter of fact Stendhal created the entire modern school of psychological fiction. Meredith, Bourget, Hewlett & the rest, while the influence of Baudelaire on poetry has been profound; without Baudelaire there would not have been the exotic note of Swinburne. . . . And Ibsen! Who changed the theatrical map of Europe! The damned asses write as if they had never allowed the great intellectual currents of the 19th century. . . . In what back alleys of the brain live our provincial critics."[22]

IV   *Joel Elias Spingarn (1875–1939)*

J. E. Spingarn received his baptism in impressionism from Lewis E. Gates at Harvard, but he was confirmed in the ranks of expressionism by Benedetto Croce, the great Italian neo-Hegelian philosopher.[23] Spingarn's credentials were impeccable. He came through Gates' courses relatively unscathed, studied under George Woodberry at Columbia, received his doctorate in comparative literature from that institution in 1899, and the same year published his dissertation, *A History of Literary Criticism in the Renaissance.* The following year he became a tutor in comparative literature at Columbia, encountered Croce's theories, and in 1902 published a not altogether favorable review of Croce's *Estetica.* In 1903 he founded and became the first editor of *The Journal of Comparative Literature.* Active in liberal political circles, he ran for Congress in 1908, and for a long number of years played a central role in the National Association for the Advancement of Colored People, from 1930 to 1939 serving as president of that organization. His *Critical Essays of the Seventeenth Century* was published in three volumes in 1908–1909. Fired from Columbia in 1911 by President Nicholas Murray Butler, Spingarn's subsequent teaching was desultory. But he continued to publish articles and books on literature, including a collection of essays entitled *The New Criticism* (1917) and *Criticism in America: Its Function and Status* (1924).[24]

Spingarn's aesthetic purism was well-nigh absolute, as he dissociated criticism from any reliance on biology, history, psychology, or tradition. Possessed of a solid background in literary history, which makes the introductions to *Critical Essays of the Seventeenth Century* first-rate discussions of the literary theory prevailing in that period, he eventually came to confirm Santayana's complaint that philosophy had lost its queenly throne when it chose to investigate knowledge as an empirical science. Imagination, he thought, must be given its due, and the work of art must be seen as singular and organic. But whereas Santayana had arrogated to poetry the office of instructor to mankind and had described the best poets as prophets in the biblical and religious sense, Spingarn resolutely restricted the discussion of poetry to the discussion of expression. It was not even necessary to know the name of the author; indeed, such knowledge could be a liability. He harped continuously on the value of the art work itself independent of all other considerations. His aesthetics gave first play to the mind, or more properly to the imagination. Criticism, like art, had but one ruling passion—to externalize and concretely realize the mind's imagined vision.

As an expressionist Spingarn engaged almost exclusively in theoretical rather than practical criticism. He criticized the impressionists for putting too much emphasis on the subjective side of experience, which reduced art to little more than "the exquisite expression of delicate and fluctuating sensations or impressions." The dogmatists, for their part, were much too rational; they sought to objectify experience and missed the subjective element altogether. Both sides failed to see that in any case they were dealing with the principles of *expression,* "an expression of something, of experience or emotion, of the external or internal."[25] Why not, then, muster attention on what the artist proposed to do, and then follow through by examining how well he had done it? The procedure was an old one. Goethe had broached it in the early nineteenth century, but had added one more provision: was the effort worthwhile? The detractors of Croce and Spingarn continually pointed out the dropping of that last provision. In doing so, they argued, Spingarn and Croce had surrendered the right of criticism to evaluate literary work.

The objection bothered Spingarn not a whit. Occupying the ground on which all criticism must necessarily meet, the literary work itself, and restricting the literary work to its expressive properties, he was relieved of the need to evaluate its intrinsic or unique merits. At the same time, by concentrating on its expressive side, he could abandon all those concerns which had preoccupied critics for so many years—for example, its moral relevance, its place in the evolutionary development of its form, its reduction to patterns of rhetoric (invention, figures of speech, and the like), its embalming in conventional models like the lyric, sonnet, or epic. All these misguided concerns led critics into the byways of literature, so that the individual work became not much more than a Rorshach card for testing their little arsenals of assumptions and expectations.

Spingarn saw that work (and the critical piece that examined it) as a totally unique existence dissociated from all considerations of past or future. Hence no single work ever conformed to an abstract "type" or "form." The literary work simply stood there, containing its own meaning and power. Since it is to little purpose to evaluate something that is, our critical energy should be devoted to understanding what it is. And the only way to do this is to forget whatever theory in which one has been trained in order to take on the work itself. He had only scorn for those academics who wrote whole books on prosody or on imagistic traditions. When they did turn to individual works the results were again spurious, for they necessarily removed all those attributes that made the work singular and worthy of attention. Technically, then, Spingarn would have little sympathy with such preoccupations as the "Elizabethan sonnet," since what made it important was not the fact that whole sums of sonnets had been produced but that Sidney, Spenser, or Shakespeare had written this or that one.

To Picasso's statement that it is as fruitless to describe the artistic wellsprings of a work of art as to understand the warblings of a bird, Spingarn would have answered that artist and critic have a common creative need to conceptualize the processes of inspiration. Obviously we can in no wise be sure of an absolute correspondence between creative impulse and finished product. But we can ally ourselves as closely as mentally possible to the artist, and attempt to recreate his action. In a sense, Spingarn's criticism envisioned a kind of boarding operation. The critic came "alongside" the work in order to grapple with and ultimately master it. Goethe, and in this country E. P. Whipple and George Allen, had urged a similar sort of approach earlier in the century. The difference is that Spingarn was more resolutely bent on working *solely* with the work of art, so that he might track the psychological processes of creation. Artists, he said, "have made it clear . . . that rhythm and metre must be regarded as aesthetically identical with style, so style is identical with artistic form, and form in its turn is the work of art in its spiritual and individual self."[26]

One understands a work of art, Spingarn said, only when one owns it: "there is no other way to possess it except to live again the vision which the artist creates."[27] He was not too specific on how one should go about reliving the creative experience. The intensity of his expression suggests that the matter is in the nature of some subjective correspondence. Later, as Robert E. Spiller suggests, the New Critics would develop the tools for analytical examination of the work as Spingarn had liberated it.[28] Spingarn's contribution was to separate the work from its ties to literary kinds and from the whole crush of incidental formulas in which it had become lost. The idealists, the realists, and historians, and the naturalists had tended to make truth the end of art. Aesthetic considerations were a sort of way station along that path. Spingarn, in concert with other aesthetes, called attention to the irreducible fact that art is art, and we had better understand it as art lest we lose it altogether.

CHAPTER 6

Aesthetic Criticism: George Santayana

GEORGE Santayana (1863–1952) has struck many Americans as exotic and overly idealistic, scarcely "relevant" to the "mainstream" of American philosophical interest. His philosophy, full of verbal felicities and jeweled phrases and references to the issues of ancient philosophy, has been disparaged as too poetical or as possessing a persuasive surface consistency which does not hold up when subjected to strict critical analysis. Centering on ideality and viewing all interpretations of ultimate realities as projected murmurs of the spirit of man, he prized poetry at a time when many philosophers were trying to dissociate its subjectivity from the philosophical quest for certainty through science and logic. Poetry, he said, is a type of "normal madness" in which the yearnings of the imagination are temporarily objectified in images that provide intermittent glimpses of perfection associated with beauty. Much of his work, then, is devoted to aesthetic and critical theory, and he wrote several memorable critical essays.

He was born in Madrid, Spain, on December 16, 1863. At the age of nine he took up residence with his mother in the United States. Except for a brief interval of study in Germany, his education, including a Harvard doctorate in philosophy, was all in this country. From 1889 to 1911 he taught philosophy at Harvard and gradually became disenchanted with the life of a university professor. England and Europe beckoned, and in January 1912, he left this country to take up permanent residence there. The departure was long and deeply meditated and became possible when he came into a small legacy from his mother. He never returned. But he confessed that the American scene had been instrumental in clearing and settling his own mind, though he disliked its "unintelligible sanctimonious and often disingenuous Protestantism."[1]

An enormously productive writer, Santayana published valuable work before leaving Harvard: *The Sense of Beauty* (1896), *Interpreta-*

tions of Poetry and Religion (1900), the five-volume *Life of Reason* (1905–1906), and *Three Philosophical Poets: Lucretius, Dante, and Goethe* (1910). Later he was to publish, among other works, the seminal *Scepticism and Animal Faith: Introduction to a System of Philosophy* (1923) and the four-volume *Realms of Being* (1936–1940). On September 26, 1952, he died of stomach cancer at the age of eighty-eight in the clinic of the Little Company of Mary overlooking the Roman Colosseum, and was buried in "neutral" ground in the Catholic cemetery reserved for Spanish citizens.

I The Naturalistic Description of Life and Mind

A. *Naturalism*

Santayana embraced the virtues of the "hard" materialist: aggressive intellectualism, dispassionate objectivity, love of one's own life, the search for truth under the "moral hue of materialism."[2] "Naturalism is a philosophy of observation, and of an imagination that extends the observable; all the sights and sounds of nature enter into it, and lend it their directness, pungency, and coercive stress."[3] When he turned to aesthetic criticism, then, it was under the "inspiration of a naturalistic psychology." The metaphysical notion that beauty and an "intrinsic rightness" exist in nature does not correspond to the fact, he argued, for nature "everywhere appears to move by mechanical law," whereas man confers beauty and rightness upon things in his experience. Animal faith tells us that things exist in nature, but they exist *for us* "by mere chance," simply because we become interested in them. Hence personal perception, understanding, and enjoyment are central to art. Once an object is perceived, the first stirrings of beauty may be observed in our response, which then increase as we come to understand and enjoy it.[4]

The world provides the artist his subject matter, but that subject matter is simply plastic in the hands of the artist. The artist's need to experience perfection sharpens his critical observation, and he notices how infrequently things correspond to what he would wish them to be. The world is "used" in order to fashion a superior second world of "logic and reflection."[5] On these grounds Santayana was critical of realism. The realist impulse to simply reflect the world of experience, he thought, condemned man to a fractured world view in which he could barely keep afloat, much less direct his course. The nominalistic positivism inherent in realism acted as a brake on man's capabilities, and prevented him from building a spiritual and transitive world view which his instincts told him was the only way of realizing "a finished life and a perfect character." When, however, poetry, science, and religion are pursued in reference to man's need to systematize experience, they become at once "more human, more conditioned, than are the senses and the common understanding themselves."[6]

Adverse to that higher optimism which commonly consisted in recounting all "the evils of existence with a radiant countenance," and viewing nature as a "conspiracy of accidents," Santayana prized art as one means for controlling his horrors. Living in a diluted, partial, unstable and often sad world, human beings can turn it to account through the imposition of form upon experience. Experience is endowed with emotional content. In its purest form, that of music, man realizes the pure feeling of joy, since "rhythms can explicate every emotion." Literature is less pure, for it must refer to the world of experience in order to be fully expressive.[7] Some poets—Poe, for example—have tried to evade the impurity of literature by converting it into musical sound. But while interesting, such attempts always fail, for the inevitable outcome is a false, spineless aestheticism lacking the means of renewal offered by experience.

B. *The Primacy of Reason*

To Santayana, human reason most distinguished man as a species and had two functions: to read life and the world in terms of their laws and constitutions; and to read the needs and desires of man through art. Under the tutelage of reason, poetry mastered the world of experience in order to describe it justly, and it selected from the world what spoke most eloquently to human interests.[8] When the imagination substituted itself for reason, poetry got out of hand. "Common sense and poetry must both go by the board, and conscience must follow after; for all these are human and relative."[9]

While Santayana was far from asserting that the end of poetry is truth, he did observe, like James, that a "failure of reason is a failure of art and taste." Art should be a "rational principle of creation and order," as much concerned with the clarification of ideas and the disentanglement of values as, say, philosophy.[10] Too often artists rejected reason because they felt it deprived them of their inspiration, and this in turn led to a decline of their art into force. To Santayana, such art was barbaric, mechanical, driven by blind impulse or tradition. The artist, thinking himself inspired, accepted everything and drove toward the splendor of achievement, but his work was really all confusion and absurdity, for he had banished reason. Unknowing readers, mistaking mystification for profundity, thought he had better insights than they. But really the work failed through want of discrimination, a charge that Santayana most frequently leveled against Whitman. [11]

II *Art and the Artist*

A. *The Nature and Value of Art*

Santayana gave art an important place, but in his mind it was no master discipline. The arts were "employments of our freedom" which come after the exigencies of life are met, and they were therefore "superadded" marginal activities which we "slip into the interstices of life."[12] Since art is instinctive, it is not the human response to a governing idea, as Emerson thought. The idea, in fact, resulted from the artistic impulse just as did form and expression. The informing idea is not known prior to the work, is not summoned, is not used in producing the work. It comes as do all parts of a work, through the process of creation itself.[13]

The art of his own day was an anomalous quality to Santayana. He thought that both science and sentiment in the nineteenth century had so disturbed our habitual modes of perception and our ideals that people had confusedly come to believe expression and not form was the end of art. The result was two popular types of literature, neither of them equal to classical expectations. The one moved toward impressionism, in which the emphasis was all on primary effects, "pure colour and caricature," the result of artists' uncertainty about the nature and function of art and their subsequent desire to get back to basics. The other type indulged readers' hunger for facts and passion rather than for beauty, but it possessed no "intrinsic" aesthetic value either, for its objective was to depict truth rather than beauty.[14]

B. *Beauty*

Santayana directed us to sexual response as the source of beauty, but its conditions begin to exist when love lacks a specific object, and we wander into religion, philanthropy, fondness for pets, or into love of nature. "We may say, then, that for man all nature is a secondary object of sexual passion, and that to this fact the beauty of nature is largely due."[15] Because beauty inheres in subjective experience, it is a "free natural gift"—its own excuse for being, as Emerson said—so that our attention should focus on how it expresses and fosters harmony within the person. It confers pleasure because it is a "pure gain which brings no evil with it," and it is fundamental in the sense that the pleasure is immediate, an "ultimate good" irrespective of its utility.[16]

Yet Santayana opposed the idea of "pure" beauty, what the romantics in the manner of Poe called "supernal," because it was too disembodied and irrelevant to our pleasure in the world. Such beauty cloyed. The better tack, he thought, was to bring to our attention the miscellaneous world of experience, which may not be altogether lovely since nature is "full of ugly, cruel and horrible things"; nevertheless, the experienced world best stimulated attention, while the desolating horrible things in the world could be psychologically neutralized through "aesthetic detachment."[17]

C. *The Nature of Poetry*

Because beauty seemed so much a condition of human life, Santayana was skeptical of the positivist hope that all "useless" ornament, such as religion or poetry, could be disposed of once the race reached maturity. Poetry was an instinctive activity, its function to repair to the common world in order to isolate and abstract those passions and sensations which underly our conventional dull world, and out of this "living but indefinite" material build new structures "truer to the ultimate possibilities of the soul"; "we revert to sense only to find food for reason; we destroy conventions only to construct ideals."[18] Because poetry was relative to the individual sensibility and inspiration of the poet, it provided no solid view into the reality of the world, and was really a kind of "makeshift" activity. In this sense poetry was to truth what myth is to science. Not necessarily a form of lying, as some philosophers have thought, poetry in its brevity and intensity provided us glimpses of the beauty of particular experiences and particular inspirations. These glimpses are intelligible, but they are not systematically interrelated in the way that truth-seekers try to systematize their observations.

Poetry cannot serve truth because it is an innocent, liberal type of perfect activity that has no end beyond itself. When poetry tries to be erotic or religious it fails, for the impulses to passion or veneration are countered by the impulse to beauty, which must win for poetry to be art. Similarly, poetry in its singular attention to beauty is superior to prose, but the "descent" into prose may be a progress because it is more informative. Poetry stimulates, prose enlightens. Poetry relies on its initial inspiration and never abandons its early "feelings and underlying appeals," so that it is "incorrigibly transcendental" in that everything revolves around the experience and is made to support the experience. The transparency of prose enables us to look through it to the reality it hopes to describe. Prose thus reassures us, whereas poetry deals in "ecstasy." Young people tend to be poets, maturer people, masters of prose.

D. *Poetry and Religion*

Santayana disliked sectarian religion, but he found that poetry and religion had similar objectives if religion was viewed as an elaborate system of spiritual symbols which substituted an ideal world for the real world of shifting atomic relationships. The best poets were religious in this sense. Once poets realized that religion was basically an "imaginative interpretation of life in which its truth consists," they donned prophetic robes and wrote their best work: for example, the early mythologists dramatized nature, the Hebrew poets forged a bond with the heavens, and the "detached philosophers of all ages" developed a natural religion in which "the imagination touches the precepts of morals and the ideals of reason."[19] Emerson was such a philosopher, and for this reason is essentially stateless and timeless, a man whose philosophic aspirations surpassed temporal bounds.

Santayana's overview of Western culture convinced him that the always tenuous bond of ancient culture and Hebraic religion which comprised it had broken down by the time of the Renaissance. Poetry opted for classical culture, religion for the Hebraic, but poetry could not regain the ancient world view and became increasingly exotic as it tried to describe a "world of passion and beauty without meaning." For Shakespeare the matter was even worse, for in Elizabethan England religion had sunk into a shallow fanatical Puritanism which meant the death of poetry. Bereft of the wholeness of vision religion provides, Shakespeare failed to achieve that unity of conception which is "an aesthetic merit no less than a logical demand."[20] In the following centuries, poetry became increasingly incoherent and indistinct. Thrust back upon themselves, writers came to trust only their own uncultivated powers, and addressed themselves to material life in the name of "realism." Ultimately, Santayana prophesied, poets would embrace the "inexperience and self-assurance of youth," mistake its didactic vein for inspiration, and celebrate the delights of raw experience. "Against such fatuity reason should raise her voice."[21]

E. *The Poet*

Writing out of his own experience, the poet paradoxically finds ground for communicating with others. Santayana does not go into the reasons for this mysterious correspondence, but two factors are obviously present: a common human nature serves as the ground for interaction between poet and public, and the better poets abide by the limitations of shared experience; and the poet's subjective response to experience finds its correlation in his public. The poet necessarily relies on personal inspiration, but if his inspiration is *too* personal he wrenches rather than masters experience, the public removes its trust, and he loses his social purpose: "Literature has its piety, its conscience; it cannot long forget, without forfeiting all dignity, that it serves a burdened and perplexed creature, a human animal struggling to persuade the universal Sphinx to propose a more intelligible riddle."[22]

The problem with most poets, Santayana thought, is that they are too wrapped up in their own inspiration. Reason must at some point be operative in the creative process to redeem inspiration and make it work. Much poetry that passes for superior literature in the modern period he thought too infected with a sense of its own importance. He was hard on Wordsworth for touching only a part of the "cosmic process" in his nature poetry. He was cordial to Dickens only because modest aims were so consummately realized. And he felt that Shakespeare was better at texture, imagery, and various happy strokes than in "integrating ideas." *Hamlet,* so often taken as one of the jewels in the canon, was to Santayana critically flawed: a Christian ghost commanding pagan revenge; a hero whose motives and actions are not clearly blocked out; a creaky structure in which various expedients are used in order to keep the play going. Worst of all was the modern epicurean poet, infatuated with his own words. Santayana admitted that there is pleasure in wordplay, but like pure music it soon palls for lack of substance.[23]

F. *Imagination*

As John Herman Randall, Jr., has pointed out, Santayana almost alone among the evolutionary philosophers at the turn of the century stressed the "imaginative vision" and the "glory of man the imaginative animal."[24] To Santayana, all our disciplines are based upon imagination in the sense that form is impressed upon "indeterminate" matter or experience. "The disintegration of mental forms and their reintegration is the life of the imagination."[25] The imagination codifies basic experience into a "single conception of reality" enriched with an order of value. Following this action, the analytical mind is able to break down this unified picture into parts, so that we formulate a physical universe of law, another of moral order, still another of logical ideas, and so forth. Thus what the imagination builds up can be dissolved into "abstract science and conscious fable," a position that Whitehead also held.

Essentially the same faculty which yields us "vulgar perception," the poetic imagination is our primary "form of sensibility." Through it we are provided "supersensible" forms with such sweep and passion and vitality that life itself becomes a joy. Its constant construction of new forms does not disprove the old ones but is a response to the "prevalent mood" of the moment. This shifting and play of expression, passions, and ideas, Santayana said, are all parts of the "realm of Spirit."[26] If imagination does no more than alienate us from the objective world, and fails to provide a model for its structure, then its purpose is defeated. Of all the poets, Homer knew the value of renewal best, and consequently became "the most poetical" of writers. Dante had a spiritual world view, but his poetry is not so vigorous. Possessing more imagination than either, Shakespeare yet lacked their consecration and rationality. As for Browning and Whitman, they spent so much of their coin on raw experience, which has its own genuine if limited delights, that their thought is "inchoate and ill-digested."[27]

G. *Literary Form*

Santayana's attitude toward form is classical, even though he consciously allowed for considerable experiment. No form can have absolute unity, as the romantics thought, for then all things dissolve into one impenetrable whole. Form is simply a combination of elements which allows us to see their interrelationships. The chief element is plot, or what we would call structure, in which the analogy is clearly to drama in the manner of Aristotle. Next, the elements of expression, including even the order and arrangement of words, require attention to their structure.[28] Finally, he thought that convention had a utility which writers should not disallow, for it offered modes of association that facilitated understanding. "The ancients found poetry not so much in sensible accidents as in essential forms and noble associations; and this fact marks very clearly their superior education."[29]

Santayana's antirealist stance was based on his belief that the mere recitation of particulars in the illusion that they constituted the "truth" was unintelligible. The mind has no alternative but to react to the forms of things if it wishes to clearly understand what is being presented. Any instability in the form, consequently, is a loss of communication and can have no advantage for art. But literary naturalism and romanticism, he argued, were so preoccupied with the indefinite and indefinable that by embodying no form but suggesting many they presented the illusion of structure without its actually being there.[30] Both schools accordingly ran the risk, often realized, of disintegrating into mere sensation.

III   Art as a Social Resource

A. Moral Value

Early in *The Sense of Beauty* Santayana listed three approaches to critical study. The first is the didactic approach, which seeks to pronounce judgment, and which is relative to the character of the judge. The second is the historical, the most popular to date, which looks at art through an anthropological lens. The third approach, favored by Santayana, is the psychological, which tries to find out why we judge some things beautiful, others not. "It deals with moral and aesthetic judgments as phenomena of mind and products of mental evolution."[31] Despite his psychologism, however, Santayana was forever casting up judgments, because he viewed man as primarily a "political" animal, and art as but one part of that complex social arrangement we call culture. Sometimes artists, unable to cope with their own social instincts, picture themselves as outcasts, alienated from society and absorbed in the pursuit of their own pleasures and happiness. In dissociating themselves from a role in society, however, they run the risk of being taken at their word and ignored, for Santayana felt that the societal moral sense determines the value of beauty and even whether it is an "aesthetic good." His concept of the moral sense was broad. It was relative to a social consensus, based on experience, of what things in life most minister to the comfort of human beings, and thereby promote an "inward harmony" which confers pleasure and happiness. Absolute standards are nonexistent. The best we do is measure the good against our personal and social needs:

Art, as I use the word here, implies moral benefit: the impulsive modification of matter by man to his own confusion and injury I should not call art, but vice or folly. The tropes of art must be concentric with those of health in the psyche, otherwise they would not, on the whole, extend her dominion or subserve her need of discharging her powers.[32]

Poetry, then, has a "universal and moral function" relative to "the ideals and purposes of life."[33] Risks are run. Moralists especially have a greater capacity to condemn than to praise, for their taste is based on the desire to control and extend presently accepted aesthetic effects without reference to those "more primitive aesthetic values" which push art continually into new areas. In general, however, moral considerations do exercise authority over the aesthetic, because our "practical reason" is dominant in the conduct of life, since it exists to "compare, combine, and harmonise all our interests, with a view of attaining the greatest satisfactions of which our nature is capable."[34]

In a sense, art is reason propagating itself. That is, any achievement of an individual dies with him unless some means has been perfected to perpetuate the achievement. Because art serves as an instrument beyond the human body for altering external matter to correspond to inner values, it serves as a "ground whence values may continually spring up."[35] Art is a part of life, and the criticism of art, a part of morals. Science and morals are "principles of ideal synthesis and safe transition," are cumulative, and build continually. But they are informed by a primordial aesthetic sense which they cannot eliminate. The aesthetic sense comes first, and it is the business of science and morals to build upon it. To proscribe the aesthetic sense as socially useless would be to proscribe utility and logic, for the sense gives to everything "a form, which, implying a structure, implies also an ideal and a possible perfection."[36]

As a "practical moralist," the intellectual realizes that he cannot change the world, much as he would like to. Whatever the origins of natural laws, we soon learn that they are "fixed and unchangeable conditions of our happiness." Thoughtful persons are attentive to those conditions which fix man in his place, and then they encourage us to use our modest abilities and powers to "the realization of our ideals in society, in art, and in science." Unfortunately, just as the intransigent moralist tends to limit the range of art, the vagueness of morals as a discipline inhibits our movement. A certain moral dullness is the consequence.[37] In this world, madness is as much a part of nature as rationality, and an unduly restrictive society often imposes its will upon the living generation. To have a genuine, native, and inevitable art, it would be necessary to abolish all those comfortable illusions which rest upon an irrational tradition. Despite the utopians, that is not likely to happen. The ideals of art, then, teach us our moral lessons and provide guidelines to conduct. But they are not capable of producing the desired effect.

Nevertheless, aesthetic value has social utility and cannot be divorced from its moral significance: "neither in the history of art nor in a rational estimate of its value can the aesthetic function of things be divorced from the practical and moral."[38] A poet such as Whitman possesses only a "sensuous sympathy" for the whole of existence, and is consequently unable to discriminate value. No matter how much he might have fancied himself the poet of democracy, Whitman's casting off of all "distinctions of tradition and reason" unfitted him to be the leader of a people. He really addressed himself to something more elementary, sensuality "touched with mysticism," a form of primitivism contrary to most people's social aspirations.

B. *The Social Utility of Art*

Whitman's problem was that he thought the value of experience lay in experience itself, whereas to Santayana its value lay in the ideals which experience can reveal. Unless the resources of reason and tradition are brought to bear on our movements in life, human beings are doomed to their endless, senseless repetition, as James also pointed out. Furthermore, the social order is in many respects stronger than art, and art can gain in strength by clinging parasitically to it: "Imagination needs a soil in history, tradition, or human institutions, else its random growths are not significant enough and, like trivial melodies, go immediately out of fashion."[39] In turn, society could gain from this close identification with art. The subject matter of art, Santayana said, ideally includes attention to "what ought to be" and to a better concept of humanity. These two subjects enable society to define its values and establish its goals. Society has been wise in recognizing the contribution art herein makes by institutionalizing art in the total social organization, so that the momentum of art can be absorbed into the social order in order to maintain cumulative cultural progress.

C. *The Relativity of Taste*

Santayana defined taste as a learned ability to rationally assess the harmonious blend of experience created by art. Because it is learned, it differs in pertinence and in breadth of appeal according to the intellectual abilities of the critic, yet its rational authority in good hands is always acknowledged. Critics of inferior ability commonly experience the beauties of a work of art in an aesthetic vacuum. More perceptive critics are also receptive to the elements of beauty in a work of art, but they go on to examine its adjustment of the pieces of experience, its expressionistic effects, and its utility for the public at large. Hence taste has a "social career." It hopes to educate people and to promote their intellectual growth. Critics do not exist to praise poets. Poets are quite capable of handling that function for themselves. Critics exist to "inquire how significant the poet's expressions are for humanity at large or for whatever public he addresses."[40] When a work of art solicits attention in the hope of becoming a "public possession," the critic's task is to estimate how worthy it is to receive that attention. He asks: "Is it humane, is it rational, is it representative?" [41]

While good taste is "friend to the whole man," it has the same "infinite range" as art and shifts just as easily in response to the "human bias" of personal thoughts, judgments, and feelings. Sometimes a certain dogmatism results, but so long as its principles are not taken to be universal or metaphysical there is little harm. Dogmatism is simply the resolute defense of personal taste.

Here as elsewhere, Santayana held to criteria of flexibility, good sense, and reasonable balance. To express a preference for one poet over another, as T. S. Eliot did in praising the superiority of the *Paradiso* to *Macbeth*, is more a "personal confession" than a critical statement.[42] Our reactions to art are relative to temperament, age, the language we know best, and the doctrines we treasure, all of which illustrate the barrenness of wrangling about the comparative merits of writers. In the heat of criticism Santayana strayed from this insight. He ranked Lucretius over Dante and Goethe, thought Homer superior to Virgil, had good words for Shelley but played down Keats, and frequently used the poets of antiquity to illustrate the cultural decline of art in his day.

D. *Romanticism*

Santayana was a political conservative, a classicist in literary taste, a philosophical materialist with leanings toward epicurean stoicism in terms of an "animal faith" in sensory impulse and inspiration, a celebrant of reason as the means to the good life of pleasure and happiness, and a hedonist of great refinement. For all these reasons he distrusted the frenetic pursuit of the absolute that he associated with the romantic temperament. This attempt to raise the ideal to the impossible status of a "central and universal power in the world" led directly to its errors of faith: trust in destined progress, the efficacy of "raw" experience, the gospel of endless human aspiration, the rejection of the past. The errors of romanticism are thus moral rather than historical, a point overlooked by such critics of Santayana's position as Irving Singer, who indicts Santayana for not taking seriously the issues with which the romantics grappled.[43] Santayana acknowledged that idealism functions as a "moral energy" for improving conditions. It thus played a necessary role in the life of man. Romanticism, however, confused the ideal description of reality with reality itself.

Thus the romantic temperament is doomed to perpetual disenchantment. It forgets that the spirit of nature is continuous, spontaneous, always changing, without goal nor end, and substitutes for it a perfect world that never existed and never will. The disintegration of stifling and confusing social conventions which inhibit perception and arrest reform is all to the good. But a dream is substituted instead of a workable project. When the dream fails, romantic vitality and pluck are invoked to pursue the dream even further, and the bitter taste of failure is repeated.[44]

Like Irving Babbitt, Santayana linked the lame and impotent conclusion of romanticism to its theory of history. To him change was simply an "unspecified flux of material forces actually carrying events forward from phase to phase."[45] The romantics attached purpose to history, and saw it as the vast progressive unfolding of universal purpose. In *The Last Puritan,* Cousin Caleb accuses German romantics of "wilful arbitrary perspectives" which are "scandalous": "Nothing else is required for them to pose as the latest leaders in the march of thought." And what a latter-day romantic like Taine does is to construct "a set of brilliant dramatic sketches or notes of moral attitudes, strung together so as to suggest a voluminous current of evolution carrying these various spiritual moments on the crest of its waves. It is a material movement sketched by romantic suggestion and wrapped in moralistic eloquence or even in prophecy."[46]

The problem with this view of history as the march of progress, according to Santayana, is that it effectively closes off for the present the history of the past. History becomes antiquarian, the study of something quaint and far distant, irrelevant to "modern" concerns. Romantics pursue history because it does not count for much. What validity does Greek wisdom have for minds that have traveled beyond its experience and wisdom? Closed off in their little niche in the past, the Greeks could be exhaustively "studied" much as one examined a specimen through curiosity alone. "But the past had not been consciously romantic; what the ancients actually thought and felt was understood much better before the nineteenth century than since; for formerly they were regarded simply as men, essentially contemporary—which comes much nearer the truth."[47]

When concerned with narrower issues, Santayana was not so prone to discount the romantics out of hand. The genius of Goethe he thought sufficiently high to include him in a book with Lucretius and Dante. In 1900 he went to great lengths to characterize Whitman as a "barbaric" poet lacking a base in the American people. Eleven years later he observed that Whitman's work "contains a beginning . . . that might possibly grow into a noble moral imagination." The essay on Shelley, primarily concerned with the poet as the sensitive revolutionist, was an attempt to refute Matthew Arnold's statement that Shelley was "a beautiful and ineffectual angel, beating his wings in a luminous void in vain." He was sympathetic to Emerson and wrote one long and two short essays on him, and there is much in Santayana himself that echoes the wisdom of Emerson.[48] In general, however, Santayana's temperament was not romantic, and his criticism of romantic writers is edged with a sense of their intellectual limitations.

E. *The Decline of Art*

Santayana thought that the nineteenth century was witness to an "era of chaos" in the arts, in which energy and actuality rather than reason were increasingly emphasized. The lack of order and discipline, both necessary for intellectual progress, signified that the period was in a state of cultural decline. Its poets and thinkers were in a state of "imaginative decadence" partly brought on by an intellectual relaxation throughout the entire culture:

> Our public, without being really trained—for we appeal to too large a public to require training in it,—is well informed and eagerly responsive to everything; it is ready to work pretty hard, and do its share towards its own profit and entertainment. It becomes a point of pride with it to understand and appreciate everything. And our art, in its turn, does not overlook this opportunity. It becomes disorganized, sporadic, whimsical, and experimental. The crudity we are too distracted to refine, we accept as originality, and the vaguenesses we are too pretentious to make accurate, we pass off as sublimity. This is the secret of making great works on novel principles, and of writing hard books easily.[49]

Part of the disenchantment Santayana felt he attributed to positivism, itself an offshoot of the romantic temperament. Positivism settled for brute facts and particular realities, failed to appreciate the past, and resigned responsibility for formulating useful cultural ideals. "The nineteenth century . . . has nourished the hope of abolishing the past as a force while it studies it as an object. . . ."[50] Consequently the age, under the auspices of positivism, had become "singular and revolutionary," deprived as it was of any recoverable past, and its imagination had "relapsed into barbarism."

This general decline had its impact upon art. Sense and passion, power, irrationality, heaps of images, and the play of mood and fancy were valued at the price of distinction and permanent values. Prizing passion for itself, the writer felt no need to break it to harness and project ideal goals. "He is the man who does not know his derivations nor perceive his tendencies, but who merely feels and acts, valuing in his life its force and its filling, but being careless of its purpose and its form."[51] James directed the same criticism toward the naturalists, and for much the same reason. Temperament was followed without discipline, energy exercised without objective, adventure pursued without plan.

Such art had simply lost the will to perfect human nature, our reason, or the world. Its only wish was to return to some "Unutterable Reality" variously thought to be God in matter, as Whitman believed, or the primary world of matter as described by the impressionists and naturalists. The problem with this kind of writing was that, while it had force and possessed considerable emotional value, the reader was dazzled by this onslaught of sheer fact and sank into confusion. In an effort to rescue himself, the reader occasionally developed the ability to assign symbolic meanings to such detached impressions in order to make them represent a greater reality. Here he did the work that rightly should be assigned to the writer. And in addition the reader had no warrant for assuming that his symbolic construction corresponded to anything that might be in the work of art.

Santayana also detected another way in which modern poets reacted to the multiplicity of experience. Some symbolist poets were "ringers of mental chimes" who waited and listened for "chance overtones of consciousness." Instead of bending their thoughts to become symbols for things, the usual process of literary creation, they played with things and made them symbols of their thought. Santayana does not supply us with names, but those of Paul Valéry and André Breton come to mind. Other symbolist poets broke up the world and fashioned symbols to describe their ideal world rather than the world we know and in which we live. Santayana cites Shelley, but the Yeats of gyres, masks, and visions would also serve.

All these writers, Santayana held, were ignorant of the "fatal antiquity of human nature." His own aesthetic theory and literary criticism reflect his belief that the elements of idealism and naturalism need to be combined in any worthwhile and socially useful art. Always averse to dogma or special pleading, he relied on the reflective powers of intelligence and imagination. Consequently, he sought less to explain or to describe literary works than to evaluate a literature of change according to the unchanging "moral identity of all ages," the source of which was in the vital poetry of Homeric times and which remained for him always "the sweetest and sanest that the world has ever known."

CHAPTER 7

Critical Naturalism

NATURALISM may be viewed from two perspectives, as a philosophical model or as a movement strictly limited to time and place. As a literary movement in this country, naturalism dates from 1890 to roughly 1920. It is sometimes viewed as the logical distention of realist theory, and in the sense that many naturalists were first encouraged and promoted by realists in positions of editorial influence that point has some justification. But there are distinct differences between the two movements. Realism was not a coherent philosophical scheme nor even a technique. It simply required writers to select from experience in the name of an uncertain nuance they called reality. The "reality" itself varied from man to man: Twain's emphasis upon autobiographical recollection; Howells' upon the moral implications of social acts; James' upon the subjective response to experience. All of them were concerned with the meaning of decision, of the shifting relations of people as they interact. Their work was empirical and implied the existence of human variables as characters sought their own answers to the problems of existence.

Naturalism was much more doctrinaire in its approach. Realism tended to be "scientific" in its approach to social and psychological phenomena for the purpose of creating the illusion of life. The naturalist use of science had a different purpose, to enlighten people on the ontogenetic nature of life, often with the object of encouraging them to a right course of conduct. Thus Donald Pizer finds two sets of "tensions or contradictions" in the naturalistic novel: the tension between the dull commonplaces of this world and the possibility of heroic and extraordinary action; and the tension between a heavy determinism and a paradoxical commitment to an "affirmative ethical conception of life."[1]

Naturalism is best viewed as an inverted romanticism resulting from a loss of faith in romantic precepts in the latter part of the century. This is the thesis of Charles Child Walcutt's *American Literary Naturalism, a Divided Stream* (1956), which suggests that optimistic and pessimistic forms of naturalism constitute separate streams whose headwaters are in Transcendentalism. Warren French makes much the same point in his book on Frank Norris.[2] One problem with this thesis is that it is difficult to think of Transcendentalism, which most people thought impractical and not worth the powder and shot, as little more than an eddy in or a tributary to the "mainstream" of American thought, though we have since come to recognize its preeminence, of course. Romantic overtones of a more general nature, however, are easily caught in naturalist thought: interest in the organic, in processes of change and development, in genetic continuity and inquiry into origins, in the role of natural law, in sweeping projects to reform people and their institutions. Even those views thought most intrinsic to romanticism, the exaltation of the determinative powers of the individual, the excellence of the world and of instinct, and the generally benign character of the universe, appear in naturalist thought just often enough to make its antiromantic bias suspect.

The scale of that thought is thus romantic, even while the naturalists felt themselves at one of those turning points in history which preclude any return to old ways of thinking and acting. The country had changed. It was urban now, with the cities drawing labor from the surrounding areas, and the whole process of living becoming more standardized. Labor organized against business and the farmers against "eastern capital," and finally in 1893 there came a paralyzing depression that was to last four agonizing years. The naturalists drifted toward a quasi-romantic world view which dwelt on the seamier side of existence to define man as a "natural" animal reacting with perfect predictability to various causes and stimuli. Man seemed a small, minute, inconclusive, and indeterminate element trying to keep his feet in the vast convolutions of cosmic processes. Science, the new god which shunted aside the old dogmas and egocentric beliefs in good and evil, provided a new paradigmatic model for man and his world. The model proved unattractive to most people, and they chiefly regarded the naturalists as a tribe of nay-sayers whose resolution to tell things as they are misled them into exaggerated fictions of reality.

Those naturalists most frustrated by the refusal of people to hear the truth found that their alienation demanded a millenarian faith, usually socialism, which would subvert established societal values and replace them with a new integration of man and nature. Hamlin Garland embraced Henry George, Jack London revolutionary socialism, Theodore Dreiser the image of Russia. Only Stephen Crane seems free of an idealism, based on discontent, which anticipated a luminous future of sweet reason and complete social acceptance of its treasured axioms. Before they could hope to act as liberated moral beings, and to fulfill themselves within the social order, however, they had to first narrow the space between their knowledge and the public's knowledge of the actual state of things, by inspecting the fissures that crisscrossed social organization. They wanted to acquaint the public with the grim, shocking indignity of having to face facts.

The naturalist world view thus converged on the ideal of a sound, rational society whose lodestar would be science. While he is speaking in a different context, George Santayana catches exactly the naturalists' moral fervor: "All their zeal is for something radically different from the actual and (if they only knew it) from the possible; it is ideally simple, and they love it and believe in it because their nature craves it."[3] Their millenarian faith gave them knowledge of the future. Their extravagant faith in science gave them their revelation of history and the tools to effect its purposes. And literature provided them the means for educating the public.

I   Hamlin Garland (1860–1940)

The realism versus naturalism versus romanticism debates were at their height in the 1890s, with American writers thoroughly embroiled in the quest for a suitable literary theory. Equally turbulent was the search for a truly "American" literature detached from all connection to tradition and other national literatures. Hamlin Garland, drawing on Spencer, Taine, Whitman, Henry George, Howells, Joseph Kirkland, the reformer B. O. Flower of the Chicago Arena, as well as others, played a key role in both controversies.

Garland was a reform-minded man whose romantic optimism and cordial good nature mark him as a transitional figure between American populism, whose inseparable characteristics are moralism and social reconstruction, and the doctrinal certainties of classic naturalism. He stressed "local color" as an essential element in an emerging national literature, associating localism with Spencer's idea of evolution toward heterogeneity. All forms of imitation were rejected. As a believer in evolutionary thought, he stressed the intimate connection of life and literature and their twin shifts as they respond to the "on-going" continuum of evolutionary change. An aversion to "Kodak" reality, evidently the result of his reading in Eugène Véron's *Aesthetics* around 1886, led him to suggest that literature should include both objective reality and subjective response. In 1891 and 1892 especially, he campaigned extensively for land reform in support of the aims of Henry George and the Populist (Agrarian) Revolt.

Born in Wisconsin in 1860, Garland was raised on a series of homesteads throughout the Midwest. The ten years between his first arrival in Boston in 1884 and the publication of *Crumbling Idols* in 1894 are marked by literary and economic concerns undergirded by his acceptance of Herbert Spencer's philosophy. Evolution, if it could be extended to society, would lead to much-needed reform. The extension of the same view to the arts led to his bold disregard for established classics in favor of what he called "veritism."

Economic reform and literary theory were in fact linked in Garland's mind. He had read Henry George's *Progress and Poverty* and accepted the main thesis that the root of social evil is in land monopoly. The insight led him to oppose collectivist remedies. "The sufferings of the victims of society," he said, "are not due, as the Socialists claim, to free competition, but to the lack of free competition—in short to monopoly."[4] With land reform there would be a rise in the standard of living, which in turn would lead to a rise in the standard of art. With leisure time and more money, "the common man would be no longer a common man, and art, genuine art, with free and happy intellects before it, would no longer be the poor, begging thing it seems now."[5]

In several very useful studies, Donald Pizer has traced the growth of Garland's attitudes toward literature. *Hamlin Garland's Early Work and Career* (1960) is especially helpful on Garland's literary creed between 1884 and 1887. And in "Herbert Spencer and the Genesis of Garland's Critical System,"[6] Pizer draws mainly on Garland's unpublished paper, "The Evolution of American Thought," written sometime during 1886–1887, to show that he argued for literary progress in analogy with supposed growth toward an integrated, heterogenous American social and intellectual life. Much later, in *Roadside Meetings of a Literary Nomad* (1930), he repeated these earlier views: "Literature, in order to be great, must be national, and in order to be national must deal with conditions peculiar to our own land and climate." In support of this view he cited such regionalists as Joel Chandler Harris, G. W. Cable, Sarah Orne Jewett, Mary Wilkins Freeman, Joaquin Miller, and Bret Harte to illustrate "varying phases of the . . . movement which is to give us at last a vital, original, and national literature."

At first Garland attacked Howells and other "so-called realists." But perhaps partly as a result of Whitman's influence, he favorably reviewed Howells' *The Minister's Charge* for the Boston *Transcript* in 1887 and came to see himself as a champion of Howells and a brand of realism which Garland preferred to call "veritism." In *Crumbling Idols*, his only book-length treatment of literary theory, he said that "This theory of the veritist is, after all, a statement of his passion for truth and for individual expression. The passion does not spring from theory; the theory arises from the love of other verities . . . and one's sincere convictions. . . ."[7] And in an essay entitled "The Productive Conditions of American Literature," he again spoke of the need for the American artist to reflect native conditions "without deprecatory shrug or spoken apology."[8]

Garland's principal objective was to stress the country's need for the iconoclastic artist, the writer who would break out of the hopeless circle of traditional authority. That authority described both the New England tradition and the sense of idolatry the tradition seemed to encourage. As the "idols" began to crumble, people would abandon what was no longer tenable. Literary practices based on imitation would cease, and the expectations of the critics would change. Garland wanted no masters. The goal of artists should be "freedom from masters." "Life, Nature,—these should be our teachers. They are masters who do not enslave."[9] A knowledge of the past was necessary, not in order to escape from the present, but to invigorate the present through our knowledge of origins.

He placed his hopes in Midwestern and Western writers. In his overview of American literary history, Garland admitted that the writers from 1776 to 1860 had reflected American taste fairly well. But they were imitative in spirit and form. The Civil War had promoted a feeling of nationality which resulted in a native literary groundswell, enabling writers to confront and break away from the influence of the English literary tradition. By 1894, however, the problem of artistic independence had taken on a new aspect. The Midwest and West were in the same position with regard to the "Eastern school" that all America had been in with respect to England earlier. The task of writers of the Midwest and West was to break away from Eastern dominance and to create American literature anew. It had scarcely begun: "the mighty West, with its swarming millions, remains undelineated in the novel, the drama, and the poem."[10]

The realism-naturalism clash was central to his discussion, as was some suggestion of Howells' influence. Naturalism, Garland felt, dealt with "crime and abnormalities" and with "diseased persons," subjects which the new literature should avoid. His vision comprehended a literature of brotherly-sisterly affection in which evil was replaced by the communal utopian dream: "It will deal, I believe, with the wholesome love of honest men for honest women, with the heroism of labor, the comradeship of men,—a drama of average types of character, infinitely varied, but always characteristic."[11] Veritism, the passion for truth and individual expression, would encourage each locality to produce its own "literary record," so that "each special phase of life" in America could "utter its own voice."[12] In a very Whitmanesque passage, Garland expressed his dream in prophetic terms:

I saw children moving along to school in the shadow of the most splendid mountains; I saw the youth plowing,—behind him rose a row of palms, against which he stood like a figure of bronze in relief; I saw young men and maidens walking down aisles of green and crimson peppertrees, and the aisles led to blue silhouetted mountains; I saw men herding cattle . . . I saw children, playing about cabins . . . and I thought "Perhaps one of these is the novelist or painter of the future."[13]

The advantage of localism, he thought, was that it encouraged the writer to handle what he knew best. The writer would be true to his knowledge, his locality, and his time. Furthermore, since literature is basically a celebration of "this" life, the grip of tradition would be weakened. Our future literature would then be "more democratic" and "more individualistic in method." His anticipation was phrased in terms of impressionism: "Impressionism in its deepest sense, means the statement of one's own individual perception of life and nature, guided by devotion to truth. Second to this great principle is the law that each impression must be worked out faithfully on separate canvasses, each work of art complete in itself."[14]

Garland thus managed to combine Howells' concern for realism with his own stress on individual impression. The combination made the writer a realist in the sense of his actually reflecting what does exist, and an idealist who can suggest what conditions ought to be. "The realist or veritist is really an optimist, a dreamer. He sees life in terms of what it is; but he writes of what is, and at his best, suggests what is to be, by contrasts."[15]

Garland's impressionism is not in the service of a finely tuned sensibility capable of exquisite responses, then. In this respect his theory is different from that of Gates or Huneker. His definition of veritism as "the truthful statement of an individual impression corrected by reference to the fact" was partly meant to serve a literary approach to experience.[16] By emphasizing singularity of perception, the writer could focus his attention and ignore subordinate matter, whereas the realist according to Howells was condemned to be a mere recorder of objective facts and things. The impressionist writer could rectify this predicament of the realist by selecting "some moment, some centre of interest" which was simple and straight-forward, but which could be worked out with "great care" while the surrounding scene faded away "into a subordinate blur of color, precisely as in life."[17] Beyond this literary intention, however, lurked another objective, and that was to enlist literature in the cause of reform, something the aesthetic impressionists had avoided.

Garland's apotheosis of progress, modernity, and reform was loosely based on his idea tha life was a "continual process of change." Change itself was "progression" through "endless but definite suc-cession," as central to art as to geology. The "statical idea of life and literature" was thus bound to slowly crumble away, growing fainter by the year. New ideas and new attitudes toward the world were emerging which contested the hold of tradition on the minds of the people. We should turn our backs on the past, he said eloquently. "It is a highway of dust, and Homer, Aeschylus, Sophocles, Dante, and Shakespeare are milestones. . . . Idols crumble and fall," but nature calls for "rebellious art."[18]

Progress, however, was not always realized in fact, and much of the subjective impulse gotten from Véron was translated into a reform-minded approach to literature intended to give cosmic processes a little human nudge. In A Son of the Middle Border (1917), Garland reminiscences about how as a youth he studied Taine's determinism, and how shortly after as the spokesman for Midwest regionalism and agrarian reform he formulated his "great principle" that a vital literature had to deal with "conditions peculiar to our own land and climate." The local colorists were the best examples of this new approach to writing. But here Garland introduced a dysfunctional element, namely, that the momentum of the new literature had been slowed because the public was dominated economically by the few, who used technological and industrial strength to frustrate the natural course of social development. Such considerations led Garland to state that "truth was a higher quality than beauty, and that to spread the reign of justice should everywhere be the design and intent of the artist. . . ."[19]

The twin aim of his subjective veritism, then, was to free art from bondage to the past through concentrating on conditions as they presently existed, and this for the purpose of promoting beneficial change through reform. One cannot change a thing until it is known. Active on the single-tax lecture circuit in 1888 and after, Garland went on to headlong involvement in a number of reform activities: populism, realistic drama, impressionist painting (he was the first president of the Central Art Association), psychic research. He threw himself into all these activities with characteristic fervor. He wrote plays, for example, he touted Ibsen as the foremost realist dramatist of the period, he championed the realism of James A. Herne and his actress wife in relation to their play *Margaret Fleming*, and he adapted some of his own stories for the stage in support of populist views.

Some of the local colorists and regionalists that Garland influenced were better artists than he. And even late in the 1890s, there still remained a highly verbal countertheory to this stress on the local. The renowned Platonist Paul Shorey opposed Garland's regional assumptions, arguing that if writers were to follow his advice and chronicle the passing parade, the changing ways of social development would soon outmode their work and it would all have to be done again. As a Platonist, Shorey argued that writers would be better advised to place more emphasis on the changeless traits of human nature in its basic unity rather than on the shifting relationships of a changing society.[20]

After his reformist period, Garland wrote a group of romantic novels about the West, such as *The Captain of the Gray-Horse Troop* (1902), and then ended his career with an autobiographical series, including *A Son of the Middle Border* (1917), which won a Pulitzer prize, *Roadside Meetings* (1930), *Companions of the Trail* (1931), *My Friendly Contemporaries* (1932), and *Afternoon Neighbors* (1934). These are books which have considerable value as presentations of a long succession of authors whom Garland vividly gives us as he recalls their personalities and their habits. He claims, for example, that in his last years Henry James told him he regretted his turn to cosmopolitanism and wished that he had done more to treat the American scene and to nourish his native roots.

II   *Frank Norris (1870–1902)*

Born in Chicago and raised in San Francisco, Norris was early trained in the more conservative tradition of French academic art as taught in the Paris schools. There, according to William B. Dillingham, who has subjected this early period to intense analysis, Norris picked up habits and attitudes that stayed with him throughout his career: interest in precise draughtsmanship and close observation; a preference for subdued colors and for animals, humans, and large historical scenes as subjects; a concern for accuracy and for a clear-cut story line; a greater interest in technique than in emotional content; and a conventional deference to the objectivity of science, especially to the formulas of Taine without Taine's determinism.[21]

Returned to this country, Norris attended the University of California, Berkeley, where he was drawn to French naturalism through Zola and to the evolutionary views of Professor Joseph LeConte, whose classes in geology Norris regularly attended. He absorbed Zola sufficiently to feel the only worthwhile art was factual. The writer's task was simply to present the truth, with the reader left to apply the diagnosis and remedy. Temperamentally attuned to impersonal observation and the positive play of natural law, Norris found these two points reinforced by his reading in Zola. He was unwilling, however, to accept Zola's determinism, preferring a more eclectic approach in line with his deep-seated romanticism.[22] His overall view was optimistic. But historically, as in the more violent scenes in *McTeacue* and *The Octopus* (where plowing is described in orgiastic terms), Norris was a stepping-stone to the kind of naturalism associated with Dreiser, whose *Sister Carrie* Norris helped to promote.

Through LeConte, Norris was given a way of shaping his insights about man and the social order in both his literary and critical practice. Greatly interested in literature, LeConte partly derived his ideas from Spencer and Fiske, then modified them to reconcile his twin interest in science and poetry. A place for ethical responsibility was allowed, the primacy of the moral order was confirmed, and the Christian dual view of man as part sensualist and part moralist was maintained. These three points were then subsumed in LeConte's theistic faith that the orderly processes of nature were good and ultimately beneficial to man.

It is uncertain just how much Norris was influenced by LeConte's views, but the evolutionary ground plan as described by LeConte appears over and over in such books as *The Octopus, The Pit,* and *Vandover and the Brute.* "The larger view always and through all shams, all wickednesses, discovers the Truth that will, in the end, prevail, and all things, surely, inevitably, resistlessly, work together for good."[23] It was a view that Emerson could have confirmed. At the center is nature as a coherent body of law governing both the physical and moral orders, active and continuous. It was, as Donald Pizer says, "above all moral":

It removes those individuals harmful to the race; it aids those who abide by its rules; and it benefits the race as a whole. Norris reaffirms the ideals of free will and of moral order, but he does so by means of an ethical scheme which finds these values in natural law rather than in revelation. Norris makes nature not only theoretically God, by means of the idea of immanence, but functionally so: within his novels nature is omnipotent, yet allows free will; it rewards and punishes; and it is cosmically beneficient.[24]

These beliefs must have given Norris a great deal of satisfaction. One of his last statements, shortly before his death at thirty-two, was to the effect that "I never truckled. I never took off the hat to Fashion and held it out for pennies. I told them the truth. They liked it or they didn't like it. What had that to do with me? I told them the truth."

There was, then, this scramble for truth. Yet it is also truthful to say that his aesthetic sense tended to dominate his intentions. Naturalism attracted him precisely because its unconventional and at that time suspect method provided dramatic intensity. Both Charles Child Walcutt and Charles Hoffman contend that naturalism interested Norris more for its fictional possibilities than for its philosophical tightness.[25] It allowed a scale of action almost cosmic in its proportions. The back-curtain of inviolable natural law neatly defined the closer and more immediate actions of men and women, so that the reader could follow with interest the vagaries of human beings and at the same time exercise that objectivity of aesthetic distance which provides a context for action and infers larger meaning.

Norris' criticism is mainly interesting for its practical approach to writing and for his attempts to work out a supportive literary theory. The essays themselves are mostly narrow slices of exposition, some only one or two pages in length, often written in haphazard fashion, and betraying a good deal of needless repetition. One of the slender threads running through this material is his skepticism toward theories of the inspirational or semimystical nature of authorship. He took writing to be a broad, plain, earthy, and quite natural thing, subject to rule and open to analysis. Writing was a business, an industry, complex, composed of many parts—the novelist, of course, and what makes or unmakes him, but also the public, the whole state of literature in the nation, retailer, publisher, and reviewer.

"In all human occupations, trades, arts, or business, science, morals, or religion," Norris wrote in "The Mechanics of Fiction," "there exists 'way at the bottom,' a homogeneity and a certain family likeness, so that, quite possibly after all, the discussion of the importance of the mechanics of fiction may be something more than mere speculative sophistry."[26] Despite his appalling inconsistencies, frequent limp writing, and failure to fully explore the implications inherent in what he said, Norris was incorrigibly speculative, and given more years his habitual tendency to systematize his experience might have led to something worthwhile. He obviously thought that even the most "ephemeral" commonplace had its latitude and longitude in relation to the whole. Formulas were not to be trusted, because they were artificial, yet "even a defective system is—at any rate, in fiction—better than none."[27] Good novels, for example, often have a pivotal point that brings together whole movements. He thus consciously created such a pivotal climax in the farmers' battle with the railroad's hired thugs in *The Octopus*. In *McTeague* the pivotal action occurs at the point where McTeague murders his miserly wife.[28] In order for such climactic action to stun or overwhelm the reader, the effect could be intensified if the style were kept simple. No burring adjectives or metaphors, no reminder of the author's presence, nothing to detract from the dramatic immediacy of the scene. He even once suggested that the amateur might find it worthwhile to treat each chapter as a unit in itself, with a "definite beginning, rise, height and end, the action continuous . . . the locality unchanged throughout."[29]

In much the same spirit of practical advice he analyzed the writing of fiction from a business standpoint. Enumerating the possible ways of making money, he chiefly laid down a series of don'ts, which included a fifteenth suggestion not to write a novel and a sixteenth warning against one's friends writing novels. Discussing various factors that helped to promote a book, he discounted newspaper reviews. The good ones nourish the ego. But they do not necessarily add to sales. The retail bookseller, after all most immediately responsive to the book-buying public, is the real literary dictator. A good insight, but Norris then spoiled the effect by glamorizing the reader: "The sham novelist . . . sooner or later meets a wave of reaction. . . . He fools himself all of the time, he fools the publisher three times, he fools the retail dealer twice, and he fools the Great American Public exactly once."[30] The mathematics is not impressive.

Actually, Norris was ambivalent about the public's ability to read perceptively. Just as architecture and painting had once been dominant forms of expression in earlier periods, so the novel had become the "great expression of modern life."[31] People took novels to heart to a degree that the aesthetic cult could not imagine nor the press or pulpit match, and consequently it was incumbent upon the novelist to measure his every statement. When a writer can reach a credulous public numbering one hundred and fifty thousand, "Is it not in Heaven's name essential that the People hear, not a lie, but the truth?"[32] The omnivorous readers of his day, Norris thought, "do not stop to separate true from false; they do not care."[33] He consequently cautioned the novelist to be earnest and sober, know his limitations, be sincere, write simply and broadly and vividly, so that the uneducated could comprehend the message the novelist was obligated "to teach."

Norris had run up against a problem American writers had faced since Hawthorne, the widening gulf between the writer's commitment to excellence and the middle-class taste for mediocrity—the latter as impenetrable as a wall.[34] His answer to the dilemma was typical of the man whose starry gaze blurred his appreciation of obstinate facts. People may confuse the false with the true, he admitted. But as time went on they would learn to discriminate. Better mediocre books than no books at all. And finally one had to admit that the people had more power than the novelist. The people, "despised of the artist, hooted, caricatured and vilified," are the "real seekers after Truth" and the court that hands down judgments.[35] Their taste quickened by quantity rather than quality, they would eventually "demand the 'something better,' and the writers will have to supply it—or disappear, giving place to those who can, and *then* the literary standards will be raised."[36] The idea gave him complete confidence that *"In the last analysis the People are always right."*[37]

When he discussed the development of the artist, Norris seems to have emphasized physical causes and training rather than the more mysterious personal attributes of the subjective self. The spark that makes the novelist is not some mysterious element called, for want of a better term, genius. Environment and training determine whether a child with average intelligence will become a minister or an engineer: "If a failure is the result, blame the method of training, not the quantity or quality of the ten-year-old's intellect."[38] Thus the external causes which mold a woman's personality really cloister her from the practical world of writing, even though leisure, a literary education, and an impressionable, emotional, and communicative temperament should be favorable factors. For the modern writer was becoming more and more the advocate not of culture but of life, which Norris identified with the emotional, the instinctual, the primitive, and the masculine.[39] He had a special antipathy toward aestheticism, writing in "Novelists of the Future" that the American muse "will lead you far from the studies and the aesthetes, the velvet jackets and the uncut hair, far from the sexless creatures who cultivate their little art of writing as the fancier cultivates his orchard . . . she will lead you straight into a World of the Working Men. . . ."[40]

His attitude toward the moral character of the writer was almost ascetic. Like most writers of the period, he demanded *sincerity,* which he described as a "nameless sixth sense" that allowed the writers to live "*in* people" rather than simply "*among* them."[41] An immoral or cruel mind could not produce "one single important, artistic or useful piece of fiction. The better the personal morality of the writer, the better his writing."[42] Success lay not in intellectual subtleties, but in humility and purity of art.

This is a very conventional picture of the writer, but it becomes complicated when Norris turns to the discussion of fiction, for his conventional writer is asked to go far beyond Howellsian realism to plumb causes, motives, and secrets beneath the visible surface of social life. Realism was concern for the normal, for surfaces, for the average, a matter of broken teacups, walks, afternoon calls, dinner invitations, all the round of social activities that serve so well to distract people from taking the "plunge," as Melville put it. To Norris, Howells' realism was about as tingly as the elegance of the magazine illustrators.

Norris' own preference was for the romance of naturalism, a combination of realistic accuracy with the truthfully bizarre or variations from the normal which he associated with Zola. Zola impressed him not so much for his materialistic determinism, which

Norris seems to have overlooked, as for his passion, violence, and fullness. Romantic fiction in the naturalist mode was not, then, a matter of daggers, moonlight, and sentiment. It was an instrument that pierced through surface wrappings to go "down deep into the living heart of things."[43] It enabled the writer to deal incisively with subjects that often included the unlovely aspects of life, and was therefore no "conjurer's trick box full of flimsy fakeries." Where realism stressed everyday life, Norris stressed variations from the normal as more expressive of life. McTeague bites his wife's fingers and dies handcuffed to a corpse. Vanamee's fianceé is raped and dies in *The Octopus*, and syphilitics and prostitutes appear in *Vandover and the Brute*.

The truth was not something to be glibly defined. As Norris saw it, the problem was that nobody really knows what truth and life are. Both are captured in strange ways: "In the fine arts we do not care one little bit about what life actually is, but what it looks like to an interesting, impressionable man." Truth may be "as concrete as the lamp-post on the corner." On the other hand, each writer had to "go down into his own heart and into his own life to find it." In the essay "The Novel with a 'Purpose,' " Norris explained that every novel must do one or more of three things: tell something, like the action-centered novel; show something, like the novel of character; or prove something, like the novel with a purpose. The last was favored by Norris, for it "draws conclusions from a whole congeries of forces, social tendencies, race impulses, devotes itself not to a study of men but man."[44] Because the novel with a purpose dealt with elemental forces in concrete terms, it also included the factors of show and tell, since the novelist proved his case not by pleading abstraction or statistics but through "pictures from life as he sees it." In this way the novel may become a "sincere transcription of life." People may complain of unhappy endings, but such complaints fail to register when the novel proves that "power is abused, that the strong grind the forces of the weak, that an evil tree is still growing in the garden, that undoing follows hard upon unrighteousness, that the course of Empire is not finished, and that the races of men have yet to work out their destiny in those great and terrible movements that crush and grind and rend asunder the pillars of the houses of nations."[45]

Norris thus had a high estimate of the function and power of the novelist as a teacher rather than a trickster. He believed the novel capable of influencing thought and action. Such optimism was based on a great assumption, that men can learn, grow, and change. If the novel is to promote the amelioration of man's condition, it must have method and purpose, it must work according to rules, be responsible and open to analysis, since the law of cause and effect is operative in literature too. The writer's search for truth has significance and reality only when he has gone deeply enough into his subject to convince people that he is telling the truth. "The thing that is to be looked for," he said, "is not the Great American Novelist but the Great Novelist who shall also be an American."[46]

III   Jack London (1876–1916)

A proletarian discontented with his "lower" origins, which included illegitimacy, and a relentless activist who fancied himself a socialist ideologue, within the relatively brief period of sixteen years Jack London showered a cascade of books on the public which added up to twelve volumes and over fifty titles in the 1917 Sonoma edition of his works. Writing was obviously a way of living, though he pretended to an heroic, ecstatic acceptance of life in which writing was but one item in his round of industry as philosopher, revolutionary, reporter, man of action, and traveler. The writing itself is woefully uneven. A small handful of stories and novels have staying power. These benefit from a strong narrative line. But even they suffer from his usual defects: an inability to draw well-rounded, deeply interesting characters; a weak structural sense; and a pretentious overwriting compounded by inverted sentences, awkward rhythms, scores of adjectives—all those things that result from a poor sense of the choice and arrangement of words.

His letters contain a good bit of material on both the theory and practice of literature, of which Earle Labor has made full use in exploring London's craft of writing.[47] Formal excursions into literary criticism, however, were rare, and were mainly undertaken to support a political point of view. That view was formulated in response to his reading in Spencer, Nietzsche, Marx, and assorted socialists. Spencer convinced him that the law of evolution was established, that the law of development was realized through the struggle for existence, that man was socially and biologically determined. Socialism confirmed him generally in the belief that the struggle for existence was at least partly a class struggle in which analysis of the reflexive social impact of economic conditions upheld a materialistic conception of history. To these beliefs he added several questionable assumptions: the elitist role of socialist revolutionary leaders, and a wretched racial jingoism which he kept only partly under control.[48]

As a revolutionary, London believed that the socialist state would emerge only after the inevitable catastrophic disintegration of capitalism had taken place. But as a believer in the brotherhood of the proletariat, and in the efficacy of cooperative association, he thought a "fair world" could be fashioned if we only understood how the processes of nature worked. At least we would know that the present savagery of the world is not decreed by "the will of God nor by any iron law of Nature." "Understanding, after all, is merely sympathy in its fine correct sense. And such sympathy, in its genuineness, makes toward unselfishness. Unselfishness inevitably connotes service. And service is the solution of the entire vexatious problem of man."[49] The common man, newly emerged, benefitted by schooling and a higher standard of living, was now in a position, he thought, to formulate a labor and political movement which would annul the "old selective law" of competition. Borrowing a page from Spencer's notion of increasing cooperation through industrialism, he pointed to the capitalist use of trusts as a means for eliminating competition, which left to labor only the task of solving problems of distribution.[50] To London, the task would be done by Western man, who had the "soul stuff" of "race egotism" to effect moral progress. Whatever the brutalities and adventuring of the white race, London detected "a certain integrity, a sternness of conscience, a melancholy responsibility of life, a sympathy and comradeship and warm human feel, which is ours, indubitably ours."[51]

For these reasons London rejected the kind of realism which dealt with the "sweet commonplaces of life." "Stress and strain are required to sound the deeps of human nature, and there is neither stress nor strain in sweet, optimistic, and placidly happy events. Great things can be done only under great provocation, and there is nothing greatly provoking in the sweet and placid round of existence."[52] Tolstoy and Turgenev were thus dismissed as "tedious," trifling realistic details were discounted, and the premium was placed upon "purpose," "ardent, passionate protest," "the tragic or terrible."[53] He wanted books flowing out of the issues of his time which would be "brutal" and free of "the rule of the dead."[54]

His reviews reflect this demand. He praised Upton Sinclair's *The Jungle* for showing "what our country really is, the home of oppression and injustice, a nightmare of misery, an inferno of suffering."[55]

"Realities" flowed from Gorky's *Fomá Gordyéeff*, a book so much the better because it interrogated "the social life of to-day" rather than "life universal"; "It is a goad, to prick sleeping human consciences awake and drive them into the battle for humanity."[56] Similarly, while he quarreled with the realistic detail of Norris's *The Octopus*, he praised the book for giving us "something more than realism" in its uncompromising "materialistic conception of history, or, more politely, the economic interpretation of history."[57] Once he observed that "The creative imagination is more veracious than the voice of life."[58] But he did not have in mind the formal superiority of art to life, or its capacity for illuminating the recesses from which motive and action emerge. Rather he was thinking of how the "romance" worked, "romance so colossal that it seems beyond the ken of ordinary mortals."[59] Romance dealt with subjects that had substance and meaning. Form was a means to an end, and had no intrinsic value in itself.[60] He wanted a good story, he said, clear and robust, written in a straightforward style free of finicky detail. The full community should be capable of enjoying an artist's work, and for this to happen it should be "work-a-day" art.[61] But London himself seldom produced "work-a-day" art. He was trapped, by his own choice, really, in his kind of fictional romance, with its stalwart posing, feverish excesses, affectations, and uncertain stylistic control.

IV   *Theodore Dreiser (1871–1945)*

This same kind of commitment to the novel as a tool for communicating the "truth" of naturalism can be found in Dreiser. After stints of newspaper work, he had settled for a short time in Pittsburgh, where he enrolled in a course of self-instruction at the Carnegie Library. There he encountered Huxley, Tyndall, Spencer, and other evolutionists, and was enlightened. Life was flux; stratification and stasis were bad; man was a complex of chemical compounds sympathetically reacting to variations in the physical environment, as subject to fluctuating tides of stimuli as his household pet. Free will was a superstition. In this welter of cross-forces, the only worthwhile wisdom attached to knowing and understanding the nature of causality. Yet wisdom would always remain partial, for causes are interrelated and man's mind incapable of pursuing "comparative study" on the cosmic scale demanded by nature.[62]

Like the other naturalists, Dreiser the mechanist strove throughout his life to transcend the limitations of mechanism.[63] He was not, in fact, exactly sure what mechanism meant. Man as animal could be presumed to act mechanically and instinctually; on the other hand, if man as animal possessed a mind then mind could be presumed to be pervasive. "Either nature is mental or there is no mind anywhere— only an inexplicable mechanical process."[64] His refuge was agnosticism, a suspension of judgment whose edge was dulled by a growing interest in Thoreau and in the occult. For the rest, conventional virtue and honesty were part of a mere system of weights and measures of dubious use. Yet a moral point of view was part of man's experience: "A metaphysical idealism will always tell him that it is better to preserve a cleanly balance, and the storm of circumstances will teach him a noble stoicism. Beyond this there is nothing which can be reasonably imposed upon the conscience of man."[65]

Dreiser had a few heroes—Spencer, Bruno, Tom Paine, Whitman, Poe, later Freud—who instructed him in the art of dissent. And he had nature. Though nature masked its forms to the point of inscrutability, he had a romantic's love for its dynamic diversity, and endowed it with purpose, vitality, power, and spontaneity. "What has impressed me most about life, always, is the freshness and newness of everything, the perennial upwelling of life in every form."[66] Prodigal in its bounty, nature veiled "the inscrutable and astounding and even wholesale cruelty of itself" and presented to man a face of animated youth and wise practicality which enchanted man even while he recognized that its passion for forms made it indifferent to the individual. Nature brought physical and mental processes into being through causally determined material forces, and to this extent Dreiser was a mechanist. But he also believed that nature was a giant organism, that as an organism it included even ourselves, and that all life processes were interconnected pulsations of the living whole.

Nature was thus the touchstone in Dreiser's theory of art and literary criticism. Because they were based on the illusion of man's separateness from nature, all the great issues in aesthetics—the function of art, the relation of the artist to society, the question of value in art—were irrelevant to "the question of art in reality."[67] Art flowed from life, and life from nature, so that to talk of great men or of creativity simply revealed ignorance of the biogenetic nature of everything that happens:[68] "before the poet was, was the world about which he poetized and which created him and his poetry. And before his thought was the chemic-dynamic compulsion to thought in him and to which he responded, as a machine—not a separate or individual creative force."[69]

This emphasis upon the seamless continuity of life and nature naturally frustrated intellectual discrimination and thus severely limited the scope and insight of Dreiser's literary criticism. Although letters and interviews indicate that he was sensitive to such matters as literary structure in his own work, he mainly prized a "true" description of the processes of life and nature, which he thought should be sincerely represented, and limited all moral consideration to the probity with which the writer presented his vision of truth and beauty. Committed to naturalism, he early took Balzac as his model, was impatient with the aestheticism of Wilde and Beardsley, dismissed the new humanism of Babbitt and More as a reversion to Transcendentalism and mid-Victorianism, and attacked writers of "problem novels" as liberal but dull-minded progressives who exploit genuine human issues but lack all knowledge of human nature. His essay on the "real" Howells illustrates his critical approach. Calling Howells "one of the noblemen of literature," Dreiser dwells less on the quality of the work than on the "honesty" of Howells' vision, the sincerity with which this vision was presented, the support extended such writers as Stephen Crane and Abraham Cahan, and the intellectual limitations imposed on Howells' novels by his ignorance of the new sociology and philosophy.[70]

On a larger scale, Dreiser thought that public disinterest in the discoveries of the social and natural sciences profoundly affected the relation of the artist to society. In a contribution to the *Nation,* he admitted that this country was probably no more boorish than any other in respect to the writer. Yet circumstances made Americans particularly vulnerable to illusion. Prosperous in a land of plenty, they were misled into thinking that they were responsible for what they had achieved: "human nature is human nature, but your American cannot be made to believe it."[71] Even worse, Americans adopted a moral code that was contrary to basic human impulses. Puritans and moralists, they repressed the sexual instinct so necessary to art, banned the books of Hardy, Freud, Kraft-Ebling, August Forel, and others who offended them, and totally unfitted themselves for appreciating the artists in their midst. Dreiser should not have blamed them, given his view that life had made them as they were. But though he felt himself displaced in society, he thought himself intact in life, and therefore in a position to instruct others.

CHAPTER 8

Epilogue

HOWEVER we choose to approach post-Civil War criticism, the most notable fact is its quantity and the general *intelligence* of the critical discussions. Though the theoretical side is scarcely original, the intellectual depth and range are immensely attractive. Some good questions were asked. What kinds of truths should be expected of literature, and how does one go about assessing their value? What is the relation, if any, between truth and beauty? How dependent should we be on the theory that authors have little choice, but write in response to place, time, and race? What causes the emergence of great writers or literary movements and their sacrificial decline as other writers or movements follow? What can be gained through study of literary forms and techniques and structural patterns as gateways to the enriched understanding of literary works? The answers were by no means in accord. A complex, often confusing mixture of voices belies any easy labeling of the period as the "rise" of realism or the "era" of the genteel tradition or any one of the shibboleths so often used to characterize it. So far from counting this commotion a shame for intellectual inquiry, the critics found it paradoxically stimulating, and while they sometimes jousted with asperity, there is little evidence that they were disheartened by all the tumult.

Like their Victorian counterparts in England, who seem positively to have drenched themselves in facts, statistical studies, charts, and tables, postwar Americans were admirers of the particular. All kinds of archival materials were collected, organized, and widely used in order to understand the vital statistics of the American population, and this same impulse affected the literary critics. Of course the particular was supposed to lead somewhere, and for a few visionaries that meant a misty region completely comprehended and systematized by the intellect, such as the synthetic philosophy of

153

Spencer. But this devotion to the particular, found nearly everywhere, did provide an underpinning for theories of regionalism and local color, studies in early literatures, and the utility of the new comparative anthropology and philology for literary history.

Believing that literature was a cultural aspect of national growth, at one with the civilization which produced it, critics used historical criticism as a kind of supplement to social-intellectual history. Works were placed in relation to their antecedents and consequents, and attempts were made to trace the full battery of causes to which a writer responded: the conditions of his nurture, the "habits" of his race, the opinions of the age, the particular blend of psychosocial factors that formed the writer's personality. Most critics left some room for individual volition; nevertheless, they prized historical inquiry as a means for giving literature a new dignity as part of the history of the nation's ideals, changing views, and aesthetic taste.

While historical critics felt that they were providing, as Lanier said in a letter to E. C. Stedman, a "scientific basis for even the most elementary of judgments," historical criticism did exact its costs. For one thing, the search for influences and explanations to some degree remained speculative rather than absolute, a point that Spingarn made. For another, the concern for establishing historical contexts gave critics less leisure to deal with a literary work in itself. And indeed, isolating the poem can be a rewarding approach to its understanding, for then we respond as much to its unique qualities as to its typicality. Historical criticism tended to discourage attention to artistry and form, as the aesthetic critics claimed, and therefore evaluation was slighted. The assumption hidden in historical criticism was that literature "grew" and "developed"; in the overview, then, contemporary literature was better than past literature. The absurdity of that position was clearly demonstrated by Santayana. The critical idealists, who provided for historical criticism in their theory, were wise in recognizing that it is possible to combine forms of criticism in the effort to find an approach most suitable to writers under consideration. Henry James, a first-rate critic, did the same. These critics never gave over the question of semiclassical universality or "perpetual modernness," and used intellectual and structural analysis to good effect when the occasion warranted. James, for example, effectively used the historical approach whether dealing with a minor writer like George Sand or a major writer of the stature of Balzac, yet remained always responsive to the aesthetic qualities of particular works and to the humane standard of intelligence in culture.

I *Some Examples of Pattern Analysis*

Formal or structural critical interpretation, concerned mainly with finding in a given work patterns of meaning, belongs in its full development to the period associated with the vogue of the "New Critics"—John Crowe Ransom, Allen Tate, Robert Penn Warren, Cleanth Brooks, and others. But as a type of criticism the method was adumbrated by a few critics in the post–Civil War period. It was essentially a quest for pattern in terms of what James called "the figure in the carpet." Henry Ruggles' *The Method of Shakespeare* (1870), for example, was a pioneer attempt to find in three plays sets of imagery which amplified and symbolized major traits of the leading characters. Ruggles' lack of accord with the critical time-spirit is illustrated by the bloodthirsty review to which he was subjected in the *Atlantic Monthly*.

Another Shakespearian, Richard Moulton, who taught at the Unviersity of Chicago, published *Shakespeare as a Dramatic Artist* (1888), which was an attempt to illustrate through plot-diagrams of twelve major plays how parallelisms in plot and subplot helped to intensify dramatic intentions. Moulton's claim that he was treating criticism as an inductive science can well be disregarded. And elsewhere we have pointed to Lanier's *Shakspere and His Forerunners* (1902) as a pioneer though flawed attempt to trace the dramatist's growth in thought through his prosodic and dramatic growth as an artist. None of these studies was solid enough to survive its first publication except for James' prefaces to the New York edition of his work.

II *The Beginnings of Humanism*

The story of humanism is dealt with in the next volume in this series, *American Literary Criticism, 1905–1965*. But the method was foreshadowed in the work of Lowell, Stedman, Woodberry, and George Santayana. Charles Eliot Norton may properly be considered an early humanist. William Crary Brownell formulated his major views before 1905. And the two leading proponents of humanism, Irving Babbitt and Paul Elmer More, published some early criticism that falls within the period: Irving Babbitt in "Brunetière and His Critical Method," "Impressionist versus Judicial Criticism," and the introduction to Taine's *History of English Literature;* More as a reviewer and literary editor of the *Independent,* 1901–1903, and of the New York *Evening Post,* 1903–1909. More began publication of his eleven volumes of critical *Shelburne Essays* in 1904.

The humanists possessed the same large historical perspective encountered so often in romantic criticism, though tempered by respect for human intelligence and for the social and moral relevance of art. As critics, they especially opposed naturalist thought and the influence of such later literary "barbarians" as Van Wyck Brooks, Randolph Bourne, and H. L. Mencken. Tradition was important to them. Their meld was a combination of Christian and classical world views in support of the transcendent nature of man and his difference from the animal world. This combination they tested by means of the critical intelligence, which they exalted, in order to find and approximate a "real" world rather than some subjectively defined world contingent upon science or some other piecemeal approach to a vast subject.

A. *The Severity of Charles Eliot Norton*

Charles Eliot Norton (1827–1908) encouraged both Babbitt and More, and was one of the guiding lights of the kind of severe critcism associated with the *Nation.* A Boston patrician of considerable substance, Norton was professor of the history of art at Harvard, an important editor who gave a number of writers, including Henry James, their first start, and one of the founders of the *American Journal of Archaeology.* According to D. C. Haskell's *Index* to the *Nation,* he wrote a very large number of remarkably incisive, frequently acerbic reviews for that periodical; and he was as well an industrious editor, publishing editions of the correspondence of Goethe and Carlyle, of Carlyle and Emerson, and of Lowell's complete works. He also published a translation of *The Divine Comedy* and a biography of Longfellow, in addition to a study of Thomas Gray as a naturalist and a book on church-building in the Middle Ages. Norton's review of E. C. Stedman's *Victorian Poets* is typical of his critical technique, in which he sought to expose Stedman's weaknesses in logic and philosophical acumen by quoting a host of badly mixed figures as a prelude to showing how logically obscure Stedman could be on the subject of "the relations between knowledge and imagination." He concluded by observing that Sted-man seemed to have "no vigorous grasp of the principles of criticism."

B. *The Critical Humanism of William Crary Brownell*

William Crary Brownell (1851–1928) was Amherst educated, a writer, critic, and journalist who for half his literary career was associated with the publishing house of Charles Scribner's Sons. In a series of books beginning with *French Traits: An Essay in Comparative Criticism* (1889) and ending with *Democratic Distinction in America* (1927), Brownell sought to mediate between the excesses of romanticism and naturalism, opting for a democratic position scornful of American individualism but receptive to a moral position established by democratic consensus. In addition, he relied on Matthew Arnold's work to delineate the ideal nature of personality as a combination of reason and intuition that provided standards and thereby meaning to human existence.

Criticism (1914) and *Standards* (1917) present his considered views, though *French Traits* and the 1901 essay on Arnold in *Victorian Prose Masters* already reveal the tack his humanism would take. Criticism, he thought, was healthy when it was grounded in tradition, in enlightened disinterestedness, and in reason as guided by history, aesthetics, and philosophy. A truly balanced critical approach was thus one which had converse with practically all areas of human thought but no exclusive debt to any one. He was nevertheless lax in clearly specifying his standards, though he continually reminds us that they are needed and that they are common to all individuals. The best one can say is that Brownell believed these standards were embedded in the moral strata of Western culture and discoverable through reason.

Brownell was opposed to the straight historical approach because it obliged critics to focus on the antecedent germination and growth of a work. He was interested in the "efflorescence" of the work, the moment it had burst, under the hands of the artist, into full bloom. Art is concrete and particular, and so the work must be objectified in order to see it "as in itself it really is." Like Spingarn and Santayana, Brownell was interested in the determinative nature of beauty relative to the single work, but he went a step further: to reconcile aesthetic interest in the work and the "academic" interest in the cultural utility of work and writer as they fit into the larger "moral" context of a society. This step was of the utmost importance to him, since it brought criticism to the point where it had to assess quality and worth, not just of the work or of the writer, but of the two together. For ultimately "criticism is the pertinent characterization of great writers, in the mind and art of whom their works are co-ordinated with an explicitness and effectiveness not to be attained by any detailed and objective analysis of the works themselves."[1]

Brownell was content to work empirically. So long as the critic's historical, aesthetic, and philosophical knowledge was sound, he could be counted on to properly analyze a work of art, grasp its controlling ideas, and relate the work to its writer in order to understand how the creative intelligence of the writer had functioned. The search for ultimate standards was a no-man's-land of fruitless inquiry. The best a critic might do is to patiently scrutinize and reflect on the commonly accepted masterpieces of art in order to assemble a working set of criteria, an inductive process first used by Aristotle in the *Poetics:*

This practice involves, let me recapitulate, the initial establishment of some central conception of the subject, gained from the specific study illuminated by a general culture, followed by an analysis of detail confirming or modifying this, and concluding with a synthetic presentation of a physiognomy whose features are as distinct as the whole they compose—the whole process interpenetrated by an estimate of value based on the standard of reason, judging the subject freely after the laws of the latter's own projection, and not by its responsiveness to either individual whims or formulated prescription.[2]

Notes and References

Chapter One

1. For a full discussion of the point, see Robert Falk, *The Victorian Mode in American Fiction* (East Lansing, 1965), pp. 3–16.
2. William R. Thayer, "The New Story-Tellers and the Doom of Realism," *Forum* 18 (1894), 470–80.
3. Floyd Stovall, "The Decline of Romantic Idealism, 1855–1871," in *Transitions in American Literary History*, ed. Harry Hayden Clark (Durham, 1953), pp. 315–78.
4. Jay Martin, *Harvests of Change* (Englewood Cliffs, 1967), p. 15.
5. E. C. Stedman, *Poets of America* (Boston, 1885), pp. 349–95.
6. For a fuller presentation of Emerson's criticism, see the chapter on Emerson and Poe in John W. Rathbun, *American Literary Criticism, 1800–1860* (Boston, 1979).
7. See Harry Hayden Clark, "Conservative and Mediatory Emphases in Emerson's Thought," in *Transcendentalism and its Legacy*, ed. Myron Simon and Thornton Parsons (Ann Arbor, 1966), pp. 25–62.
8. *The Complete Works of Ralph Waldo Emerson*, Centenary Edition (Boston, 1903–1904), VII, 190.
9. Ibid., XII, 305.
10. See especially the essay on Lowell's critical theory in Harry Hayden Clark and Norman Foerster, *James Russell Lowell: Representative Selections* (New York, 1947), pp. c–cxi.
11. James Russell Lowell, "Dante," in *Writings*, Standard Library Edition (Boston, 1891), III, 247.
12. James Russell Lowell, *Writings*, VII, 320. See also III, 252–53. For full discussion of Lowell's relation to the classicists, see the studies of J. P. Pritchard, *Return to the Fountains* (Durham, 1942) and Norman Foerster, *American Criticism* (Boston, 1928).
13. James Russell Lowell, *Writings*, VII, 84–85. Lowell was one of the few men of his time to recognize that Coleridge was more indebted than he should be to Lessing, Schiller, the younger Schlegel, and others. But he evaded the conclusion to be drawn and said instead that Coleridge "owed most to his own sympathetic and penetrative imagination."
14. James Russell Lowell, *Writings*, II, 62–63.
15. Richard H. Fogle, "Organic Form in American Criticism: 1840–1870," in *The Development of American Literary Criticism*, ed. Floyd Stovall (Chapel Hill, 1955).

16. James Russell Lowell, *Writings*, VII, 191, 193.

17. E. C. Stedman, *The Nature and Elements of Poetry* (Boston, 1892), p. 216.

18. Hamilton Wright Mabie, *Books and Culture* (New York, 1886), p. 252.

19. Ibid., p. 123.

20. Charles Dudley Warner, *The Relation of Literature to Life* (New York, 1897), pp. 135–36.

21. Quoted by Jay B. Hubbell, *Who Are the Major American Writers?* (Durham, 1972), p. 100.

22. Hamilton Wright Mabie, *Books and Culture*, pp. 257–58.

23. Hamilton Wright Mabie, *Essays in Literary Interpretation* (New York, 1910), p. 74.

24. Ibid., p. 85.

25. Robert Falk, "The Genteel Decades: 1879–1900," in *The Development of American Literary Criticism*, ed. Stovall, p. 154.

26. George Woodberry, *The Torch* (New York, 1905), p. 123.

27. George Woodberry, *The Appreciation of Literature* (New York, 1907), p. 8.

28. Ibid., p. 172. See also George Woodberry, *The Inspiration of Poetry* (New York, 1910), pp. 26–28.

29. George Woodberry, *Nation* 43 (1886), 525–27.

30. George Woodberry, *Makers of Literature* (New York, 1890), pp. 2–3.

31. Julia Power, *Shelley in America* (New York, 1940), p. 137.

32. Brander Matthews, *These Many Years* (New York, 1919), p. 266.

33. Brander Matthews, *Inquiries and Opinions* (New York, 1908), p. 61.

34. *Inquiries and Opinions*, pp. 4–5.

35. Brander Matthews, *Shakespeare as a Dramatist* (New York, 1915), pp. 295–96.

36. Brander Matthews, *Literary Style and Other Essays* (Chicago, 1881), pp. 7, 45.

37. See Charles Dudley Warner, "Modern Fiction," *Atlantic Monthly* 51 (1883), 464–74.

38. Willard Thorp, "Defenders of Ideality," in *Literary History of the United States*, ed. Robert E. Spiller et al. (New York, 1948), II, 816. See also Hubbell, *Who Are the Major American Writers?* pp. 99–101, and Falk, *The Victorian Mode in American Fiction*, pp. 96–8.

39. Edmund Clarence Stedman, *The Nature and Elements of Poetry* (Boston, 1892), p. 199.

40. Ibid., pp. 45, 44.

41. Ibid., p. 216.

42. Ibid.

43. Walt Whitman, *Prose Works*, ed. Floyd Stovall (New York, 1964), II, 388.

44. Ibid., p. 408.

45. Ibid., p. 412.

46. Partly as a result of Whitman's refusal to tone down his "sex program," Emerson omitted all of Whitman's poems from his anthology *Parnassus* (1874).

47. Walt Whitman, *Works* (New York, 1902), II, 570.

48. Ibid., pp. 256–57.

49. Ibid., p. 516.

Chapter Two

1. Jay Martin, *Harvests of Change: American Literature 1865–1914* (Englewood Cliffs, N.J., 1967), pp. 13–14. For sales figures see Hubbell, *Who Are the Major American Writers?*, pp. 80–82.

2. The entire poem is quoted by Edwin H. Cady, *The Realist at War* (Syracuse, 1958), p. 31.

3. The literature on the movement is extensive. See especially Walter Blair, *Native American Humor* (New York, 1937; San Francisco, 1960); Claude Simpson, *The Local Colorists* (New York, 1960); Everett Carter, *Howells and the Age of Realism* (Philadelphia, 1950); Jay Martin, *Harvests of Change: American Literature 1865–1914;* and for a particular genre writer John R. Adams, *Harriet Beecher Stowe* (New York, 1963).

4. Donald Pizer, *Realism and Naturalism in Nineteenth-Century American Literature* (Carbondale, 1966), pp. 4 and 6, makes a different point. He argues that realism and romanticism disagreed on such matters as verisimilitude of detail, the representative nature of experience, and the stress on objectivity, but that realism was "ethically idealistic" in emphasizing "a private belief in what should be rather than a depiction of what usually is."

5. Bret Harte, *Stories and Poems and Other Uncollected Writings* (New York, 1914), pp. 126–27.

6. Ibid., p. 231.

7. Bret Harte, "The Rise of the Short Story," *Cornhill Magazine*, n.s. 7 (July, 1899), 3.

8. Ibid.

9. Bret Harte, *Stories and Poems and Other Uncollected Writings*, p. 267.

10. Ibid., p. 275.

11. Ibid., p. 24.

12. Bret Harte, *Representative Selections*, ed. Joseph B. Harrison (New York, 1941), p. 20.

13. "The Rise of the Short Story," p. 8.

14. Cf. *The Autobiography*, ed. Albert Bigelow Paine (New York, 1924), I, 183, 182, 76; and II, 324.

15. Joseph Gardner in "Mark Twain and Dickens" has admirably surveyed the complex ups and downs of their relations in *PMLA* 84 (1969), 90–101.

16. See Paul Fatout, *Mark Twain on the Lecture Circuit* (Bloomington, 1960).

17. *The Love Letters of Mark Twain* (New York, 1949), p. 162.

18. *The Writings of Mark Twain,* Stormfield Edition (New York, 1929) XXII, 153.

19. Bernard DeVoto, *Mark Twain's America* (Boston, 1932), p. 283.

20. *The Love Letters of Mark Twain,* p. 187.

21. Fred Lorch, *The Trouble Begins at Eight* (Ames, Iowa, 1968), pp. 205–6.

22. *The Portable Mark Twain,* ed. Bernard DeVoto (New York, 1946), p. 751.

23. *Mark Twain-Howells Letters,* ed. Henry Nash Smith and William Gibson (Cambridge, 1960), II, 534.

24. *The Writings of Mark Twain,* XXXV, 525–26.

25. To Rudolf and Clark Kirk, "Understanding flowed from Howells to Twain, rather than from Twain to Howells—perhaps this is the secret of their long and varied friendship" (*William Dean Howells* [New Haven, 1962], p. 89).

26. See Walter Blair, "The French Revolution and Huckleberry Finn," *Modern Philology* 55 (1957), 21–35.

27. See Louis Budd, *Mark Twain: Social Philosopher* (Bloomington, 1962), and Philip Foner, *Mark Twain: Social Critic* (New York, 1958), both of whom explore the way in which satire is used for constructive and humanitarian objectives.

28. Mark Twain, "About Play Writing," *Forum* 26 (1898), 215.

29. "Mr. Howells as a Critic," in Kenneth Eble, ed., *Howells: A Century of Criticism* (Dallas, 1962), pp. 67, 69.

30. W. D. Howells, *My Literary Passions and Criticism and Fiction* (New York, 1900), p. 573.

31. Ibid., pp. 257–58.

32. Quoted by Donald Pizer, *Realism and Naturalism in Nineteenth-Century American Literature,* p. 43. See also Harry Hayden Clark, "The Role of Science in the Thought of W. D. Howells," *Transactions of the Wisconsin Academy of Sciences, Arts and Letters* 42 (1953), 263–303.

33. *My Literary Passions,* p. 201.

34. Ibid., p. 198.

35. Quoted by G. E. De Mille, *Literary Criticism in America* (New York, 1931), p. 186.

36. *My Literary Passions,* p. 54.

37. William Dean Howells, "Lyof N. Tolstoy," *North American Review* 188 (1908), 847, 855.

38. In Delmar Cooke, *William Dean Howells* (New York, 1922), p. 50.

39. *My Literary Passions,* p. 215.

40. Quoted by Cooke, *William Dean Howells,* p. 50.

41. Ibid., pp. 50–51.

42. See especially the study of J. M. Robertson, "Howells," in *Essays Toward a Critical Method* (London, 1889), pp. 149–99.

43. See, for example, Hamlin Garland's *Crumbling Idols* (1894); H. H. Boyesen's many books of criticism; C. D. Warner's *The Relation of Literature to Life* (1896); W. M. Payne, "American Literary Criticism and the Doctrine of Evolution," *The International Monthly* 2 (1900), 26–66, 127–53; and H. W. Mabie, "The Significance of Modern Criticism," in *Essays in Literary Interpretation* (New York, 1892), pp. 46–70.

44. W. D. Howells, "Recent Literature," *Atlantic Monthly* 42 (1878), 118–19.

45. Everett Carter, *Howells and the Age of Realism*, pp. 185–90.

46. Howells took pride in his depiction of women, and many critics have credited him here for his art. But some perceptive men like W. C. Brownell were skeptical, pointing to the "case history" tone and "cuteness" associated with the women. See Brownell, "The Novels of Mr. Howells," in Edwin Cady and David Frazier, eds., *The War of the Critics over William Dean Howells* (Evanston, 1962).

47. Edwin Cady, *The Realist at War* (Syracuse, 1958), passim, especially chap. 2.

48. See, for example, Howells' "Poems of Emily Dickinson," *Harper's Magazine* 82 (1891), 318–21; his preface to Hamlin Garland's *Main-Travelled Roads* (Chicago, 1893); "Mr. Garland's Books," *North American Review* 196 (1912), 523–28; and "Frank Norris," *North American Review* 175 (1902), 769–78.

49. *My Literary Passions*, p. 252.

50. W. F. Taylor, "William Dean Howells and the Economic Novel," *American Literature* 4 (1932), 113.

51. See Howells' review of *Looking Backward* in *Harper's* 77 (1888), 154–55, and the general appraisal in the *Antlantic Monthly* 92 (1898), 253–56.

52. Everett Carter, *Howells and the Age of Realism*, p. 192.

53. Quoted in *Howells: Representative Selections,* ed. Clara and Rudolf Kirk (New York, 1950), p. 382.

54. Quoted by Jay B. Hubbell, *Who Are the Major American Writers?* p. 92.

55. Larzer Ziff, *The American 1890's* (New York, 1966), pp. 47–48.

Chapter Three

1. Henry James, "Miss Prescott's 'Azarian,' " *Notes and Reviews*, ed. Pierre de Chaignon la Rose (New York, 1968), p. 27.

2. "A French Critic," in *Ibid.*, pp. 102, 104.

3. Henry James, "Matthew Arnold's Essays," in *Views and Reviews*, ed. Le Roy Phillips (New York, 1968), pp. 89, 87, 94. Actually, those qualities that James prized in a critic he also prized in a writer. For a good solid study of James' development from 1864 to 1881, see Cornelia Pulsifer Kelley, *The*

Early Development of Henry James (Urbana, 1965), and for an overall view of his criticism see Rene Wellek, "Henry James's Literary Theory and Criticism," *American Literature* 30 (1958), 293–321.

4. Review of T. Adolphus Trollope's *Lindisfarn Chase,* in *Notes and Reviews,* p. 33.

5. "Miss Prescott's 'Azarian,' " in ibid., p. 22.

6. Review of M. E. Braddon's 'Aurora Floyd,' in ibid., p. 115.

7. Review of *The Belton Estate,* in ibid., p. 130.

8. Review of *Miss Mackenzie,* in ibid., p. 74.

9. Review of *The Belton Estate,* in ibid., p. 130.

10. Review of Charles Kingsley's *Hereward,* in ibid., p. 140.

11. Review of Mrs. Craik's *A Noble Life,* in ibid., p. 169.

12. Review of Julian Hawthorne's *Idolatry, Literary Reviews and Essays,* ed. Albert Mordell (New York, 1957), p. 251.

13. Ibid.

14. Lyall H. Powers for his part says that James' emphasis on the imagination was strong in his early criticism, but that following 1875 there was a "de-emphasizing of the role of the imagination in favor of accurate factual presentation" (*Henry James and the Naturalist Movement* [Ann Arbor, 1971], p. 35).

15. "Miss Prescott's 'Azarian,' " in *Notes and Review,* p. 32.

16. Review of Trollope's *Can You Forgive Her?,* in ibid., p. 87.

17. Reviews of Trollope's *Miss Mackenzie* and Alcott's *Moods,* in ibid., pp. 71, 58.

18. "Later Lyrics of Julia Ward Howe," in *Literary Reviews and Essays,* p. 228.

19. "Tyndall's Hour of Exercise in the Alps," in ibid., pp. 309–10; "Swinburne's 'Chastelard,' " in *Notes and Reviews,* p. 135.

20. "George Sand's Mademoiselle Merquem," in *Literary Reviews and Essays,* p. 123.

21. Ibid., pp. 124–25.

22. Henry James, "Middlemarch," in *The Future of the Novel,* ed. Leon Edel (New York, 1956), p. 88.

23. "The Novels of George Eliot," in *Views and Reviews,* p. 25. Oddly enough, these same characteristics, when transferred to her poetry, James thought inappropriate. Her poetry lacked "the hurrying quickness, the palpitating warmth, the bursting melody of such a creation." He is obviously thinking in terms of lyricism. But he is hardly helpful when he defines a "genuine" poem as "a tree that breaks into blossom and shakes in the wind."

24. "Octave Feuillet's Camors," in *Literary Reviews and Essays,* p. 17.

25. "Can You Forgive Her?" in *Notes and Reviews,* p. 86.

26. "Miss Braddon," in ibid., p. 114.

27. "The Novels of George Eliot," in *Views and Reviews,* pp. 33–34.

28. "A French Critic," in *Notes and Reviews,* p. 103.

29. Ibid., pp. 101–2.

30. Ibid., p. 106.

31. Henry James, "Emerson," in *Partial Portraits* (London, 1888), p. 3.

32. "Alphonse Daudet," in ibid., p. 205.

33. "Guy de Maupassant," in ibid., p. 272.

34. American reception of the book was hostile, prompting James to write Elizabeth Boott in February, 1880, that the reaction was a "melancholy revelation of angry vanity, vulgarity and ignorance" (quoted in *The Notebooks of Henry James*, ed. F. O. Matthiessen and Kenneth Murdock [New York, 1961], I, 29).

35. Howells in his review of the book took exception to James' characterization of Americans as provincial. In his reply in a letter of January 31, 1880, James defended his position vigorously, arguing that "It is on manners, customs, usages, habits, forms, upon all these things natural and established, that a novelist lives . . ." (*The Letters of Henry James*, ed. Percy Lubbock [New York, 1920], I, 72). His point and tone are very close to those of early nineteenth-century Americans, such as Irving, who lamented the lack of "associations" for writers in a nation so recently established.

36. Henry James, *Hawthorne*, ed. William M. Sale, Jr. (Ithaca, 1967), p. viii.

37. Ibid., p. 22.

38. Ibid., pp. 50–51.

39. Ibid., p. 3.

40. Ibid., p. 24.

41. Ibid., p. 46.

42. Ibid., pp. 20, 131, 144.

43. Henry James, "Ivan Turgenieff," in *French Poets and Novelists* (New York, 1878), pp. 250–51.

44. Ibid., pp. 216–17.

45. Ibid., p. 246ff.

46. "Anthony Trollope," in *Partial Portraits*, pp. 99, 104, 102.

47. "Theophile Gautier," in *French Poets and Novelists*, p. 33.

48. "Charles de Bernard and Gustave Flaubert," in ibid., passim.

49. "Emerson," in *Partial Portraits*, p. 7.

50. "George Sand," in *French Poets and Novelists*, pp. 156, 169.

51. "Charles Baudelaire," in ibid., p. 64.

52. "George Sand," in ibid., p. 172.

53. Ibid.

54. "The Life of George Eliot," in *Partial Portraits*, p. 49.

55. "Ivan Turgenieff," in *French Poets and Novelists*, p. 221.

56. "Alphonse Daudet," in *Partial Portraits*, p. 208; "Alfred de Musset," in *French Poets and Novelists*, p. 29.

57. "Honore de Balzac," in *French Poets and Novelists*, p. 74.

58. Ibid., p. 80.

59. "Anthony Trollope," in *Partial Portraits*, p. 116.

60. "Theophile Gautier," in *French Poets and Novelists*, p. 44.

61. "Ivan Turgenieff," in ibid., p. 219.

62. "Guy de Maupassant," in *Partial Portraits*, p. 246.

63. *Henry James and Robert Louis Stevenson*, ed. Janet Adam Smith (London, 1948), p. 102. In "Henry James and Walter Besant: 'The Art of Fiction' Controversy," Mark Spilka (*Novel* 6 [1973], 100–119) provides a detailed account of the intellectual and social context within which James moved at the time.

64. "The Art of Fiction," in *Partial Portraits*, p. 376.

65. Ibid., p. 388.

66. Ibid., p. 390.

67. Ibid., p. 392.

68. Henry James, "The New Novel," in *Notes on Novelists* (New York, 1914), p. 315.

69. Henry James, "Henrik Ibsen," in *Essays in London and Elsewhere* (New York, 1893), p. 231.

70. "Journal of the Brothers de Goncourt," in ibid., p. 193.

71. Ibid., p. 215.

72. *Notes on Novelists*, pp. 14, 114, 100.

73. Henry James, *The Art of the Novel*, ed. R. P. Blackmur (New York, 1937), p. 340.

74. "Robert Louis Stevenson" and "George Sand," in *Notes on Novelists*, pp. 18, 204.

75. "The New Novel," in ibid., pp. 341–42.

76. "Honore de Balzac," in ibid., p. 125. Philip Grover in *Henry James and the French Novel: A Study in Inspiration* (London, 1973), points out some useful parallels between James' art and that of the French naturalist and art-for-art's-sake schools, though the question of influences is not really settled.

77. The entire case is handled with precision by Powers in *Henry James and the Naturalist Movement*.

78. "Emile Zola," in *Notes on Novelists*, p. 26; preface to *The Spoils of Poynton*, in *The Art of the Novel*, p. 120.

79. "Honore de Balzac" and "The Novel in 'The Ring and the Book,' " in *Notes on Novelists*, pp. 118, 394.

80. "Matilde Serao," in ibid., p. 313.

81. Preface to *The Altar of the Dead*, in *The Art of the Novel*, p. 256.

82. Preface to *The Lesson of the Master*, in ibid., p. 5.

83. "Henrik Ibsen," in *Essays in London and Elsewhere*, p. 231.

Chapter Four

1. This chapter is substantially based on Harry Hayden Clark, "The Influence of Science on American Literary Criticism, 1860–1910, Including the Vogue of Taine," *Transactions of the Wisconsin Academy of Sciences, Arts and Letters* 44 (1955), 109–64.

2. For background, see chapter 6, "Historical Criticism," in John W. Rathbun, *American Literary Criticism 1800–1860*.

3. See, for example, the bibliography in C. C. Regier's *Era of the Muckrakers* (Gloucester, Mass., 1957), and the bibliographies of Lisle A. Rose in *American Literature*.

4. Donald Pizer, *Realism and Naturalism in Nineteenth-Century American Literature* (Carbondale, 1966), p. 80.

5. Richard Burton, *Forces in Fiction and Other Essays* (Boston, 1902), p. 34.

6. In *Life and Letters of Edmund Clarence Stedman*, ed. Laura Stedman and George M. Gould (New York, 1910), II, 388, Stedman remarks that "Nature is signing the wondrous story of her progress through Evolution, from star-dust up to sentient Man."

7. Donald Pizer, "Herbert Spencer and the Genesis of Hamlin Garland's Critical System," *Tulane Studies in English* 7 (1957), 153–68.

8. Hamlin Garland, *Crumbling Idols* (Chicago, 1894), p. 374. See also Ruth M. Raw, "Hamlin Garland, the Romanticist," *Sewanee Review* 36 (1928), 202–10.

9. From an editorial by Dreiser as "The Prophet" in the magazine *Ev'ry Month* 3 (1897); quoted by John F. Huth, Jr., "Theodore Dreiser: 'the Prophet,' " *American Literature* 9 (1937), 208–17.

10. John Hoskins, "Biological Analogy in Literary Criticism," *Modern Philology* 6 (1909), 407–34; 7 (1909), 61–83; and "The Place and Function of a Standard in a Genetic Theory of Literary Development," *PMLA* 25 (1910), 379–402.

11. Kuno Francke, *Social Forces in German Literature* (Boston, 1896), p. 400.

12. John Fiske, *The Unseen World and Other Essays* (Boston, 1876), p. 207. In "The Genesis of Language," *North American Review* 109 (1869), 305–67, Fiske explores the origins of language, and its relation to myth and prehistoric fancies as these flower into literature.

13. Quoted by Robert Falk, "The Literary Criticism of the Genteel Decades: 1870–1900," pp. 123–24.

14. T. S. Perry, *John Fiske* (Boston, 1906), p. 32.

15. T. S. Perry, *English Literature in the Eighteenth Century* (Boston, 1883), p. vi.

16. In *Realism and Naturalism in Nineteenth-Century American Literature*, p. 41, Donald Pizer says that Perry borrowed Symonds' view that literary genres go through growth, development, and decline as do species, which allowed Perry to reconcile his faith in progress with the obvious fact that some periods in literary history are richer than those that follow.

17. T. S. Perry, *English Literature in the Eighteenth Century*, p. ix.

18. T. S. Perry, "William Dean Howells," *Century Magazine*, n.s. 1 (1882), 682. See also "Science and the Imagination," *North American Review* 137 (1883), 55.

19. T. S. Perry, "William Dean Howells," p. 684.

20. See John S. White, "Taine on Race and Genius," *Social Research* 10 (1943), 76–99; and F. C. Roe, "A Note on Taine's Conception of the English Mind," in *Studies in French Language, Literature and History* (Cambridge, England, 1949), pp. 243–49.

21. Hippolyte Taine, *History of English Literature* (Edinburgh, 1873), I, 18.

22. Sholom Jackob Kahn, *Science and Aesthetic Judgment: A Study in Taine's Critical Method* (New York, 1953), pp. 43–44.

23. Ibid., p. 22.

24. Martha Wolfenstein, "The Social Background of Taine's Philosophy of Art," *Journal of the History of Ideas* 5 (1944), 332–58.

25. Quoted by Robert W. Stallman, *Critiques and Essays in Fiction* (New York, 1949), p. 428.

26. Quoted by Edgar Pelham, *Art of the Novel* (New York, 1933), p. 232.

27. David Wasson, *Essays* (Boston, 1888), p. 368.

28. Alfred Fouillée, "The Philosophy of Taine and Renan," *International Quarterly* 6 (1902), 260–80.

29. James T. Bixby, Review of Taine's *On Intelligence*, *North American Review* 117 (1873), 401–38.

30. William Kingsley, Review of Taine's *On Intelligence*, *New Englander Magazine* 31 (1871), 366–67.

31. John Bascom, Review of *History of English Literature*, *Bibliotheca Sacra* 30 (1873), 646.

32. H. W. Boynton, "Taine," *Atlantic Monthly* 91 (1903), 830–31; Percy Bicknell, "The Taine Memoirs," *Dial* 37 (1904), 104–7.

33. Lowell, "Rebellion," *Works*, V, 124; Mabie, *My Study Fire*, 2d ser. (New York, 1894), pp. 156, 158; Stedman, *Victorian Poets* (New York, 1875), pp. 1, 410, 434, 194–96, 143; Tourgee, *Murvale Eastman* (New York, 1889), p. 113.

34. T. S. Perry, Review of *Notes on England*, *Atlantic Monthly* 29 (1872), 370–71.

35. Lewis Gates, *Studies and Appreciations* (New York, 1900), p. 204.

36. Ralph Rusk, ed., *Letters to Emma Lazarus* (New York, 1939), p. 6. See also Rusk's *Life of Emerson* (New York, 1949), p. 473.

37. R. M. Bucke, *Whitman* (Philadelphia, 1883), p. 12.

38. Quoted by Howard Mumford Jones, *Theory of American Literature* (Ithaca, 1948), p. 124.

39. Traubel, *With Walt Whitman in Camden* (Boston, 1906), II, 160–62.

40. Hamlin Garland, *A Son of the Middle Border* (New York, 1914), pp. 307, 387.

41. Edward Eggleston, preface to the Library Edition of *The Hoosier Schoolmaster* (New York, 1892), p. 8.

42. Edward Bellamy, "Literary Notices," *Springfield Union*, April 29, 1876, 2.

43. W. D. Howells, Review of the *History of English Literature, Atlantic Monthly* 29 (1872), 241.

44. Ibid., p. 242. A more positive view of Howells' response to Taine is provided by Everett Carter in "Taine and American Realism," *Revue de Littérature Comparée* 26 (1952), 357–64, which also contains some material on Eggleston.

45. Henry James, Review of Taine's *Italy, Nation* 6 (1868), 374. See also Jeremiah J. Sullivan, "Henry James and Hippolyte Taine: The Historical and Scientific Method in Literature," *Comparative Literature Studies* 10 (1973), 25–50, which covers Taine in terms of James' book on Hawthorne, the early reviews, and James' art and travel books.

46. Henry James, Review of *Notes sur Angleterre, Nation* 14 (1872), 58.

47. Henry James, Review of *History of English Literature, Atlantic Monthly* 29 (1872), 470.

48. See the chapter on "The Approach to Taine" in Max Baym, *The French Education of Henry Adams* (New York, 1951).

49. Howard Mumford Jones, *Theory of American Literature*, p. 101. See also Jones' references to Tyler, pp. 103, 107, 105, 142.

50. E. C. Stedman, *Victorian Poets*, p. 4.

Chapter Five

1. *The English Novel and the Principle of its Development*, ed. W. H. Browne (Baltimore, 1883), pp. 35–36.

2. *The Centennial Edition of Sidney Lanier*, ed. Charles R. Anderson (Baltimore, 1945), V, 172–73.

3. Ibid., II, 193–95.

4. Ibid., II, 53.

5. Joseph Hendren, "Time and Stress in English Verse with Special Reference to Lanier's Theory of Rhythm," *Rice Institute Pamphlet* 46 (July, 1959).

6. Ibid., p. 18.

7. *Centennial Edition*, IV, 359.

8. Ibid., III, 389, 402–3.

9. Ibid., IV, 167–68, 239. As Elmer A. Havens points out, for Lanier "the artist is the moral super-man" ("Lanier's Critical Theory," *Emerson Society Quarterly* 55 [1969], 83).

10. Allen, "Sidney Lanier as a Literary Critic," *Philological Quarterly* 17 (1938), 121–38; Havens, "Lanier's Critical Theory," p. 83.

11. For my biographical details I am indebted to John S. Coolidge, "Lewis E. Gates: The Permutations of Romanticism in America," *New England Quarterly* 30 (1957), 23–38.

12. Lewis E. Gates, *Studies and Appreciations* (New York, 1900), p. 209.

13. Ibid., pp. 216–17.

14. Ibid., pp. 221–22.

15. Ibid., p. 227.

16. Ibid., p. 233.

17. See H. L. Mencken, *Prejudices* (New York, 1922), pp. 74–83, for an enthusiastic review of Huneker's work. The standard critical study of Huneker is Arnold T. Schwab, *James Gibbons Huneker* (Palo Alto, 1963).

18. James Gibbons Huneker, *The Pathos of Distance* (New York, 1913), p. 340.

19. Ibid., p. 281.

20. Schwab, *James Gibbons Huneker*, pp. 80–81.

21. See the discussion of Huneker in Arnold Goldsmith, *American Literary Criticism 1905–1965* (Boston, 1979).

22. Quoted in *James Gibbons Huneker*, p. 196.

23. For biographical data and Spingarn's general intellectual progress, I have relied upon Marshall van Deusen's fine and useful book, *J. E. Spingarn* (New York, 1971).

24. These books, based on ideas Spingarn absorbed early, are discussed in detail by Arnold Goldsmith, *American Literary Criticism 1905–1965*.

25. J. E. Spingarn, *Creative Criticism and Other Essays* (New York, 1931), p. 14. The title essay was given at Columbia University in 1910.

26. Ibid., pp. 36–37.

27. Ibid., p. 100.

28. *Literary History of the United States*, II, 155–56.

Chapter Six

1. For Santayana's criticism of the United States, see James C. Ballowe, "*The Last Puritan* and the Failure of American Culture," *American Quarterly* 18 (1966), 123–35. Maurice Brown deals with his indebtedness to his American experience in "Santayana's American Roots," *New England Quarterly* 33 (1960), 147–63.

2. George Santayana, *Three Philosophical Poets: Lucretius, Dante, and Goethe* (New York, 1953), p. 37.

3. Ibid., p. 38.

4. George Santayana, *The Sense of Beauty* (New York, 1936), p. 121.

5. George Santayana, *Reason in Art*, in *The Works of George Santayana* (New York, 1936), IV, 260.

6. George Santayana, *Interpretations of Poetry and Religion* (New York, 1957), p. 13.

7. *Reason in Art*, pp. 250–51.

8. Ibid., p. 287.

9. *Interpretations of Poetry and Religion*, p. 226.

10. *Reason in Art*, p. 358.

11. Ibid., pp. 350–51.

12. *The Sense of Beauty*, p. 166.

13. Ibid., p. 210.

14. Ibid., p. 174; "Penitent Art," in *Essays in Literary Criticism of George Santayana*, ed. Irving Singer (New York, 1956), pp. 234, 236.

15. *The Sense of Beauty*, pp. 47–48.

16. Ibid., p. 177.

17. George Santayana, *The Realm of Truth*, in *Realms of Being* (New York, 1942), p. 522. In *The Sense of Beauty*, p. 195, he points out that we experience some pleasure in recognizing and comprehending evil in a work of art, but the beauty of the medium and the expression of evil are both aesthetic pluses that remove its immediacy.

18. *Interpretations of Poetry and Religion*, p. 270.

19. Ibid., p. 24ff.

20. Ibid., pp. 161, 164. For Santayana's lifelong ambivalent attitude toward Shakespeare, see John M. Major, "Santayana on Shakespeare," *Shakespeare Quarterly* 10 (1954), 469–79.

21. Ibid., p. 170.

22. *Reason in Art*, p. 266.

23. Ibid., p. 268.

24. John Herman Randall, Jr., "George Santayana—Naturalizing the Imagination," *Journal of Philosophy* 51 (1954), 52.

25. *The Sense of Beauty*, p. 185.

26. Preface to *Realms of Being*, pp. ix–x.

27. *The Sense of Beauty*, p. 117; *Interpretations of Poetry and Religion*, pp. 167, 188, 194.

28. Part of Santayana's quarrel with literary naturalism and romanticism is that the two schools so often seemed to think expression could not be formally rendered without loss. See Katherine Gilbert, "Santayana's Doctrine of Aesthetic Expression," *Philosophical Review* 35 (1926), 221–35.

29. *Interpretations of Poetry and Religion*, p. 276.

30. *The Sense of Beauty*, p. 110.

31. Ibid., p. 6.

32. *The Realm of Matter*, p. 353.

33. *Interpretations of Poetry and Religion*, p. vi.

34. *The Sense of Beauty*, p. 164.

35. *Reason in Art*, p. 214.

36. Ibid., p. 335.

37. *Interpretations of Poetry and Religion*, pp. 249, 250, 143.

38. *Reason in Art*, p. 216.

39. "Hamlet," in *Essays in Literary Criticism of George Santayana*, p. 120.

40. *Reason in Art*, p. 352.

41. Ibid., p. 353.

42. "Tragic Philosophy," in *Essays in Literary Criticism of George Santayana*, p. 266; *Three Philosophical Poets*, p. 181. See also *Reason in Art*, p. 296: "Art has an infinite range; nothing shifts so easily as taste and yet nothing so presistently avoids the directions in which it might find most satisfaction."

43. See Maurice Cohen's discriminating discussion in "Santayana on Romanticism and Egotism," *Journal of Religion* 46 (1966), 264–81.

44. *Three Philosophical Poets*, pp. 141, 60.

45. *The Realm of Essence*, in *Realms of Being*, p. 144.

46. Ibid.

47. "Penitent Art," p. 236.

48. See for background Paul C. Wermuth, "Santayana and Emerson," *Emerson Society Quarterly* 31 (1963), 36–40; John Crowe Ransom, "Art and Mr. Santayana," *Virginia Quarterly Review* 13 (1937) 420–36.

49. *The Sense of Beauty*, p. 101.

50. *Interpretations of Poetry and Religion*, p. 199.

51. Ibid., pp. 176–77.

Chapter Seven

1. *Realism and Naturalism in Nineteenth-Century American Literature* (Carbondale, 1966), pp. 12–14.

2. Charles Child Walcutt, *American Literary Naturalism, a Divided Stream* (Minneapolis, 1956), passim; Warren French, *Frank Norris* (New York, 1962), passim.

3. *Character and Opinion in the United States* (New York, n.d.), p. 109.

4. Quoted by Walter Taylor, *The Economic Novel in America* (New York, 1964), p. 156.

5. "The Land Question and its Relation to Art and Literature," *Arena* 9 (1894), 174.

6. *Tulane Studies in English* 7 (1957), 153–68.

7. *Crumbling Idols*, ed. Jane Johnson (Cambridge, 1960), pp. vii–ix, 3–18.

8. "The Productive conditions of American Literature," *Forum* 17 (1894), 698.

9. *Crumbling Idols*, p. 16.

10. Ibid., p. 16.

11. Ibid., p. 29.

12. Ibid., p. 21.

13. Ibid., pp. 23–24.

14. Ibid., p. 42.

15. Ibid., p. 43.

16. "Productive Conditions of American Literature," p. 690.

17. *Crumbling Idols*, p. 98.

18. Ibid., p. 190.

19. *A Son of the Middle Border* (New York, 1917), p. 307; also pp. 387, 374.

20. "The Present Conditions of Literary Production," *Atlantic Monthly* 78 (1896), 164–65.

21. William B. Dillingham, *Frank Norris: Instinct and Art* (Lincoln, Nebr., 1969), introduction.

22. Arnold Goldsmith states that Norris was a full-blown determinist for only a brief period, between 1895 and 1899, and that while he never fully mastered a comprehensive statement on determinism versus volition he came to the point of allowing man limited free will in a world of necessity; see "The Development of Frank Norris's Philosophy," in *Studies in Honor of John Wilcox*, ed. A. Dayle Wallace and Woodburn O. Ross (Detroit, 1958), pp. 175–94.

23. *The Octopus* (New York, 1901), p. 652.

24. *The Novels of Frank Norris* (Bloomington, 1966), p. 22.

25. Walcutt, *American Literary Naturalism, a Divided Stream*, p. 125; Hoffman, "Norris and the Responsibility of the Novelist," *South Atlantic Quarterly* 54 (1955), 515.

26. *The Complete Works of Frank Norris* (New York, 1899), p. 313; drawn from Norris' *The Responsibilities of the Novelist*.

27. Ibid., p. 316.

28. See Donald Pizer's quotation of a letter of Norris written in 1900 concerning the climactic and accelerated plan of action for *The Octopus* (in *The Literary Criticism of Frank Norris* [Austin, Texas, 1964], p. 46).

29. *The Responsibilities of the Novelist*, p. 316.

30. "The Retailer: Literary Dictator," in *Works*, p. 331.

31. *The Responsibilities of the Novelist*, p. 255.

32. Ibid., p. 258. Norris wrote to Isaac Marcosson in March, 1899: "What pleased me most in your review of *McTeague* was the 'disdaining all pretensions to style.' It is precisely what I try most to avoid. I detest 'fine writing,' 'rhetoric,' 'elegant English'—tommyrot. Who cares for fine style! Tell your yarn and let your style go to the devil. We don't want literature, we want life" (quoted by Joseph J. Kwiat, "Frank Norris: The Novelist as Social Critic and Literary Theorist," *Arizona Quarterly* 18 [1962], 324).

33. *The Responsibilities of the Novelist*, p. 257.

34. This point is discussed by Charles Hoffman in "Norris and the Responsibility of the Novelist," pp. 508–9.

35. *The Responsibilities of the Novelist*, p. 257.

36. "Salt and Sincerity," in *Works*, p. 361.

37. Ibid., p. 379.

38. "Novelists to Order—While You Wait," in *Works*, p. 307.

39. In *The Literary Criticism of Frank Norris*, pp. xiii–xvi, Donald Pizer suggests that Norris valued life over literature, seeing them in masculine and feminine roles respectively, and that he sought to combine an "intense thematic primitivism" with conscious literary craftsmanship.

40. "Novelists of the Future," in *Works*, p. 340.

41. "The True Reward of the Novelist," in *Works*, p. 263.

42. "Salt and Sincerity," in *Works*, p. 376.

43. "A Plea for Romantic Fiction," in *Works*, p. 346.

44. *Works*, p. 265.

45. Ibid., pp. 268–69.

46. "The Great American Novelist," in *Works*, p. 292.

47. *Jack London* (New York, 1974), especially chap. 3.

48. For example, see "The Yellow Peril," in *Jack London Reports*, ed. King Hendricks and Irving Shepard (New York, 1970), pp. 340–50.

49. Introduction to *The Cry for Justice*, in *Jack London, American Rebel*, ed. Philip Foner (New York, 1946), p. 525.

50. "Wanted: A New Law of Development," in *Jack London, American Rebel*, p. 439.

51. "The Yellow Peril," in *Jack London Reports*, p. 347.

52. "The Terrible and Tragic in Fiction," in ibid., p. 334.

53. Review of *Fomá Gordyéeff*, in *Jack London, American Rebel*, p. 516.

54. "Revolution," in ibid., p. 490.

55. "The Jungle," in ibid., p. 518.

56. "Fomá Gordyéeff," in ibid., p. 515.

57. "The Octopus," in ibid., p. 508.

58. "Stranger than Fiction," in *Jack London Reports*, p. 340.

59. "Revolution," in *Jack London, American Rebel*, p. 490.

60. Earle Labor, *Jack London*, p. 86.

61. "What Communities Lose by the Competitive System," in *Jack London, American Rebel*, p. 429.

62. *Notes on Life*, ed. Marguerite Tjader and John McAleer (University, Ala., 1974), p. 111. These notes were written between 1927 and 1945.

63. See Charles Walcutt, "Three Stages of Theodore Dreiser's Naturalism," *PMLA* SS (1940), 273; James T. Farrell, "Some Aspects of Dreiser's Fiction," New York *Times Book Review*, April 29, 1945, pp. 7, 28.

64. *Notes on Life*, p. 51.

65. *The Financier* (New York, 1912), p. 250.

66. *Hey Rub-A-Dub-Dub* (New York, 1920), p. 201.

67. *Notes on Life*, p. 179.

68. Ibid., pp. 177–78, 112–13.

69. Ibid., p. 114.

70. See the essays collected by Donald Pizer, ed., *Theodore Dreiser: A Selection of Uncollected Prose* (Detroit, 1977).

71. *Hey Rub-A-Dub-Dub*, p. 273.

Chapter Eight

1. W. C. Brownell, *Victorian Prose Masters* (New York, 1901), p. 167.

2. W. C. Brownell, *Criticism* (New York, 1914), p. 82. Note Edith Wharton's apotheosis of Brownell at his death: "The most discerning literary critic of our day is dead" ("William C. Brownell," *Scribner's* 84 [1928], 596).

Selected Bibliography

1. General Discussions

ALLEN, GAY WILSON. *American Prosody.* New York: American Book Co., 1935. Chapters on the prosodic theory of Emerson, Whitman, Lowell, and Lanier.

BECKER, GEORGE, ed. *Documents of Modern Literary Criticism.* Princeton: Princeton University Press, 1973. International selections, but includes Howells, Garland, James, Mabie, and twentieth-century Americans, with brief prefaces, and a "Short Bibliography."

BROOKS, VAN WYCK. *New England: Indian Summer.* New York: World Publishing Co., 1940. Covers the period 1865–1915, with several chapters on Dickinson, James, and the Adamses.

BROWN, CLARENCE. *The Achievement of American Criticism.* New York: Ronald Press, 1954. Anthology with long documented selections to the various periods and a selected bibliography.

CLARK, HARRY HAYDEN, ed. *Transitions in American Literary History.* Durham: Duke University Press, 1953. Excellent well-documented studies of the rise and decline of literary movements in the United States.

COWIE, ALEXANDER. *The Rise of the American Novel.* New York: American Book Co., 1951. The best study of the subject.

CURTI, MERLE. *The Growth of American Thought.* New York: Harper, 1943. Invaluable for knowledge of the intellectual background of the period.

DeMILLE, GEORGE E. *Literary Criticism in America.* New York: Russell and Russell, 1967. Contains a chapter on the *North American Review* and one each on Lowell, Poe, Emerson and Margaret Fuller, Stedman, James, Howells, Huneker, and Sherman.

FALK, ROBERT. *The Victorian Mode in American Fiction 1865–1885.* East Lansing: Michigan State University Press, 1964. Reassessment of the cultural and literary history of "Victorian realism" through chronological narrative and literary interpretation.

FOERSTER, NORMAN. *American Criticism.* New York: Russell and Russell, 1962. Extended essays on the criticism of Poe, Emerson, Lowell, and Whitman, with a survey of critical principles they advocated.

GETTMAN, ROYAL. *Turgenev in England and America.* Illinois Studies in Language and Literature, vol. 27, no. 2 (1941). Responses of James, Howells, G. P. Lathrop, and T. S. Perry to Turgenev. Good bibliography.

HUBBELL, JAY. *Who Are the Major American Writers?* Durham: Duke University Press, 1972. Literary opinions of dozens of major and minor critics, with some useful information on the various polls "ranking" United States authors.

JONES, HOWARD MUMFORD. *Theory of American Literature.* Ithaca: Cornell University Press, 1948. Provides solid background material.

KNIGHT, GRANT C. *The Critical Period in American Literature.* Chapel Hill: University of North Carolina Press, 1951. Study of the controversies of the 1890s.

MCMAHON, HELEN. *Criticism and Fiction; a study of trends in . . . The Atlantic Monthly 1857–1898.* New York: Bookman Associates, 1952. History of the magazine, with a helpful appendix that lists about 600 book reviews.

MAHIEU, ROBERT. *Sainte-Beuve aux Etats Unis.* Princeton: Princeton University Press, 1945. Detailed analysis of American response to Sainte-Beuve.

MARTIN, JAY. *Harvests of Change: American Literature 1865–1914.* Englewood Cliffs, N.J.: Prentice-Hall, 1967. Literary-cultural history of the period, with attention to realism, regionalism, early and later naturalism, and ending with a section on Henry James.

PARRINGTON, VERNON LOUIS. *The Beginnings of Critical Realism in America.* In *Main Currents in American Thought.* New York: Harcourt, Brace, 1930. Three-part history of American thought of the period, using American literature to arrive at a synthesis. Left incomplete at Parrington's death, but still a forceful reappraisal from the point of view of American liberalism.

PIZER, DONALD. *Realism and Naturalism in Nineteenth-Century American Literature.* Carbondale: Southern Illinois University Press, 1966. Part of the Crosscurrents series, views realism and naturalism in terms of evolutionary theory.

PRITCHARD, JOHN PAUL. *Criticism in America.* Norman: University of Oklahoma Press, 1956. Chapters 7 through 9 deal with the post–Civil War period and discuss the New England tradition, realism, and the impressionist and regionalist movements.

————. *Return to the Fountains.* Durham: Duke University Press, 1942. Standard study of classical influences on American writers.

RALEIGH, JOHN. *Matthew Arnold and American Culture.* Berkeley: University of California Press, 1957. General chapters on Arnold in America 1865–1895, with separate chapters on the responses of James and Brownell.

SIMON, MYRON, AND PARSONS, THORNTON, eds. *Transcendentalism and Its Legacy.* Ann Arbor: University of Michigan Press, 1966. Scholarly articles on the continuing grip of Transcendentalism on thinkers in the period.

SMITH, BERNARD. *Forces in American Criticism.* New York: Harcourt,

Brace, 1939. Broad but sparsely documented survey from a Marxist point of view.

SPENCER, BENJAMIN. *The Quest for Nationality, an American Campaign.* Syracuse: Syracuse University Press, 1957. Standard study of nationalism among United States authors.

STEIN, ROGER. *John Ruskin and Aesthetic Thought in America, 1840–1900.* Cambridge: Harvard University Press, 1967. Standard. Ruskin was widely used by Americans partly because he opposed art for art's sake and sought to use art to reinforce morality and religion.

STOVALL, FLOYD, ed. *The Development of American Literary Criticism.* Chapel Hill: University of North Carolina Press, 1955. Richard Fogle's essay on organic form and Robert Falk's on criticism 1870–1900 are both fine interpretations of criticism in the period.

TUCKER, MARTIN, ed. *The Critical Temper: A Survey of Modern Criticism on English and American Literature from the Beginnings to the Twentieth Century.* 3 vols. New York: Ungar Press, 1969. Volume 3 contains Victorian and American literature.

WIMSATT, JR., WILLIAM K., AND BROOKS, CLEANTH. *Literary Criticism, A Short History.* New York: Alfred A. Knopf, 1957. Excellent background to the period, with some reference to American critics.

ZIFF, LARZER. *The American 1890's: Life and Times of a Lost Generation.* New York: Viking Press, 1966. Attention to major figures, but also includes informative chapters on newspapers and magazines, Western writing, late romantic fiction, and the early E. A. Robinson.

2. Critical Schools and Individual Authors

Chapter One

ADAMS, R. P. "Emerson and the Organic Metaphor." *PMLA* 69 (1954), 117–30. Full discussion of the importance of the organic principle to Emerson.

CARPENTER, F. I. "The Genteel Tradition: A Re-Interpretation." *New England Quarterly* 15 (1942), 427–43. The tradition is often reactionary because of its gentility and conservatism, but derives strength from humanistic ideals which provide standards in a democracy.

CLARK, HARRY HAYDEN. "Emerson and Science." *Philological Quarterly* 10 (1931), 225–60. Full discussion of the importance of science in Emerson's thought.

————, AND FOERSTER, NORMAN, eds. *Lowell: Representative Selections.* New York: American Book Co., 1947, Introduction argues that Lowell is America's greatest critic.

FLANAGAN, J. T. "Emerson as a Critic of Fiction." *Philological Quarterly* 15 (1936), 30–45. Emerson tended to ignore intermediate novelists like Hawthorne, Jane Austen, and Dickens.

HOPKINS, VIVIAN. *Spires of Form: A Study of Emerson's Aesthetic Theory.*

Cambridge: Harvard University Press, 1951. One of the standard studies of the subject, well-documented.

HOWARD, LEON. "For a Critique of Whitman's Transcendentalism." *Modern Language Notes* 47 (1932), 79–85. Whitman against his intellectual background.

PAUL, SHERMAN. *Emerson's Angle of Vision.* Cambridge: Harvard University Press, 1952. Seminal study of Emerson's epistemology and aesthetic theory.

ROBERTSON, J. M. "Lowell as a Critic." *North American Review* 209 (1919), 246–62. Starts out to refute charges of impressionism in Lowell's criticism but ends in partial agreement.

SHACKFORD, M. H. "George Edward Woodberry as Critic." *New England Quarterly* 24 (1951), 510–27. Woodberry developed a standard of criticism which valued independence, intelligence, and discrimination, rendered fresh assessments of writers, and relied on personal insights rather than traditional generalizations.

WEST, R. B. "Truth, Beauty, and American Criticism." *University of Kansas City Review* 14 (1947), 137–48. Tenets of critical idealism with attention to George Woodberry.

WILLSON, LAWRENCE. " 'The Body Electric' Meets the Genteel Tradition." *New Mexico Quarterly* 26 (1956–1957), 369–86. The question of good taste was among the issues raised about Whitman even by generally sympathetic critics such as E. C. Stedman.

Chapter Two

BAETZHOLD, HOWARD. *Mark Twain and John Bull: The British Connection.* Bloomington: University of Indiana Press, 1970. The appendices round out this standard study with data on Twain's reading and attitude toward English authors.

BLAIR, WALTER. *Native American Humor: 1800–1900.* New York: American Book Co., 1937. Standard treatment of the subject, with extensive selected bibliography.

BUDD, LOUIS. "W. D. Howells' Defense of the Romance." *PMLA* 67 (1952), 32–42. Howells distinguished between the novel and romance and tended to stress the virtues of the latter.

————. *Mark Twain: Social Philosopher.* Bloomington: University of Indiana Press, 1962. Twain's social and political criticism, with bibliographical references included in notes.

CADY, E. H. *The Road to Realism.* Syracuse: Syracuse University Press, 1956.

————. *The Realist at War.* Syracuse: Syracuse University Press, 1958. With *The Road to Realism*, the standard biography and critical analysis of Howells's career.

————, AND FRAZIER, D. L., eds., *The War of the Critics Over William*

Dean Howells. Evanston: Northwestern University Press, 1962. Useful anthology of the travails of realism during the period.

CARTER, EVERETT. *Howells and the Age of Realism.* Philadelphia: Lippincott, 1954. Full discussion of the critical debate over realism.

CLARK, HARRY HAYDEN. "The Role of Science in the Thought of W. D. Howells." *Transactions of the Wisconsin Academy of Sciences, Arts and Letters* 42 (1953), 263–303. Includes the role of science in Howells' literary criticism.

DICKASON, D. H. "Benjamin Orange Flower, Patron of the Realists." *American Literature* 14 (1942), 148–56. Background to the realist controversy.

EBLE, K. E., ed. *Howells: A Century of Criticism.* Dallas: Southern Methodist University Press, 1962. Anthology of critical responses to Howells as writer, critic, and social and political theorist.

HARLOW, VIRGINIA. "William Dean Howells and Thomas Sargeant Perry." *Boston Public Library Quarterly* 1 (1949), 135–54. Howells credited Perry with helping him to adopt a realistic view and to study the Russians.

KIRK, CLARA. *W. D. Howells and Art in His Time.* New Brunswick: Rutgers University Press, 1965. Howells' development as writer and critic and his role in literary controversies.

KOLB, JR., H. H. "In Search of a Definition: American Literary Realism and the Clichés." *American Literary Realism* 2 (1969), 165–73. The realists continued to think of fiction as illusion, but developed an aesthetic and craft which would lead readers to believe that the fiction was objective reporting.

————. *The Illusion of Life: American Realism as a Literary Form.* Charlottesville: University Press of Virginia, 1969. Analysis of five novels of three realists, with useful bibliography.

KRAUSE, SYDNEY. *Mark Twain as Critic.* Baltimore: Johns Hopkins Press, 1967. The standard study, with bibliography of Twain's criticism, literary essays and miscellaneous critical comments.

Chapter Three

BARRETT, LAURENCE. "Young Henry James, Critic." *American Literature* 20 (1949), 385–400. Young James was primarily a critic dedicated to the increasing clarification of critical principles in which morality is converted into a tool for the analysis of personality.

GROVER, PHILIP. *Henry James and the French Novel: A Study in Inspiration.* New York: Barnes and Noble, 1973. James' knowledge of French literature and parallels in his work to French naturalism and art.

KELLEY, CORNELIA. *The Early Development of Henry James.* rev. ed. Urbana: University of Illinois Press, 1968. Incisive coverage of James as writer and critic, including discussion of Goethe among early influences.

POWERS, LYALL. *Henry James and the Naturalist Movement*. Ann Arbor: University of Michigan Press, 1971. James increasingly turned from imagination to accurate factual presentation in the manner of the French naturalists.

ROBERTS, MORRIS. *Henry James's Criticism*. Cambridge: Harvard University Press, 1929. Illuminating in finding four successive periods in the criticism and in showing how James developed from dogmatic judicial standards to a much more flexible and sympathetic impressionism.

SPILKA, MARK. "Henry James and Walter Besant: 'The Art of Fiction' Controversy." *Novel* 6 (1963), 100–119. The social and intellectual issues that prompted James' response to Besant's article.

WEGELIN, CHRISTOF. "Henry James and the Treasures of Consciousness." *Studia Neophilologica* 9 (1973), 484–91. Analysis of the centrality of consciousness to James throughout his career.

WELLEK, RENÉ. "Henry James's Literary Theory and Criticism." *American Literature* 30 (1958), 293–321. Solid analysis, which views James' criticism as a bridge from organicism to formalism.

Chapter Four

CLARK, HARRY HAYDEN. "The Influence of Science on American Literary Criticism, 1860–1910, Including the Vogue of Taine." *Transactions of the Wisconsin Academy of Sciences, Arts and Letters* 44 (1955), 109–64. Evolutionary theory through Herbert Spencer is the subject of the first half, with Taine's influence taking up the second.

HOFSTADTER, RICHARD. *Social Darwinism in American Thought*. Boston: Beacon Press, 1955. Standard study of the influence of Darwin and Spencer on American thought from approximately 1860 to 1915.

SULLIVAN, JEREMIAH. "Henry James and Hippolyte Taine: An Historical and Scientific Method in Literature." *Comparative Literature Studies* 10 (1973), 25–50. Gathers together all pertinent references of James to Taine.

Chapter Five

ALLEN, GAY WILSON. "Sidney Lanier as a Literary Critic." *Philological Quarterly* 17 (1938), 121–38. Judicious treatment of Lanier's strengths and weaknesses as a critic.

COOLIDGE, JOHN S. "Lewis E. Gates: The Permutations of Romanticism." *New England Quarterly* 30 (1957), 23–38. Gates argued for a synthesis of impressionism and historical criticism.

HAVENS, ELMER. "Lanier's Critical Theory." *Emerson Society Quarterly*, no. 55 (1970), 83–89. Lanier's linking of morals to aestheticism, his concept of etherealization, his prizing of individual autonomy.

HINDREN, JOSEPH. "Time and Stress in English Verse with Special Reference to Lanier's Theory of Rhythm." *Rice Institute Pamphlets* 46 (1959), 1–72. An argument for quantitative measure.

PARKS, EDD WINFIELD. *Lanier: The Man, The Poet, The Critic*. Athens: University of Georgia Press, 1968. Lamar Lectures at Wesleyan College which bring together all relevant matter in the three categories.

SCHWAB, ARNOLD. *James Gibbons Huneker, Critic of the Seven Arts*. Palo Alto: Stanford University Press, 1963. Standard biography of Huneker, with full attention to his literary pursuits.

VAN DEUSEN, MARSHALL. *J. E. Spingarn*. New York: Twayne Publishers, 1971. Very useful study of Spingarn's career and theory of criticism, bringing together much material either unknown or difficult to obtain.

Chapter Six

AIKEN, HENRY DAVID. "George Santayana, Natural Historian of Symbolic Forms." *Kenyon Review* 15 (1953), 337–56. Despite an unwillingness to explore matters more fully, Santayana has presented us with one of the best explanations for the role of symbolic forms in clarifying and justifying reason in art.

ARNETT, WILLARD. *George Santayana*. New York: Washington Square Press, 1968. A fine introduction to the life and thought of Santayana.

———. "Santayana and the Poetic Function of Religion." *Journal of Philosophy* 53 (1956), 773–87. Santayana knew that the value of religions lies in their actions, symbols, and beliefs, but he did not sufficiently develop the implications of these aspects.

———. *Santayana and the Sense of Beauty*. Bloomington: University of Indiana Press, 1955. Analysis of aesthetic value and its relation to individual, social, and intellectual concerns and to Santayana's naturalistic humanism.

ASHMORE, JEROME. *Santayana, Art, and Aesthetics*. Cleveland: Western Reserve University Press, 1966. Emphasis on the theoretical structure of his aesthetics rather than its moral and idealist implications.

BALLOWE, JAMES. "*The Last Puritan* and the Failure of American Culture." *American Quarterly* 18 (1966), 123–35. Santayana felt the United States was too materialistic and would not mature culturally until it began to cultivate the intellect and will.

BROWN, MAURICE. "Santayana's American Roots." *New England Quarterly* 33 (1960), 147–63. Exploration of Santayana's Harvard years to 1912 to show that he belongs to an American tradition.

COHEN, MAURICE. "Santayana on Romanticism and Egotism." *Journal of Religion* 46 (1966), 264–81. Santayana uses the traditional idea of God to explain the generative power of matter, and criticizes romanticism on the grounds that romantics like Lucifer think they can circumvent the limitations of matter.

COMSTOCK, W. RICHARD. "Aspects of Aesthetic Experience: Kierkegaard and Santayana." *International Philosophical Quarterly* 6 (1966), 189–213. Both are "hard" exponents of the need for clarity through "either-or" rather than the "soft" vagueness of "both-and."

GILBERT, KATHERINE. "Santayana's Doctrine of Aesthetic Expression." *Philosophical Review* 35 (1926), 221–35. Criticism of his aesthetic theory of expression from the point of view of Croce's expressionism.

HARRISON, CHARLES. "Santayana's 'Literary Psychology.' " *Sewanee Review* 61 (1953), 206–20. Criticism of Santayana's materialism, which fails him in his effort to develop a philosophy of humanistic naturalism.

KALLEN, H. M. et al. "Conversation on Santayana." *Antioch Review* 19 (1959), 237–70. Personal recollections and opinions of Kallen, Corliss Lamont, John H. Randall, Jr., Herbert W. Schneider, James Gutmann, Ernest Nagel, and Milton Munitz.

KIRKWOOD, M. M. *Santayana: Saint of the Imagination.* Toronto: University of Toronto Press, 1961. Intellectual and chronological history of Santayana's mind.

MAJOR, JOHN. "Santayana on Shakespeare." *Shakespeare Quarterly* 10 (1959), 469–79. Citation of all relevant references, concluding that Santayana was finally reconciled to Shakespeare late in life.

RANSOM, JOHN CROWE. "Art and Mr. Santayana." *Virginia Quarterly Review* 13 (1937), 420–36. Santayana was a latter-day version of Schopenhauer whose doctrine of essence in art is a salvation amounting to the death of art.

SINGER, IRVING. *Santayana's Aesthetics.* Cambridge: Harvard University Press, 1957. Discussion of Santayana's aesthetics and philosophy of art, and an attempt to formulate an aesthetic based on Santayana and pragmatic thought.

————, ed. *Essays in Literary Criticism of George Santayana.* New York: Scribner, 1956. Useful introduction covering major points in Santayana's criticism.

Symposium on Santayana. *Journal of Philosophy* 51 (1954), 29–64. Entire issue devoted to aspects of Santayana's thought, with the articles of Randell and Olafoon most pertinent to Santayana's criticism.

Chapter Seven

ÄHNEBRINK, LARS. *The Beginnings of Naturalism in American Fiction.* Cambridge: Harvard University Press, 1950. Useful, but some points need modifying in the light of subsequent scholarship.

————. *The Influence of Emile Zola on Frank Norris.* Cambridge: Harvard University Press, 1947. Norris consciously modeled his novels on those of Zola.

DILLINGHAM, WILLIAM. *Frank Norris: Instinct and Art.* Lincoln: University of Nebraska Press, 1969. Norris' career as an artist.

EDWARDS, HERBERT. "Herne, Garland, and Henry George." *American Literature* 28 (1956), 359–69. Study of their mutual interrelationships in terms of economic theory and reforming zeal.

————. "Zola and the American Critics." *American Literature* 4 (1932), 114–29. Frank Norris figures largely.

FONER, PHILIP. *Jack London: American Rebel.* New York: Citadel Press,

1947. Collection of London's social writings together with an extensive study of London and his times.

FRIERSON, W. C., AND EDWARDS, HERBERT. "Impact of French Naturalism on American Critical Opinion, 1877–1892." *PMLA* 63 (1948), 1007–16. Zola was initially condemned by American critics, but his humanitarian principles influenced many to accept him by 1888, and this helped in the reception of American naturalists.

GOLDSMITH, ARNOLD. "The Development of Frank Norris's Philosophy." In *Studies in Honor of John Wilcox*, edited by A. D. Wallace and W. O. Ross. Detroit: Wayne State University Press, 1958. Assigns four periods to the development of Norris' views.

HOFFMAN, CHARLES. "Norris and the Responsibility of the Novelist." *South Atlantic Quarterly* 54 (1955), 508–15. Norris mixed different literary practices according to his intent, theme, and content, and shows no consistent development as a writer.

KWIAT, JOSEPH. "Frank Norris: The Novelist as Social Critic and Literary Theorist." *Arizona Quarterly* 18 (1962), 319–28. Norris belongs to the school of experience because he distrusted "literary" purposes.

LABOR, EARLE. *Jack London*. New York: Twayne Publishers, 1974. Life and intellectual history of London, using extensive manuscript materials.

LEHAN, RICHARD. *Theodore Dreiser: His World and His Novels*. Carbondale: Southern Illinois University Press, 1969. Intellectual orientation of Dreiser's mind and his novels based on manuscript materials.

PIZER, DONALD. *Hamlin Garland's Early Work and Career*. Berkeley: University of California Press, 1960. Covers 1884–1895 and explores Garland's interest in local color, theater, populism, and the arts.

———. *The Literary Criticism of Frank Norris*. Austin: University of Texas Press, 1964. Uncollected criticism 1895–1903, together with valuable introductions to different types of criticism by Norris.

———. *The Novels of Frank Norris*. Bloomington: Indiana University Press, 1966. Analysis of the novels, with attention to Norris' attitudes and plans while writing them.

RAW, RUTH. "Hamlin Garland, The Romanticist." *Sewanee Review* 36 (1928), 202–10. Garland became increasingly a romantic in his work, although even before 1895 evidences of romanticism can be found.

SALVAN, ALBERT J. *Zola aux Etats-Unis*. Providence: Brown University Press, 1943. Documented survey, followed by useful year-by-year tabulation of American reviews of Zola.

VIVAS, ELISEO. "Dreiser, an Inconsistent Mechanist." *Ethics* 48 (1938), 498–508. Conflict between mechanist views and reforming impulse.

WALCUTT, CHARLES CHILD. *American Literary Naturalism, A Divided Stream*. Minneapolis: University of Minnesota Press, 1956. Begins with Zola and ends with the generation of Hemingway. Sees both "soft" and "social" naturalism as stemming from Transcendentalism, and provides good explications of naturalistic novels.

Index

184

Randall, Jr., John Herman, 125

Realism, 23, 24, 36, 41–42, 94, 103, 119–20, 134, 138, 140, 149

Realism, critical, 41–61; as a movement, 41–42; Harte and, 43–46; Howells and, 52–61; James and, 62–83; theory of, 42–43; Twain and, 46–51

Richardson, Charles Francis: *American Literature 1607–1885*, 102

Roberts Morris: *Henry James's Criticism*, 63

Ruggles, Henry: *The Method of Shakespeare*, 155

Sainte-Beuve, Charles, 42, 62, 69, 70, 108

Sand, George, 62, 67, 70, 74, 75

Santayana, George, 17, 27, 85, 104, 115, *118–33*, 136, 154, 155, 157; art as social resource, 126–33; art and the artist, 121–26; background, 118–19; beauty, 121–22; decline of art, 132–33; form, 125–26; imagination, 125; moral value of art, 126–28; naturalism, 119–20, 126; nature of poetry, 122–23; the poet, 124; poetry and religion, 123–24; reason, 120–21, 127; romanticism, 130–31; taste, 129–30, value of art, 121; *Interpretations of Poetry and Religion*, 85, 119; *The Last Puritan*, 131; *Life of Reason*, 119; *Realms of Being*, 119; *Scepticism and Animal Faith*, 119; *The Sense of Beauty*, 118, 126; *Three Philosophical Poets*, 119

Scherer, Edmond, 42, 62, 69

Schwab, Arnold, 113, 114

Scudder, Vida: *The Life of the Spirit in the English Poets*, 89

Sears, Lorenzo: *American Literature in the Colonial and National Periods*, 101

Shaw, George Bernard, 112, 114

Sherman, Stuart, 102

Sill, Edward Rowland, 88

Sinclair, Upton, 149–50; *The Jungle*, 149

Singer, Irving, 130

Spencer, Herbert, 85, 100, 136, 137, 142, 148, 149, 151, 154; academicians and, 90–91; Fiske and, 91–92; influence on historical criticism, 86–94;

naturalism and, 89–90; Perry and, 93–94; "soft" Spencerians, 88–89

Spiller, Robert, 117

Spingarn, Joel Elias, 26, 27, 37, *114–17*, 154, 157; ahistoricism, 116; background, 114–15; expressionism, 115–16, 117; *Critical Essays of the Seventeenth Century*, 115; *Criticism in America*, 115; *A History of Literary Criticism in the Renaissance*, 114; *The New Criticism*, 115

Stedman, Edmund Clarence, 21, 24, 26, *34–38*, 88, 97, 101, 154, 155, 156; career, 35; on didacticism, 38; perspicuity, 35–36; principles, 35; on realism, 36; on rhythm and inspiration, 37; squeamishness, 36; *An American Anthology*, 35; *A Library of American Literature*, 35, 101; *The Nature and Elements of Poetry*, 37; *Victorian Poets*, 35, 89, 102, 156

Stendhal (Marie Henri Beyle), 68

Stevenson, Robert Louis, 76

Stovall, Floyd, 18

Strindberg, August, 112, 114

Taine, Hippolyte, 42, 55, 69, 70, *94–102*, 108, 131, 136, 140; American writers and, 97–98; academicians and, 100–102; Adams and, 100; criticism of, 96–97; historical theory, 94–96; Howells and James on, 98–100

Taylor, Bayard, 19

Taylor, Walter Fuller, 59

Thackeray, William, 60, 67

Thayer, William, 17–18, 59

Thompson, Vance, 103

Trent, William: *A History of American Literature 1607–1865*, 102

Trollope, Anthony, 65, 66, 68, 73, 75

Truth in literature, 103, 136; critical idealism and, 24, 25; Dreiser on, 90, 150–51; Garland on, 90, 138, 139; James and, 63–64; London on, 90; Norris on, 90, 143, 145, 147; realism and, 42–43; Stedman on, 37

Turgenev, Ivan, 34, 42, 60, 62, 73, 74, 75, 93

Twain, Mark, 18, 32, 34, 41, 42, 43, 44,